"The Big Book on Starting Your Own Auto Detailing Business!"

SUCCESS TRAINING MANUAL

Copyright © 2012 Greg Dumond

Written by: *Greg Dumond*
Auto Detailing Veteran of 25 Years

Library of Congress Cataloging-in-Publication Data Dumond, Greg
The Big Book on Auto Detailing
Printed in the United States
Registration #28292529

COPYRIGHT 2012

All rights reserved by the author. No part of this publication can be reproduced, soldered in a retrieval system or transmitted in any form or by any means, electronic, mechanical, photocopying, recording or otherwise, without the prior permission of the publishers and/or authors.

"The Big Book on Starting Your Own Auto Detailing Business!"

SUCCESS TRAINING MANUAL

Copyright © 2012 Greg Dumond

All rights reserved. Except as permitted under U.S. Copyright Act of 1976, no part of this publication may be reproduced, distributed or transmitted in any form or by any means, or stored in a database or retrieval system, without the prior written permission of the publisher.

Exterior Book Design by www.JHGrafix.com

Book compilation by KV@ - Virtually Everywhere www.kva4u.com

"A special thanks goes out to Ugur Sahin for the use of his Dino Ferrari illustration"
UgurSahinDesign www.ugursahindesign.com

Printed in the United States of America

Third Edition
Paperback:
ISBN

While every attempt is made to ensure that the information in this book is correct, no liability can be accepted by the authors or publishers for loss, damage or injury caused by any errors in, actions, or omissions from, the information given.

Table Of Contents

Section 1 12
Introduction 12

Section 2 16
Setting Up Your Work Area 16

Detailers Canopy 17
Canopy Instructions 18
Setting Up Work Area 20
Customer Greeting 21
Equipment 22
Accessories And Chemicals 23
Car Set-Up 24

Section 3 27
Glossary Of Auto Detailing Terms 27

Detailing Terms*1 29

Section 4 40
Chemical Information 40

Cleaning And Polishing Chemicals 41
Be Professional Always Use The Highest Grade Products 42
Chemical Reference Guide 44

Section 5 50

Greg Dumond – Success Training Manual

Equipment And Maintenance Information	50
Maintenance	51
Orbital Polisher	51
Safety Instructions	52
Other Orbital Polisher Options	53
Maintenance Instructions	53
Fabric Guard Applicator	54
The Immersion Heater	54
Carpet And Upholstery Extractor	56
Operating Instructions	57
Cleaning Process And Procedures	58
Cleaning Carpets And Upholstery	58
Cleaning Methods	59
Highlights To Remember:	59
Care And Maintenance	60
Detailer's Vacuum	60
Vacuum Care And Maintenance	61
Gas And Electric Pressure Washers	62
Safety Precautions	62
Care Of Your Equipment	63
Setting Up	64
How To Clean	65
Water Tank	66
Safeguards And General Safety Instructions	67
Electric Pressure Washers	68

Important Freeze Protection 69

Section 6 71

Engine Cleaning 71

The Motor 72

Steps For Engine Cleaning 73

Section 7 85

Basics Of Prep Work 85

Prep Work 86

Washing The Car 87

Washing The Paint 88

Automatic Car Washing Facilities 89

What Is Acid Rain And How Does It Affect An Automobile? 92

What Causes Acid Rain Spots? 93

Prepping For The Car Wash 93

Prep Work Includes: 95

The Initial Pressure Washing Sequence For: 98

Wheels, Tires, And Undercarriage 98

Rubber Tires And White Walls 102

Grill Body And Undercarriage 104

Road Tar And Sap Removal 106

The Pressure Washing Sequence 108

Vinyl Tops 109

Convertible Tops 111

Power Up The Suds! 112

Hand Body Wash 113

Power Rinsing 115

Drying The Car 116

Section 8 121

Detailing The Interior 121

Interior 121

Vacuuming 124

Animal Hair 130

Shampooing The Interior 132

Headliner - Shampooing 133

Cloth Upholstery Seats 136

Sun Rot 137

Carpets And Mats 137

Removing Carpet Stains 140

Extreme Circumstances 140

Shampooing/Extraction Method 142

Operating Instructions For The Carpet And Upholstery Cleaner Solution 143

Cleaning Vinyl Headliners 144

Sunroof 144

General Area Cleaning 145

Dashboard And Gauges 145

Vents And Recessed Areas 146

Steering Wheel 148

Ashtrays 148

Seat Belts 149

Floor Mats 150

Fabric Guard 151

Cleaning Interior Vinyl 152

Door Jambs 154

Vinyl Upholstery And Trim 155

Vinyl Dressing 156

Leather Upholstery And Trim 157

Section 9 161

Exterior Polishing 161

Polishing 162

Automotive Paint Technology 163

What Is A Natural Sealant? 163

What Is A Synthetic Sealant? 164

Silicones 164

Waxing - Sealing - Glazing 164

Saving Time With Combo Or One Step Products 165

What Is POLISHING? 166

Achieving Perfect Paint Is Possible 169

Technical Glossary And Illustrations 170

What Is Crazing 171

What Are Fisheyes 171

Cobweb Paint 171

What Is Oxidation? 172

Can Oxidation Be Cured? 173

What Is Compounding? 174

Consistent Paint Cleaning 174

The Importance Of A Paint Thickness Gauge 176

Paint Measuring Gauge 177

Polish: Non-Abrasive And Abrasive 179

Directions For Applying A Polish. 179

Compounding And Buffing Procedures 180

Divide And Conquer Procedure 181

Keeping Bonnets And Towels Clean 185

Sealing 186

Combination One Step Products 187

Base Coat/Clear Coat Paint 189

Paint Type Analysis 190

Compounding Base Coat/Clear Coat 191

Water Spots 193

Treating Chemical Fallout, Acid Rain And Water Spots 194

Industrial Fallout 194

Paint Overspray Removal 195

Paint Transfer 195

Wood Grain And Aerodynamic Body Parts 196

Section 10 199

Exterior Polishing 199

Finishing Touches 200

Wheel Polishing 202

Chrome Work 203

Antennas 204

License Plates 204

Toothbrushing 205

Section 11 207

Selling Paint Sealant For More Profit 207

Long Term Paint Sealant Application.. 208

Some Tips On Cleaning Wool Bonnets And Foam Pads.......................... 209

Section 12 212

Window Cleaning 212

Glass Cleaning 213

Plastic Rear Windows 217

Cleaning And Polishing Diagram For Windshields And Windows 218

Section 13 220

Vehicle Detailing Summary Steps 220

Setup Area And Equipment... 221

Engine Cleaning 221

Initial Pressure Washing... 221

Detailing The Interior 223

Exterior Polishing.. 224

Window Cleaning 224

Section 14 227

Special Tips And Techniques 227

Special Tips Section 228

Section 15 236

Recreational Vehicles 236

Rv's 237
Interior Cleaning Will Consist Of: 237
Potential Customers Are: 239

Section 16 241

Boats And Airplanes 241

Marine 242
Potential Customers Are: 246
Price List For Detailing Boats 247
Overview Of The Steps For Detailing Aircraft: 248
Suggested Price Schedule For Aircraft Detailing 251

Section 17 253

Checklist And Retail Service Price List 253

Vehicle Checklist 254

Section 18 258

Equipment And Supply Check 258

Supply And Equipment 259
Final Walk-Around 260
Inspection And Payment 260
Sample Invoice 262

Section 19 264

Recommended Aftermarket Add-On Services 264

Add-On Repair And Restoration Services For Extra Profits 265

Section 20 270

Conclusion 270

Congrats 271

Section 21 273

Resource Guide 273

Product And Equipment Resource Guide 274

Section 1

Introduction

Welcome to the world of professional automotive detailing and restoration. Now more than ever, with the increasing complexity of today's automobiles, the business of automotive detailing requires skilled professionals to maintain and preserve the life and longevity of their customer's vehicles.

Professional auto detailing requires specialized knowledge and training. It will also require hard work, determination, and a yearning to be the best in the business! This is what will set you apart from your competition.

We have compiled a comprehensive Training Manual to guide you in all aspects of the automotive detailing business. By following these procedures, the chain of events we have outlined for you will assist you in growing your detailing operations. We have pulled together one of the finest and most thorough training programs ever developed for professional detailing. All the information contained in your Operations/Training Manual will be an invaluable guide for yourself and your employees. You will learn all the correct methods for detailing everything from automobiles to RV's, as well as how to run the business; hiring employees; advertising techniques; and how to find customers. It doesn't matter if you are a seasoned veteran or new to the detailing business, the information found within this Training Manual will be invaluable instructional information.

Even though you may be familiar with the automotive detailing business, there is more to detailing than just washing and waxing a car. This Training Manual will help give you the confidence to make old car's look new and new car's look like a showroom model. You will learn in depth and painstaking procedures that will ensure that even the most discerning customer will be satisfied with the outcome of their vehicle and your detailing services.

Through a variety of special detailing processes we will show you how to achieve the best results and ensure professional quality work.

It is recommended that you become familiar with the detailing industry through subscriptions and related trade journals. By doing so, you will have an advantage over many of your competitors and gain the latest tips, techniques, and changes within the industry. There are several detailing forums on the internet, which may keep you in touch other professionals who are growing their business just like you.

One final word:

The utmost important principal for running your business is to provide excellent value for your customer. By being fair with your pricing, developing an honest customer relationship, and providing excellent service you will have a customer for life!

Congratulations on making the decision to operate your own detailing business. Very few people have both the drive and entrepreneurial spirit to start their own business. Your desires and motivation for success will take you to the top of your field.

I truly hope that all your entrepreneurial dreams of success come true, and look forward to assisting you on the path to a successful business.

Much Success,
Greg Dumond

Special Notes Page

Section 2

Setting Up Your Work Area

Detailers Canopy 18

Canopy Instructions 19

Setting Up Work Area 21

Customer Greeting 22

Equipment 23

Accessories And Chemicals 24

Car Set-Up 25

Detailers Canopy

The multi-function and usefulness of the portable shade canopy will simulate the effects of having a detail shop, and will give you the ability to detail your customers' vehicle under a protected shelter. The most important functions of the canopy will provide protection in varying weather and shade for both the operator and vehicle. Even though many of the chemicals and polishes perform well in direct sunlight, more optimum results can be achieved by working on a cooler surface.

By using a portable shade canopy you will receive both visibility and attention allowing for a more professional appearance for your detailing company. Of course, the purpose is to attract new customers, receive more inquiries, and book more jobs!

The detailer's canopy is portable and constructed of an aluminum single frame accordion assembly which sets up and folds down in minutes. The cover is made with a denier nylon oxford cloth that's made of a waterproof urethane coating. However, the cover is not fire retardant so use caution when storing your canopy.

Illustrated on the next page are simple procedures to help with setting up the canopy. Please read these instructions carefully before setting up your canopy.

Canopy Instructions

1. Read Instructions carefully and completely before proceeding with each step.
2. Always handle the unit with care. Use no excessive force while setting up or folding.
3. Although this unit can be set up by one person, we suggest that two or more people be involved.
4. A proper securing of this unit to the ground after set up is **Always** a must. (Some suggestions below.)
5. In windy situations, please use this unit with discretion. Remember, **THIS UNIT IS NOT WINDPROOF.**
6. This unit is specially designed to be used as an instant, portable sunshade, **not a weather shelter**. Therefore, it is not recommended to use while it is raining or snowing. When there is a sudden downpour, the water must be pushed off the fabric to prevent it from stretching.
7. This fabric **does not have Flame Retardant Treatment**.
8. Be careful not to catch any part of your hands in the frame when setting up or closing.
9. Keep children away from this canopy while it is folded in the upright position. For safety reasons, lay the unit down when folded.

SETTNG UP

Step 1: Holding the posts, lift the unit up and slowly move backwards as you spread your arms in an outward direction as shown in Figure 1.

Step 2: When your arms are fully extended, set the unit down. Place your hands on position A and B (Figure 2) and while moving backwards away from the canopy, slowly draw both hands toward each other until the lower beam becomes almost horizontal (Figure 3). **Note:** While spreading the canopy, all the posts must be clearly off the ground to ensure free mobility.

Step 3: Proceed to a corner of the canopy. While holding the post down from the top raise the slider up with the other hand until it locks into place. You will hear a "snap" sound when the slider locks. Make sure that the snap under the leather tab is in a locked position (Figure 3). Do the same for the other three posts. When the canopy is locked in place, straighten the canvas corner by gently pulling it down.

Step 4: Now is the time to raise the canopy to a desirable height. In each of the four posts, you will find an inserted lower post. Slide the lower post out until the lock button is released through one of the holes in the upper post. **Note:** There is a dotted line on the lower post and the lock button is found on the line. Also, the two posts on either of the narrow side should be extended first. Do not start on the wider side.

Step 5: Secure all four posts to the ground. Some suggestions are below.

FOLDING: (Folding is the reverse of setting up)

Step 1: Free the four posts from the anchors. When there is a strong wind, it is recommended that more than one person be invoked during the folding process. One person on each post would be ideal.

Step 2: Release the post lock buttons and telescope the lower posts into the upper post. Once again, begin with the two posts on the narrow side. **Note:** In windy situations, lower the side which is facing the wind first.

Step 3: After all four legs are inserted into the upper post, release the sliders by pressing the leather tabs. **Do Not Remove The Leather Tabs** for they are there to prevent your fingers from being pinched.

Step 4: Place your hands at position A as found in Figure 3 and press down about four inches.

Step 5: Holding the lower beam at position D with both hands (Figure 3), lift the unit up and slowly collapse it towards the center by moving inward. Be careful that your hands or fingers do not get caught in the frame.

INSTRUCTIONS

Please read each step before you attempt to set up. Save these instructions for future reference.

How To Set Up

Note: First time attachment is required.
Top and frame are shipped unattached to avoid damage. A first time set up requires that fabric top be attached to the frame. This first-time will take longer than future set ups. Once top is permanently attached to frame, set up and take down are easily accomplished within seconds.

1. Place your frame in the center of area to be used. With partner on opposite side, grasp two outer legs, slightly lift off the ground, and step backwards, stopping at full arms length – approximately 1/2 its total size.

2. Gently unfold the fabric top and place it over the open frame.

3. Attach the fabric top to the frame by matching the quick attachment strips on the fabric top with the quick attachment strips on the frame. Pull the corners down fully. Push the strips firmly together at each corner.

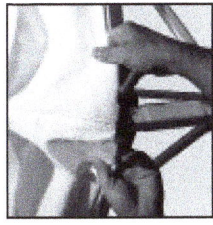

4. Grasp the bottom of the diamond shaped area of trusses on opposite sides. Lift up and step backwards until shelter is fully opened, being careful not to pinch fingers.

5. To engage the slider at each corner, first lift the fabric top off of the slider, then with one hand hold the top of the leg while pushing up on the slider with the other hand. The pull pin will engage the hole. Pull down the fabric top over the slider. Repeat on remaining three corners.

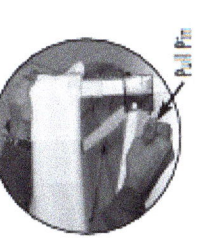

6. Lift the two adjacent outer legs and slide out the inner legs until the snap button locks into the hole in the outer leg. Repeat on the opposite legs – make sure to do two legs at a time.

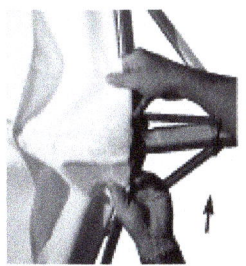

Note: Once top is permanently attached only perform steps 1, 4, 5 and 6 to set up.

How To Take Down

1. With a partner, slightly lift up two adjacent outer legs, depress snap button and telescope inner legs into outer legs. Repeat on the opposite legs - making sure to do two legs at a time.

2. Release the pull pin at each corner by first lifting fabric away from slider. With one hand push up on the truss near the pull pin, pull the pin out to release.

Pull Pin

3. Grasp the top of the diamond shape areas of trusses on opposite sides by "close" stickers. Lift the shelter up slightly and shake it while stepping towards your partner until the unit is 3/4 closed. With each partner grasping two outer legs, slowly push frame together to fully close it - Be careful not to pinch fingers. Store shelter in cover bag in upright position.

Setting Up Work Area

The best method is to be consistent and decide what works best for you when setting up your operation, by doing so you will save valuable time and energy. Many of the procedures outlined in this manual are how we operate our own detailing service and will help you to develop your own system. We recommend you develop a consistent system and stick with it, especially if you plan on operating a multiple crew.

We recommend you keep all of your tools, equipment, chemicals, and accessories as close to the car you are detailing as possible. You want to have everything you need at hand to keep yourself organized, which will help save you time. You may want to invest in a detailer's tool bag to hold your tool brushes, razor blades, business cards, towels, bottles, and more.

I have found that in my years of detailing vehicles that a one-on-one situation is more productive than having a whole team work on one vehicle. It is important to run a smooth and efficient operation based on the TQ PC motto **("Time-Quality-Pride-Consistency")**. As your experience increases you will experiment with different approaches which will help to speed up your production. When you start hiring on staff members remember to compliment every angle of operation with your employees and their abilities.

By hiring on employees you may want to consider having one member work on the inside as another member works on the outside of the car. In most cases, each member should finish roughly around the same time. Each employee should be consistent in their work and it's a good idea to double check each other to ensure quality work each and every time. Be sure to have each member switch positions to conduct a final inspection helping each other be consistent with their work.

You will find the excitement and appreciation of your customers is infectious pushing you to provide quality work in order to satisfy your customer every time.

Remember this is your detailing service and the pride of ownership will filter down to your employees and your customers, but it must first start with you.

Let's proceed on how to approach your customer's vehicle one-on-one and how to perform the services.

Customer Greeting

First impressions are very important and it's best to approach your customer with a helpful and positive

attitude. You want to ensure each customer feels special, so it's best to show enthusiasm and excitement when you're talking about their car. We highly suggest you treat your customer, as you would want to be treated. Think to yourself, what impresses you and makes you want to come back as a loyal customer? This will give a huge advantage over your competitors, as customer service is even more important in today's world. Remember, your customer has choices and can always go somewhere else. By treating your customer with respect, patience, and enthusiasm you create a loyal following. Always be kind when you review their car, after all an automobile is a big commitment and most of your clients will only expect the best for their pride and joy. Ensure you review the car with your customer and find out specifically what their needs are.

Some examples you may ask your customer:

- Do they have children or dogs? If this is the case, you may ask if they would be interested in your fabric protection program.

- Perhaps they have a brand new car. This would be a great opportunity to sell them your premium paint sealant.

- Find out the main use of their cars. Do they use it for business or only personal use?

- Do they prefer that glossy, oily look on their upholstery or the soft satin finish?

- What types of smells do they prefer? That natural leather smell or an air freshener scent. It is paramount that you have a good rapport with your customer.

Be sure to ask your customer where they would prefer you do the work. It's best that you are aware of obstacles and unforeseen issues upfront to help prevent having to move the vehicle during your detailing process.

Equipment

We recommend you use a GFI (Ground Fault Interrupter) for your safety and protection. The GFI is a device designed to protect people from electrical shock. The GFI will automatically open the protection circuit if there is a difference of more than 5 milliamps (.005 amps). The GFI has a six foot cord that can be used as an extension cord when placed between the machine and the outlet. We highly recommend purchasing the Ground Fault Interrupter since you will be working around water.

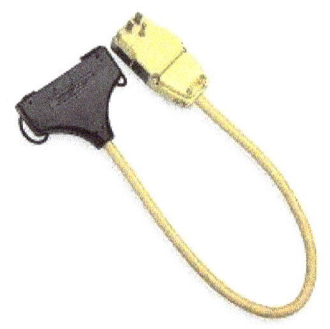

We suggest you also purchase a multiple plug power block, found at any local hardware store, to have the ability to plug in multiple machines at the same time. Note: We highly recommend you use your GFI should you plug into a home outlet. Many times, having too many pieces of equipment running at the same time could trip off a circuit breaker. Should you be operating out of a self-contained vehicle, using a generator, the procedures for setting up the GFI and multi plug are the same.

Accessories And Chemicals

Let's discuss setting up your work area. It's best practice to bring your work vehicle as close as possible to the vehicle being detailed. When detailing customer car's at the office, we suggest you contact the customer in advance to have them move their car to the far corner of the parking lot away from other cars. This will help to show good sense on

your part, should you ever be approached by the Property Manager of the building.

Be sure to have all your supplies close by and at hand to the vehicle as possible, by doing so you will save yourself valuable time. We recommend you purchase a detailer's pouch and keep it stocked with Q-Tips, Razor Blades, Toothbrushes, Towels, and a bottle or two of

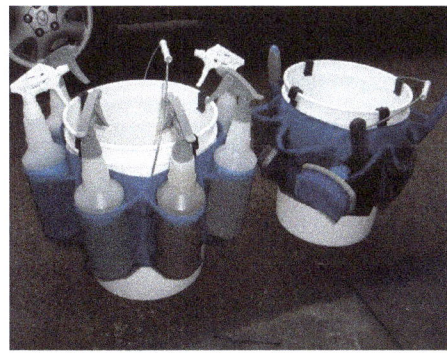

your cleaners. Ensure you dispose of any contaminated towels or bonnets that have fallen on the ground, since fine sand or grit particles could scratch the surface you are trying to clean. Have ample towels at hand for back-up should this happen. It's a good idea to carry a minimum of 6 towels or bonnets and 6 Micro Fiber Towels per vehicle. We suggest you clean your towels or bonnets at commercial Laundromats, due to the slight chemical odor, which could affect your regular clothes if washed in the same washing machine.

Car Set-Up

We recommend you locate the cleanest possible area to detail the vehicle. Asphalt and concrete provide the flattest area and drain much better than areas of grass or dirt. Be cautious of where the vehicle is placed during an engine cleaning or when you clean the wheels. Acids and solvents are very strong cleaners and could permanently stain a concrete driveway.

With this said, we suggest you park the vehicle out on the street. It is best practice to rinse your work area down thoroughly after you have completed the detail.

In a separate box or container place all the customers' belongings left in the vehicle, making a mental note where they came from. You always want to ensure you replace anything removed to the same position they were found. Put these items aside, or in your work vehicle, so they will not be damaged or stepped on. Take a moment to observe the original positions of the control knobs on the dash; seat and seat positions; radio volume control, emergency or road tools in the trunk of the car, so that these can be put back in place as they were. Should the car have an antenna, check to see if it can be lowered by turning the ignition key on, then switching the radio volume knob to the off position. Lower manual antennas carefully to help avoid snapping it off during your detailing. In the Finishing Touches Section, we will cover the procedure for properly detailing the antenna.

Now remove the floor mats and place them away from the car, on a clean surface, to be scrubbed later. Remove all debris on the floor and empty out all the ashtrays into a trash bag. Once all obstacles have been cleared from the car it is time to prep the car for detailing.

Special Notes Page

Section 3

Glossary Of Auto Detailing Terms

Detailing Terms*1 30

Section 3

Fallout

OSHA

Blushing

Glaze

Auto Detailing Terms

Sealer

P.S.I.

Clear Coat

Wax

Teflon

Adhesion

Dwelt Time

RPM

Detailing Terms*1

Abrasive - Natural or synthetic particles (grit or media) found in polishes or compounds which cut the paint surface to remove imperfections.

ACGIH - American Conference of Government Industrial Hygienists.

Acid - A substance below 7 on a pH scale. Cleaning products containing acids must be used with care on certain surfaces and in some cases should not be used at all.

Acid Rain - Rain contaminated with acidic compounds from industrial pollution. May cause damage to automotive finishes and glass.

Adhesion - How well a product bonds to the surface to which it is applied.

Alkaline-Alkalis - Substances above 7 on a pH scale classified as basic or caustic. Caustic compounds are used in cleaning products such as soap. Cleaning products containing alkalis must be used with care on certain surfaces and in some area it should not be used.

Appearance Reconditioning - The cosmetic restoration of a vehicle to a like new condition.

Base Coat - The foundation layer in the basecoat/clearcoat automotive finishes comprised of a layer of dense pigment applied over primer coat.

Bath Tubber - A slang term used to refer to a manufacturer who mixes his own chemical products in large drums or 'bath tubs', usually of low price and poor quality.

Biodegradable - Capable of being broken down into safe, stable sub-compounds by natural forces.

Blushing - Paint finish turns milky or cloudy shortly after polishing new paint. Solvents have not finished evaporating from the paint. Wait 30 days to rebuff.

Body Shop Safe - A generic term used to refer to products for the body shops which contain no silicone or components that interfere with the painting system.

---

1 *Information obtained from Professional Detailing Association.

Buffer - A piece of equipment used by skillful technicians to apply products to a vehicle. Reduces the time spent, and improves the quality of work performed.

Buffer Marks - Circular marks which remain in the paint when abrasive cleaners or compounds are used. Comprised of unevenly distributed oils and or scratches, also called swirls and wheel marks.

Buffing Compound - A strong cleaning substance which may contain grit designed to remove severe oxidation or other major finish imperfections from painted surfaces. Not all buffing compounds are compatible with all paint finishes (such as clear-coats) and must be used carefully or not at all.

Burn - Damage to a surface by fire. (Interiors) Damage to paint surface by a polisher, i.e., to unintentionally scar or remove paint from a vehicle.

Burnish - Polishing with a tool to make the surface smooth or glossy by friction; increases distinctness of image by smoothing the paint.

CAS No. - Chemical Abstracts Services registration number.

Chemicals - A term to categorize a group of products, i.e., Polishing Chemicals, Chemical Cleaners, Cleaning Chemicals.

Citrus - A cleaning agent of similar chemical composition to oranges and lemons (d-Limonene). Also a fragrance added to cleaners or air fresheners.

Cleaner/Glaze - A product which removes some minor finish imperfections and gives a protective gloss or shine to the paint surface.

Cleaner/Polish - A product which removes some minor finish imperfections, especially those caused by compounding. Contains little or no wax or sealers.

Cleaner/Wax - A product which removes light to medium oxidation and scratches from the paint surface. Leaves a protective shine.

Clear Coat - A thin transparent layer of paint (may be enamel or lacquer based) applied over a pigmented layer of paint (basecoat) to provide a deep, rich, shiny finish. Highly abrasive waxes, polishes, and compounds are not compatible with clear coat.

Combustible Liquid - Any liquid having a flashpoint at or above 100 deg. F.

Compound Scratches/Swirls - Small visible scratches left after compounding an automotive finish. May be removed with a cleaner/polish.

Concentrate - A product that requires thinning with an appropriate reducer, water, solvent, thinner, etc.

Conventional Paint - More traditional ways of finishing automotive surfaces. Generally recognized as lacquered, acrylic, enamel, and acrylic enamel paint finishes.

Co-Polymer - A chemical compound of two polymers which are compatible and stable when joined.

Cosmoline - A heavy grade petroleum by-product or paraffin applied to automobile exteriors as a protective coating during transit. Requires special chemicals and procedures to be removed.

Checking - Cracking - Crazing - Paint looks like shattered glass. Paint dries out and loses its elasticity. Repeated extreme temperatures cause the paint to expand and contract and pulls the paint apart.

Cutting Pad - Most often a natural wool pad with fiber strands that resemble shag carpet. May also be coarse foam pads.

D.A. Polisher/Sander - Duel Action rotates with a double elliptical movement.

D.O.T. - Department of Transportation. Government agency which regulates the transport of goods.

Degradable - Capable of being broken down by natural forces. Resulting products may not necessarily be safe or stable.

Detailing - To clean item by item each minor part of a vehicle to the completeness of the work.

Detergents - Cleaning products for auto interiors and exteriors with different chemical formulations as the active cleaning agent. Differentiated by thickness and cleaning ability.

Dilute - To reduce by thinning with appropriate reducer; water, solvent, thinner, etc., in accordance with directions.

Dressed/Dressing - The application of a coating applied to vinyl, leather, plastic, and rubber to protect or make shiny.

Durability - The power of long term resistance to decay or change.

Dwell Time - A time period in which a product is encouraged to remain in an active state during application. During cleaning a product may be required to sit or dwell for several minutes before being rinsed.

E.P.A. - Environmental Protection Agency. Government body which helps protect the environment. Has jurisdiction over the manufacturer through the end user of a product.

Emollient - A substance designed to add moisture or increase softness. Found in hand cleaners or leather and vinyl conditioners.

Emulsion - The suspension of a solid or liquid within another solution preventing it from settling to the surface.

Enamel Paint - Type of O.E.M. paint used for many years. (Acrylic enamel.)

Exposure - Having been subjected to a hazardous chemical through any route of entry. (Inhalation, ingestion, skin contact or absorption.)

Extractor - A machine used to clean carpets and cloth seats. Applies cleaning solution in fan spray and removes moisture and dirt with vacuum action.

Fabric Protector - A product applied to fabric or cloth seats and carpets. Repels moisture and food soils. Allows textiles to be cleaned easier. There are resin and silicone types.

Fallout - Contamination which settles out of the air onto automotive finishes and imbeds itself into the paint, such as industrial stack fallout, air craft fuel and volcanic ash.

Finishing Pad - A combed wool pad normally yellow in color. Also soft foam pad normally white or black in color.

Fish Eye - Complications which occur during repainting. Whereas paint is repelled from a spot because grease, oil, or silicone is present on the paint surface.

Flammable Liquid - A chemical that has a flash point below 100 deg. F.

Flash Off - Dwell time for solvent to evaporate from the paint surface.

Flash Point - The temperature at which a product, when heated, will release a combustible vapor.

Foam Pad - A round foam disk made of various designs and textures for polishing vehicles.

Glaze - A product when applied with a polisher produces a glossy appearance by burnishing and coating the paint surface. Used by hand to protect the surface and hide wheel marks.

H.M.I.S. - Hazardous Material Identification System. A system of numbers, symbols, and letters which gives information about health, flammability, reactivity, and personal protection for chemicals and products.

Hazardous Chemicals - Products or chemical components that may pose a health risk to the user if used improperly or if proper safety equipment is not used. READ MSDS for each product you use. Warnings are normally written as if hazardous product were at 100% solution.

Haze - State where a product is dry on the surface and appears dull or milky. A dull film of imbedded dirt or oxidation on the paint surface.

Hi Tech Paints - Clearcoat and urethane paint finishes.

IHRC - International Agency for Research of Cancer.

IDLH - Immediately Dangerous to Life or Health.

Industrial Fallout - Airborne pollutants from heavy industry or railroads which settle onto automotive surfaces and become embedded in the finish. Gradually the particles oxidize and appear as dark specks in the paint. Requires special products and procedures to be removed.

Lacquer Thinner - A solvent combination used to thin lacquer or acrylic paints.

MSDS - Material Safety Data Sheet. Standardized sheet which systematically describes a product and its chemical components. Distributors are to provide customers with a MSDS sheet for every product they buy. Distributors should also have a full set of MSDS sheets on their truck.

Metallic - A type of automotive finish which produces a glittery or metal looking appearance.

Metering System - A system which mixes chemicals with water as it uses them, e.g., automatic or coin operated car washes.

Micro Fiber Towels - Microfiber is a man-made material that combines two fibers, polyester and polyamide. The polyester gives the material strength and durability, the polyamide allows the fabric to be tremendously absorbent and quick drying.

Mottling - Paint color appears streaked, with light and dark areas. Cause, heavier film thickness in some areas than others. Excessive wetting of some areas when painted. Uneven disbursement of metallics in the paint.

Multiple Step Process - When three or more polishing steps are required to properly process the painted surfaces of the vehicle. Example; overspray on paint may require sanding, compounding, polishing, and sealing.

OSHA - Occupational Safety and Health Administration. Government agency which sets standards for worker's safety.

Oil - Viscous liquids of natural plant and animal oils which are mixtures of terpenes and simple esters or mineral oils which are mixtures of hydrocarbons, used in paint and auto polishes.

One Step - Polishing a vehicle with one product that both cleans and seals at the same time. Sometimes uses as a short cut to speed production of dealer's vehicles.

Orange Peel - The nubbly rough appearance of paint; looks much like the texture of an orange skin; surface lacks clarity of reflected image. Caused by paint being applied too dry, resulting in poor flow out.

Orbital Buffer - A mechanical buffer with a pad that travels ellipse's instead of rotating on a fixed axis. Used when waxing to simulate the movement of the human hand.

Original Finish - The paint finish applied by the manufacturer.

Overspray - Substance such as paint mist that settles out of the air onto automobile surface appearing as tiny speckles.

Oxidation - Chemical substances within an automotive finish that collect and bond with oxygen molecules causing the paint to become dry, dull, and lifeless. Condition may be remedied by using suitable polishing materials.

PDA - Professional Detailing Association formed for the betterment of the Auto Detailing Industry.

Pad Washer - A mechanical device used to remove accumulations of compounds and cleaners from buffing pads. Uses water spray and spur action while the pad is on the buffer.

Paint Film Thickness - The amount of paint film on the vehicle. Measured in millimeters.

Paint Cleaner - Product used to remove oxidation and light surface imperfection from the paint surface.

Paint Sealer - A product applied to a clean surface to protect the paint. Durability and degree of gloss will vary.

Paint Burn - To unintentionally scar or remove paint from a vehicle with a polisher.

PEL - Permissible Exposure Limit.

PH Scale - A scale used to determine the nature of water soluble chemicals.

Petroleum Solvents - Liquids derived from crude oil through the refining process.

Polish/Polishing - A product normally applied by machine polisher to produce a smooth, bright, and glossy paint surface. May remove minor surface imperfections and light to medium oxidation. Normally contains no durable coating material. Term is often used to describe the action of using a machine to buff or wheel a vehicle.

Polisher - A piece of equipment used by skilled technicians to apply products to the painted surface of a vehicle. Typically turn at 1000 to 3000 R.P.M.

Polishing Pad - A wool or foam covered disk that attaches to a machine polisher or buffer, for application, and removal of cleaner and sealers on the painted surfaces.

Polymer - A naturally occurring or synthetic substance consisting of large molecules formed by smaller molecules of the same substance with a definite arrangement. Used in the production of durable waxes and polishes.

Polyurethane - A catalyst type of paint known for exceptional durability.

Pressure Washer - A mechanical device that steps up city water pressure 50-65 P.S.I. anywhere from 500 to over 1200 P.S.I. A system used to clean surfaces with cleaning solutions under pressure.

Professional - A person fully educated, trained, and skilled in all aspects of his profession.

Pre-Wash - First step in preparing a vehicle for detailing.

Procedure/Processing - To put through the steps of a prescribed method of application techniques.

Primer - Material applied to the surface to seal, fill scratches, and improve adhesion of paint.

P.S.I. - Pounds Per Square Inch - a measure of air and water pressure.

Quality - Degree of excellence or relative goodness of work performed.

RPM - Revolutions Per Minute, number of complete turns made in one minute.

Rail Dust - Small metallic particles attributed to railroads which settle onto automotive surfaces and become embedded in the finish. Gradually, the particles oxidize and appear as dark speckles in the paint. Requires special products and procedures to be removed. Also known as industrial fallout.

Resin - A synthetic or naturally occurring polymer.

Respiratory Distress - A physical condition caused by inhaling toxic vapors characterized by shortness of breath, inability to breath, dizziness, and sometimes unconsciousness. This condition requires immediate medical attention.

Sealer/Sealant - A protective product applied by hand or machine to automotive paint finishes. Normally contain silicones to maximize attention.

Shine - To brighten or increase luster by polishing. Highly reflective gloss.

Silicate - A hard glossy compound; usually some form of the dioxide of silicone (Si 02) used in waxes, polishes, and dressings.

Silicone - Any group of polymerized semi-inorganic compounds comprised of silicone items, oxygen and possibly organic compounds. Characterized by high resistance to heat and water. Silicone can create complications during repainting in body shops. Non-silicone products are preferable for body shop applications.

Solvent - A substance, usually liquid that dissolves or can dissolve another substance.

Spur - A small, hand held tool with a spoke wheel used to clean a buffing pad of accumulation of wax or polish.

STEL - Short Term Exposure Limit.

Surfactant - A compound which helps lift substances from a surface so they may be removed. Usually found in cleaners to improve rinsing.

Swirls - Circular scratch marks in the paint surface caused by abrasive buffing products, heavily contaminated polishing pad or poor buffing technique.

TCC - Tagliabue Closed Cup - Test used to determine flammability of a product.

Technician - A person skilled and knowledgeable of the duties he is to perform.

Teflon - Nonstick coating applied to cooking pans at over 700 degrees F. Teflon powder may be in used in polishes, waxes, and sealers as a leveler to ease application and removal of excess material.

Throw off - Product which is thrown from the surface or tool due to centrifugal force. For buffing this appears as tiny speckles of product on other surfaces. Also used when discussing lubricants for spinning or turning machinery.

TLV - Threshold Limit Value.

Transit Coating - A protective coating applied to auto exteriors prior to transportation to prevent damage to the exterior surfaces.

TWA - Time Weighted Average.

Two Step - A term to describe the process of cleaning or polishing the paint surface followed by a separate finishing application of a durable coating of wax or sealer.

Ultra-Violet Ray - A component of ordinary light which cannot be seen by the human eye. Deteriorates automobile surfaces by causing fading, cracking, peeling, and discoloration. Some products contain ingredients that guard against UV damage.

Urethane Paint - A catalyst activated paint known for exceptional durability.

Wash Mitt - A large, soft pouch worn on the hand used to wash automobile surfaces.

Water Based - A compound whose primary liquid ingredient is water.

Water Soluble - Characterized by the ability to mix completely in or with water.

Wax - A natural or synthetic that contains little or no silicone. May be in paste or liquid form for application by hand or polisher.

Weathering - The change or failure in paint caused by exposure to weather.

Wet Sanding - A procedure of simultaneously sanding and rinsing an automotive finish to remove imperfections. Regarded as complicated and should only be attempted by professionals.

Wheel Marks - Circular scratch marks in the paint surface. Also called buffer marks or swirls

Special Notes Page

Section 4

Chemical Information

Cleaning And Polishing Chemicals 42

**Be Professional Always Use
The Highest Grade Products** 43

Chemical Reference Guide 45

Cleaning And Polishing Chemicals

It is very important to be aware of all the safety concerns when using chemicals. Be aware of all possible hazards to yourself, employees, and the environment. Each chemical should be clearly identified and understood to help ensure complete safety.

Agencies like the Environmental Protection Agency (EPA) and the Occupational Safety and Health Agency (OSHA), have been put into place to study the cause and effects of today's chemicals. There are over a half a million chemicals used in the work place nationwide causing a growing concern in the process of manufacturing or distributing these chemicals.

OSHA standards were put into effect in every company and individual business that use hazardous materials in the work place. These laws were put into place to keep everyone safe and healthy on the job. It's your responsibility to ensure anyone that works for you is made aware of any hazardous materials and taught how to protect themselves should they be exposed.

A hazardous material is defined as; any material which, because of its quantity, concentration, physical or chemical characteristics, poses a threat to human health or the safety of the environment. Even dishwasher soap can be dangerous. To get more information on chemicals and methods of application contact your local Hazardous Materials Office. These types of agencies can be located by contacting your Fire Department or County Hazardous Waste Department.

Any company offering a complete detailing service will generally use these products that fall under OSHA regulations. For example: Acid Wheel Cleaners, Engine Degreasers, Tar, and Gum Removers, just to name a few examples of products that could be harmful to employees if not properly used or stored.

In order to avoid any possibility of exposure or accidents we highly recommend you identify your products using the Material Safety Data Sheets (MSDS) provided by your chemical supplier. Ensure you study these information sheets and don't forget to review them with your employees. It is everyone's obligation to be concerned about safety.

Be Professional Always Use The Highest Grade Products

With today's chemical breakthroughs, mankind is finding easier and more timely ways to accomplish detailing tasks. There are hundreds of manufacturers, wholesalers, and distributors that offer a variety of products. Please refer to the reference guide in the back if this manual for a list of several suppliers where you can purchase your chemicals.

Let's discuss the differences and why all chemicals are not the same. A study done by E. L. Nemous DuPont Co. revealed that when a typical low grade Carnuba wax (over-the-counter type), was exposed to temperatures of 73 degrees and higher, these products melt or break down at a rate of 1 1/2% per day. Which means that if you were to apply wax to the surface of a car, under normal circumstances, the wax job will last approximately 20 days using these types of products.

Many automotive detailing products are made up of a water base. The difference in the durability is actually caused by the active ingredients combined with the water. Another inert (non-active ingredient) that is combined with water is a certain type of food coloring. Another base product, used in inferior wax products, is beeswax which is an extremely soft material that looks shiny when applied, but breaks down at a highly rapid rate. A superior type of wax has no beeswax but rather contains a high ratio of carnauba wax (the hardest wax known to mankind).

Be aware that there are hundreds of suppliers and manufacturers, some better than others and always follow the recommended use for each product. We recommend starting out detailing your own vehicle and getting familiar with the variety of products and their potential hazards if used improperly.

For example: Certain glue and tar removal products on the market are fast drying because of the higher concentration of dissolving solvents. These may be too strong for some factory paint finishes. It's best to obtain products that are silicone based from a professional distributor designed to be safe for all types of paint finishes both factory and after factory paint.

Be aware that most vinyl conditioners are made up of either a petroleum or silicone base and can cause discoloration and premature disintegration of the materials being treated, such as some over-the-counter products.

A good Vinyl Conditioner is made up of a high ratio of silicone oil which is not harmful to leather, vinyl or rubber. Silicone is the best conditioning oil for this type of purpose.

Keep in mind that silicone type products can either be your adversary or your enemy; dependent on its use. Silicone is a very complex oil used for both conditioning, adding depth, and/or gloss within the paint. A high ratio of silicone used in a vinyl dressing makes for an excellent conditioner, however too high a ratio used in a wax product can turn into a messy and difficult situation to remove.

Due to the fact that there is a complex world of chemicals, we suggest you use the proper grades and balances. There is a huge difference between products found over the counter versus a professional line of products. Over the years we have found that there is no one manufacturer that makes the best of everything.

It is our fundamental belief to give your customer first rate quality every time. When you substitute quality to save a few dollars, you cheat yourself and your customer losing them - **FOR GOOD!** You will build a foundation for success by repeat customers. Ensure you treat them well.

In today's high overhead, smart operators research every way to save money. One easy way to significantly save is to order your liquid products in 4 gallon lots. By doing so you can save from $4.00 to $4.50 per gallon. That is a 22% savings per gallon as opposed to paying in 1 gallon lots. Where else can you earn 22% on your money legally? Another thing to remember is that UPS charges less for one case weight of 39 lbs. than it does for 4 individual cartons weighing in at 9 to 10 lbs. each. When you add up the savings it makes buying by the case the only smart way to go.

Chemical Reference Guide

The knowledge and use of cleansers and polishes are an important fundamental in establishing your service as more than just another auto detailing company. Below, you will see how we have covered each of the unique detailing formulas you will likely use as well as the best way to apply each one. These are general guidelines. Always use manufacturers recommended directions.

PETROLEUM DISTILLATES - What is a petroleum distillate? Simply put it is a solvent based product found in the petrochemical family. Petroleum distillates are used in connection with polishes and waxes alike. It is used as a carrier to keep waxes and polishes in a ready to use soluble state. Once a distillate product is applied to a painted surface, the chemical evaporates through oxygenation leaving the product polish or wax to cure and dry on the surface.

ALL PURPOSE CLEANER is a concentrated multi-phase cleaner for removal of grease, dirt, insect stains, carbon, stains from metal, leather, and vinyl. All-purpose cleaner cleans vinyl tops and white walls. All-purpose cleaner contains a powerful foaming cleaning agent. Apply this product with a spray bottle applicator and a clean soft micro fiber towel for interiors or with a carpet brush or wire wheel brush for tires.

ALUMINUM CHROME POLISH cleans wheels, polishes, beautifies, and protects mag wheels, aluminum and chrome. Apply this product by hand, using a soft clean micro fiber towel or wax pad and a squeeze dispenser bottle.

CAR WASH SHAMPOO is a pH balanced soap concentrate and a blend of surface active ingredients, detergents, water softeners, and soil suspending agents. It removes road film and leaves a clear bright surface. Car wash shampoo is concentrated for economy and is instantly soluble with water. Apply car wash shampoo by mixing in one once of product into a full wash bucket. When using a pressure washer with soap nozzle, mix two ounces of product per gallon of water. You may also apply soap directly to a wash mitt if preferred.

CARNUABA CREME WAX is made from the Brazilian carnauba plant. Using a special blend of the best grade of carnauba and polymers will make for a hard durable finish. Its creamy consistency makes application smooth and easy. Carnauba creme wax is effective on all paint finishes including clear coat finishes and is used as a final protectant sealer. Carnauba creme wax may be applied by hand or with your orbital polisher using a squeeze dispenser bottle. Carnauba creme wax should be used on cool-to-the-touch surface. Be sure to apply the product in small 3 x 3 foot sections. Allow the product to cure for approximately 2 - 5 minutes before wiping it off with your micro fiber towel or buffer pad.

CARPET AND UPHOLSTERY SHAMPOO is a semi-dry sudsing foam shampoo formula concentrate. It is safe for both manmade and natural fibers; it contains a blend of sophisticated synthetic, detergents, and brightening agents. Carpet and upholstery shampoo is used on rugs, floor mats, headliners, and door panels. Mix this concentrated product in a bucket of water and scrub upholstery or carpet with cleaning tool or carpet brush. **Caution: This product is not meant for use in extractor type machines as it has very high foaming properties.**

CLAY BAR is a revolutionary product for removing surface paint overspray, tree sap, rough surface contaminants and industrial fallout easily and safely. This incredible product makes old methods of using heavy abrasive compounding or the use of harsh solvents obsolete. Clay bars are sold in block form. Simply tear off a small piece and flatten it like a pancake, wet the surface with the recommended liquid surface spray or soapy water and agitate back and forth until surface is smooth. Clay bars are safe for all types of paint finishes.

CLEAN AIR FRAGRANCE leaves a "clean interior air scent". It is a multi-phase odor neutralizer for control of organic malodors. Its complex formula contains a wider range of effective deodorization than traditional single dimension products. The clean car fragrance lasts for days, leaving a pleasant lingering air freshening scent. Apply this product by misting the vehicle with a spray bottle applicator.

COMPOUND (MILD CUT) contains a special blend of solvents, wetting agents, non-abrasive cleaners, detergents, and emulsifiers. It easily removes wax buildup, hairline polishing scratches, and paint blemishes. Mild cut compound provides a clean, smooth surface for subsequent polishing or paint sealant applications. Apply it by hand or with your orbital polisher. Apply this product with a squeeze dispenser bottle and **do not apply on hot surfaces.** Work the product into a 3 x 3 foot section and allow the product to dry to a light haze, about 1 to 2 minutes. Then buff off the residue before going on to the next section of the vehicle.

COMPOUND (MEDIUM CUT) is a mildly abrasive liquid cleaner that removes heavy oxidation and dead paint. It clears faded finishes and is a good paint leveler. Medium cut compound is a very mild compound and may leave hairline polishing scratches. It is ideal for all colors - especially on metallic finishes and dark colors because it won't stain or discolor. Apply this product by hand or with your orbital polisher using a squeeze dispenser bottle. **Do not apply this product on hot surfaces**. Work the product into a 3 x 3 foot section and allow it to cure to a light haze before buffing it off.

COMPOUND (HEAVY CUT) is designed to prepare for polishing older vehicles whose finish is badly weathered and oxidized. It contains a special blend of heavy abrasives, emulsifiers, and agents. Heavy cut compound, although tough, is gentle enough to bring back the gloss to an old, dull finish. **Do not apply this product in the direct sunlight or on freshly painted surfaces**. Apply heavy cut compound by hand or with your orbital polisher. Follow up by removing fine polishing scratches using the medium, then mild cut compounds using a squeeze dispenser bottle, work this product into a 3 x 3 foot section and allow the product to cure to a light haze before buffing it off.

ENGINE DEGREASER – Water Based is an effective nonflammable and non-solvent degreaser which eliminates the hazards of combustible solvent based cleaners. It removes oil, grease, dirt, and road grime from all engine compartments. It is safe on all painted surfaces and rubber hoses. Certain engine degreasers that contain citrus ingredients can also be used to clean automotive interiors. Apply this product with a spray bottle applicator.

FABRIC GUARD provides protection for interior fabric, upholstery, and velour. It prevents permanent staining due to spills from coffee, soda, milk, and other liquids. Fabric guard contains the active ingredient, DuPont Teflon protector. Apply this product with a sure shot spray applicator or pressurized sprayer and allow approximately 2 hours drying time.

FENDERWELL DRESSING is a non-flammable, non-solvent chassis coating formulated to give automobiles and trucks the detailed look right down to the fenderwells, undercarriage, and chassis. Simply pre-clean areas to be treated and let the area completely dry. Apply Fenderwell dressing with a spray bottle over entire surface to be covered for a showroom protective finish. Fenderwell dressing will restore the color and beauty of all the surface blemishes and hard to remove left over dirt marks and abrasions normally ignored under the vehicle.

GLASS AND CHROME POLISH a thick liquid that restores the new shine and look to chrome and glass surfaces and will not streak. Glass and chrome polish works especially well on heavily smoke stained windows. Apply this product by hand with a soft clean micro fiber towel or applicator pad and a squeeze dispenser bottle.

GLASS CLEANER is an economical blue glass cleaner ready for fast cleanup. It dissolves and removes film, smudges, bugs, and cleans glass and chrome to sparkling shine. Apply the product with a spray bottle and a soft clean micro fiber towel. Also check out glass cleaner in aerosol cans.

LEATHER CONDITIONER is scientifically formulated to preserve the strength, beauty, and supple feel of leather - old and new. Its formulated pH balanced conditioner is specifically designed to protect and enhance fine leather interiors. It conditions and replenishes lost oils in leather, lubricating it for pliability and high luster. Apply this product by hand with a squeeze dispenser bottle using a soft clean micro fiber towel or applicator pad. After 30 minutes, buff to a shine with a separate dry micro fiber towel.

LIQUID SPEED WAX is a special blend of solvents, polymers, and silicones. It is a quick and easily applied sealant and the answer for that "get the new car ready" for any automotive dealership and showroom car. Liquid speed wax also works great as a swirl remover for removing left over glaze on the car as well as a lubricant for your clay bar application. Apply this product by hand or with your orbital polisher, using a squeeze dispenser bottle. This may be used in direct sunlight with no adverse effects.

MACHINE EXTRACTOR CLEANER is a liquid or powder formula mixed in the extractor machine for deep cleaning of interior carpets and upholstery. For carpets cleaned previously with shampoo or spray foam, use an anti-foam solution to prevent suds from building-up in the vacuum recovery tank.

ONE STEP CLEANER WAX is uniquely formulated with carnuaba and micro fine clay powders to clean and wax all domestic and foreign car finishes in one easy step. It is especially formulated for light to medium color cars and removes stubborn stains such as water spots, road tar, dirt stains, bird droppings, and more. One step cleaner wax may be applied by hand or with your orbital polisher using a squeeze dispenser bottle. It may be used in direct sunlight with no adverse effects.

POLYMER PAINT SEALANT is formulated for long term protection. It is a polymer based sealer and polishing agent. Polymer fuses with paint or fiberglass to form a diamond hard shield and will outlast ordinary wax or other typical sealants. This product is ideal for all vehicle colors. Apply polymer by hand or with your orbital polisher using a squeeze dispenser bottle and <u>do not apply on a hot surface</u>, work the product into a 3 x 3 foot section. Allow it to cure for approximately 2 - 3 minutes before buffing it off.

PREP SOLVE is a special blend of solvents and silicones that quickly dissolves road tar, grease, glue, gum, window stickers, road oil, and cosmolene. It prepares the surface for excellent paint adhesion and polishing. Prep Solve also removes grease from door jambs and left over residue from bumper and window stickers. Apply this product with a spray bottle applicator and a clean micro fiber towel.

SOLVENT TIRE DRESSING is a solvent-based dressing designed to give old rubber a new look formulated as a long-lasting tire and bumper dressing. Liquid rubber dressing is ideal for removing old waxy residue from rubber trim and bumpers. For bumpers and trim, apply with a lint-free micro firer towel or applicator pad and allow the product to air dry. Wipe off excess as needed. **Caution: Liquid rubber dressing is solvent-based and must not be used on the interior of the vehicle or as an engine dressing.**

STONER TRIM SHINE conveniently restores the shine and color back to dull or faded rubber, vinyl, plastic, and other surfaces, quickly shines and brightens tires, bumpers, exterior trim, dashboards, gearshift boots, vents, hoses, side door panels, tops, and other interior and exterior surfaces. This will bring back a like-new, low luster showroom finish. It hides wax marks and old white hazing on dark automotive trim. Easy to use and saves you time. Simply spray on - no wiping or rubbing needed just buff off excess if used on interior dash.

TRAFFIC LANE CLEANER is a mild cleaner for all color fast fabrics and sensitive leathers. It is used as a pre-cleaner or spot remover before shampooing or conditioning leather. Traffic lane cleaner does not contain butyl; therefore, it leaves no foamy residue.

Apply this product with a spray bottle applicator and a soft clean towel or with your carpet and upholstery brush.

VINYL PROTECTANT is a water based emulsion of silicone fluids and wetting agents designed to impart a durable, glossy, detergent resistant protective film to vinyl surfaces, leather interiors, vinyl tops, tires, engine hoses, and rubber bumpers. It enriches colors and returns a natural gloss finish to old weathered surfaces. Apply this product with a spray bottle applicator and a clean micro fiber towel or applicator pad.

WHEEL AND MAG CLEANER is a specially formulated acid based cleaner for wire wheels. It removes surface rust on chrome plated finishes, metal, and is an excellent remover of brake dust build-up. It is <u>**not**</u> intended for use on aluminum, anodized wheels, or painted wheels. <u>**Caution:**</u> **this product is extremely caustic; always wear protective goggles, gloves and a face shield.** Apply this product with a spray bottle applicator, allowing product to dwell for approximately 30 seconds to 1 minute before rinsing off.

Special Notes Page

Section 5

Equipment And Maintenance Information

Maintenance	52
Orbital Polisher	52
Safety Instructions	53
Other Orbital Polisher Options	54
Maintenance Instructions	54
Fabric Guard Applicator	55
The Immersion Heater	55
Carpet And Upholstery Extractor	57
Operating Instructions	58
Cleaning Process And Procedures	59
Cleaning Carpets And Upholstery	59
Cleaning Methods	59
Highlights To Remember:	60
Care And Maintenance	61
Detailer's Vacuum	61
Vacuum Care And Maintenance	62
Gas And Electric Pressure Washers	63
Safety Precautions	63
Care Of Your Equipment	64
Setting Up	65
How To Clean	66
Water Tank	67
Safeguards And General Safety Instructions	68
Electric Pressure Washers	69
Important Freeze Protection	70

Maintenance

You will realize that by using only the best equipment in the industry, you will have an advantage over your competitors. After all, a craftsman is as good as his tools. Keep in mind that each piece of equipment is designed to save you time. And as we all know, "Time is Money".

Within this manual, we have provided you with many resources, techniques, and equipment examples to bring you confidence in your abilities to perform professional work with maximum efficiency. We will also go into more detail in the following pages on how to maintain your equipment.

Orbital Polisher

The Gem Orbital Polishing Machine is virtually maintenance free. Many of the features are:

- A tough cast aluminum housing
- Has a strong ball bearing motor
- There are no gears to grind or strip
- Or any armatures winding and burning out
- As well as no carbon brushes
- It has a removable shaft system that buffs compounds and scrubs.

This Polisher has been proven to not leave swirls and gouges nor will it burn or mar delicate surfaces. The orbital action buffs, polishes, and sands with a human touch, but hundreds of times faster. It is completely stable allowing complete operator control. In contrast high speed rotary polishers can gouge and leave unsightly swirl marks.

This Polisher is perfect for use with autos, vans, campers, aircraft, trucks, boats, fiberglass molds, and even furniture. The orbital action and buffing pad will not create damaging heat regardless of the pressure applied. Due to the 11" polishing pad surface, it cuts your detailing work in half compared to work done by the hand polishing method.

There is only one accessory needed for the Gem Orbital Polisher, and those are the Orbital Bonnets. Ensure you use clean Bonnets every time when polishing the vehicle. Discard any damaged Bonnets with holes or heavily absorbed materials that could scratch the paint surface. Most Bonnets can be reused for roughly 200 washings.

Safety Instructions

1. Remove Bonnet from the drive pad after each use to allow the drive pad to dry out.

2. You can also turn Bonnets inside out to use the other clean side, should it get too dirty, instead of using another clean Bonnet.

3. We recommend you wash your Bonnets in cold water with a small amount of detergent setting it to a short wash cycle. Your Bonnets can wear out by over washing much faster than waxing or polishing. Dry your Bonnets in a dryer set at medium heat until dry or wring them out and hang dry.

4. By using too much pressure on the Orbital Polisher you will slow down the orbiting oscillating motion which can affect the quality of your work. Also, excess pressure can overwork and overheat the motor causing it to burn out.

5. Always store the Orbital Polisher with the drive pad face up.

* * * * * * * * **CAUTION** * * * * * * * * *

Be sure to eyeball the polisher for any Bonnet threads or material that may become entwined around the motor shaft. Any build-up that goes unchecked will overload the motor causing damage to the armature, VOIDING THE MAUNUFACTURER'S WARRANTY.

6. To protect the operator from electrical shock, we suggest you use an electrical ground fault interrupter. We recommend you use only the three prong grounding plugs and three hole receptacle. For 50 feet we recommend a 16 gauge wire, and 14 gauge wire extension cord for 100 to 200 feet.

7. Ensure you keep your cord away from heat, sharp edges, and overloads.

8. When changing accessories, (i.e., Bonnets) or new Drive Pads we highly suggest you disconnect the Polisher first to prevent any injuries.

9. By maintaining a good flat drive pad edge and keeping your Polisher clean will ensure a better performing machine that will last longer.

Other Orbital Polisher Options

There are a variety of (DA) Dual Action orbital polishers on the market. The procedures and safety instructions are very similar. The differences are:

1. They are lighter in weight than the Gem polisher.

2. They operate using a foam sponge type of polishing pad for applying wax or sealants and use microfiber bonnets for removal of these products.

Maintenance Instructions

1. Be sure the Polisher is turned off and unplugged before you inspect it or perform maintenance. Keep in mind that the motor is only made for a 115 voltage outlet. If for some reason the unit stops operating, we suggest you check for a blown circuit breaker and ensure the unit is properly plugged in. The Orbital Polisher requires no additional lubrication or maintenance.

2. The only necessary replacement will be the Polishing Pad. When the edges are worn to the pad becoming overly rounded, replace it. Otherwise the orbital polisher is maintenance free. Supplied in the Resource section in the back of this manual you will find the suppliers that carry all three types of orbital polishers. Our favorites are the Portor Cable and Cyclo orbital polishing machines.

Fabric Guard Applicator

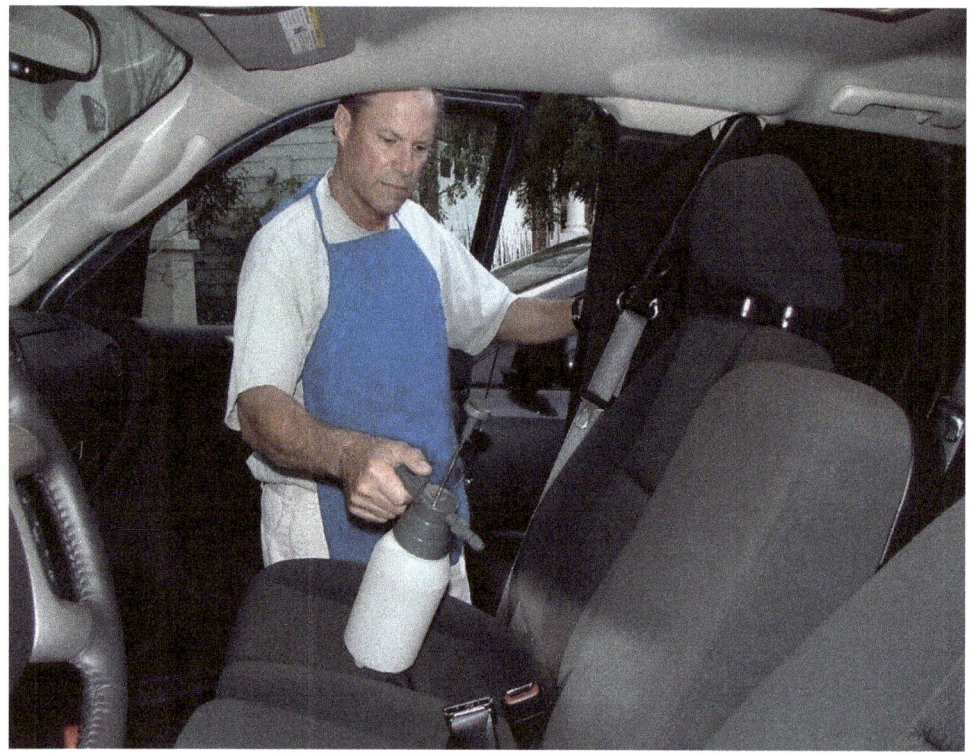

There are 2 methods to apply fabric protectant to the interior fabrics and carpets inside the vehicle, a pressurized pump sprayer applicator or a spray bottle. For best results we recommend investing in a better quality pump sprayer. It will spray liquids evenly and effortlessly.

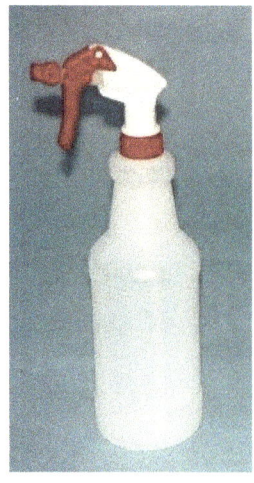

The Immersion Heater

An Immersion Heater is used for one purpose, in conjunction with your Carpet & Upholstery Extractor to create a hot water extraction system. This method of purchasing a less expensive cold water extractor along with a separately purchased Immersion water heater will save you money as opposed to purchasing an extractor with a heater already built into it.

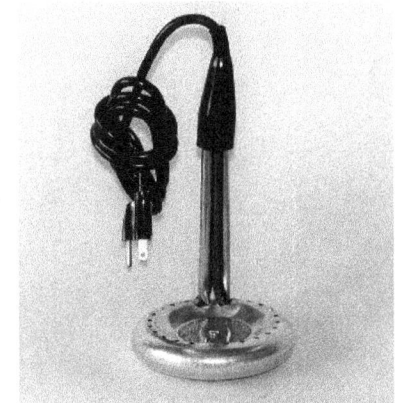

In order to operate the Immersion Heater, place the unit into a bucket of cold water for roughly 10 to 15 minutes or until water is hot. Ensure you set the heater base flat on the base of the container, a 5 gallon bucket for example. After the heater has been placed in the container, the proper water level should be slightly above the bottom edge of the rubber shaft.

* * * * * * * * * **CAUTION** * * * * * * * * *

To avoid injuries, never allow the extension cord to fall into the container of water. Plug the cord into the nearest outlet or extension cord, once the Immersion Heater is in place and the proper amount of water has been added. The heating process should take roughly 7 to 10 minutes to complete. Should you be using a generator, we suggest you plug the unit into the generator using an extension cord. Once the water is sufficiently heated, pour the water into the holding bucket of the extractor in order to mix with the proper cleaning detergent used with the extractor. Follow the procedures mentioned in the Carpet & Upholstery Extractor Directions, noted in this manual.

TIP: **The Immersion Heater could be simultaneously heating the water in the bucket while washing the car. This can help you save time when setting up. Once the car is washed and dried, your extractor will be ready to use in the next phase of detailing the Interior.**

Carpet And Upholstery Extractor

You will find the Carpet & Upholstery Extractor to be one of your most valuable pieces of equipment. By using the extractor over the standard hand scrubbing method, you will be able to obtain professional results. The extractor cleans by using a chemical pressure spray in conjunction with a powerful suction hose for removing deeply embedded dirt in both car interiors and in residential homes.

By combining the effectiveness of the convenient hot water maker (the Immersion Heater), you will have a very efficient and cost effective extractor. A good fact to note: When you heat water up to 120 degrees Fahrenheit it will multiply your cleaning force over the conventional cold water systems by 300%! However, we recommended that you use the temperature in your Owner's Manual as close as possible.

Operating Instructions

PROCEEDURE FOR SET UP (Depending on the Manufacturer - directions may vary)

1. Pour the recommended amount of extractor detergent into a clean container and fill the bucket of water up to the MAX line on the handle of the Immersion Heater.

2. Connect the spray/suction hose to the machine and suction pipe. Connect the couplings to the pressure hose.

3. Put the container for dirty water into tank and close the cover.

4. Connect the water line fitting to the main outlet socket.

5. Pour the heated water and cleaning solution from the bucket into the holding tank of the machine. Use only lukewarm not too hot roughly 50 to 100 degrees C.

6. Turn on the "Suction and Spray" buttons at the same time.

AFTER USE

1. Remove any cleaning solvent not used from the tank with a suction hose.

2. Refill the tank with clean water and flush out the machine including the spray nozzle.

3. Switch off all on/off buttons and unplugging the unit.

4. Empty the dirty water container.

5. Wipe clean the inside and outside of the machine.

Note: Depending on the model of extractor you choose to purchase, directions may vary.

Cleaning Process And Procedures

1. Switch on the suction blower by pushing the "suction" and pump "spraying" button.

2. By squeezing the valve lever on the blower nozzle or hand nozzle the cleaning solvent will then spray. This will cause the dirty water to immediately be sucked back into the machine through the suction nozzle.

3. With the nozzle lifted, move it over the surface to be cleaned in overlapping passes while moving forward and back cleaning the surface as you move. Use short even strokes.

4. Switch off the washer suction cleaner, when the cleaning solution is used up, by pressing the off button. Remove cover, lift out dirty water container, and empty the water out.

5. Repeat the process as often as necessary.

Cleaning Carpets And Upholstery

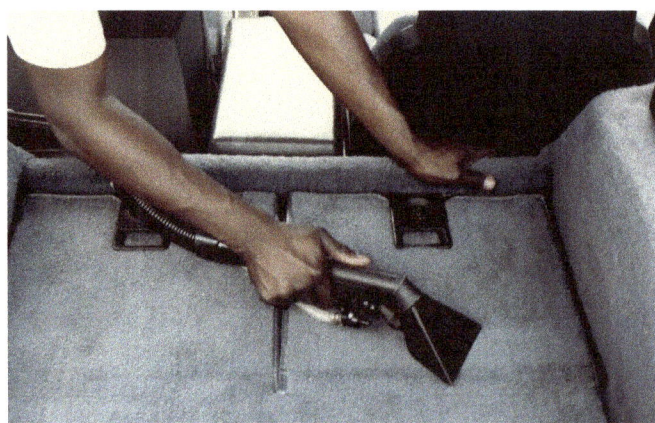

1. Use the floor nozzle attachment shown here if available to clean flat fitted carpets found in RV's or in homes.

2. Use the hand nozzle to clean upholstery, interior carpets, stairs, wall hangings, tapestries or the interiors of motor vehicles. When cleaning upholstery with sensitive fabrics, the amount of detergent should be reduced and the nozzle should be held at a distance when spraying.

Cleaning Methods

1. During the normal spray extraction process the detergent solution is sprayed on and then suctioned off immediately. By repeating the suction without spraying reduces the drying time.
Application: Normally soiled carpets

2. With heavily soiled areas and spots be sure to spray with the detergent solution first before suction takes place.

Wet the surface generously by moving the nozzle at a distance of about 6 inches away from the surface while actuating the valve lever. Wait for about 3 – 5 minutes to allow for the detergent to activate then clean the surface as described below.

If possible, allow the surface to dry overnight. Work over the surface again with clean warm water according to Method #1. This with reduce the detergent residues and completely wash out the loosened dirt.

Highlights To Remember:

- As a result of wet cleaning, fitted carpets with jute backing can shrink and discolor.

- Be sure to pre-spray heavily soiled areas on carpets and upholstery with a colorfast spot remover.

- Always start from the cleaned to the non-cleaned areas.

- The more sensitive the covering i.e., (oriental rugs, Berber carpets, sensitive upholstery fabrics) the less detergent should be used.

- Do not walk or place furniture on cleaned surfaces until they are completely dry.

- Stop working if the spraying pattern is not satisfactory. Instead, turn it off and clean the nozzle mouthpiece with a toothbrush.

- In the case of household carpets that have been shampooed, the foam must be dissolved in the dirty water tank by adding a de-foaming solution.

- Continue working until the detergent solution or the clean water in the tank has become dirty.

********* **CAUTION** *********

Do not use any detergent or cleaning agent that has not been tested and approved by the manufacturer. You can purchase compatible detergents at your local Janitorial Supply Store.

Care And Maintenance

On a regular basis we suggest you flush out the unit with clean warm water to ensure no chemical residue remains in the pumps, valves, hose or nozzle mouthpiece. The unit should also be cleaned externally. Ensure you also check the hoses and power connection cables for any damage. We also suggest you lightly oil any rapid action hose couplings now and then so that they engage properly.

********* **CAUTION** *********

As with any piece of equipment, always follow manufacturer's safety and warning instructions. The appliance must be unplugged before conducting any cleaning, maintenance, and repair work. We highly suggest you have any repair work carried out by an approved service depot who is familiar with all the safety regulations.

Detailer's Vacuum

A good Heavy Duty vacuum is the best way for achieving clean, plush looking carpets, and upholstery. Be sure to purchase a compact and lightweight one for easy maneuverability around vehicles. Most high quality powerful vacuums come with a minimum of a 1.5 horsepower motor with suction power of 250 c.f.m. of water lift.

Wet/Dry vacuums come with a Heavy Duty Bypass Motor allowing cooler air to flow to the motor head, opposed to the old conventional filtered air models. Due to the Wet/Dry design feature of the top mounted bypass motor, the Vacuum is capable of picking up dirt and excess moisture after shampooing.

Look for a vacuum that comes equipped with a heavy duty 10 foot crush proof hose, a wide pick-up floor tool, and a long nose crevice tool for hard-to-reach areas such as, underneath seats, seat pleats and in between window sills.

Vacuum Care And Maintenance

To keep your vacuum operating in peak performance, ensure you do a routine cleaning. If you allow the holding tank to overfill with debris, papers, dirt or water could cause the motor to overwork and burn out quickly. Open the top portion of the vacuum, separate the holding tank, pour the contents out, and flush out the tank with water. It's a good habit to routinely inspect the air filter and replace it, if necessary. Should your vacuum be equipped with a foam filter, remove it, and rinse it with clean water. Be sure to allow the foam filter to dry thoroughly before replacing it on the vacuum. We recommend you do this maintenance once a week.

Follow the below procedures should you experience a loss of power:

1. Heavy debris will restrict the air flow dropping suction power, so we recommend you check the tank for an overabundance of debris.

2. Check for debris that may become trapped at the connection point of the hose or trapped in the hose.

3. Check for debris blocking the crevice or floor tools.

4. Check the paper filter and/or foam filter to be sure that they are not restricting air flow or torn or falling apart.

5. Take a long wooden pole and push it through and out the opposite end of the hose or flush it out with water, should the hose or crevice tools be blocked with debris.

Gas And Electric Pressure Washers

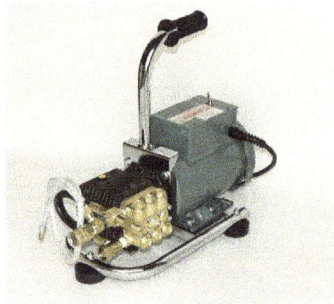  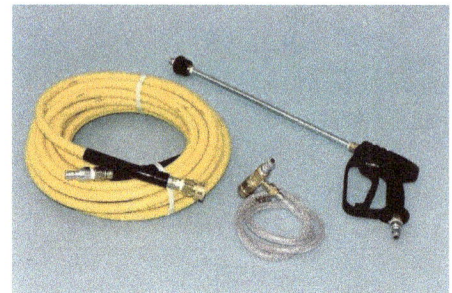

The only real difference between each Pressure Washer is the psi rating and motor performance. The 1000 psi electric pressure washer is lightweight and compact, and has all the professional features you would expect, while the gas gives you more independence because of its unlimited maneuverability. Most pressure washers are fully adjustable from 50 pounds of pressure for a gentle flutter wash, up to 3000 pounds of pressure to produce a powerful blast of water for cleaning tough areas like engine blocks, undercarriages, wheels, door jambs, etc.

Many pressure washers feature a chemical injection system for soap displacement and a clear plastic tube attached to a chemical tube strainer for dipping into a premixed cleaning solution. Included with a pressure washer is a trigger gun, high pressure steel braided hose, and a soap injector control knob usually located at the top of the pressure wand.

Safety Precautions

The gasoline Pressure Washers are independently-driven and therefore do not require an electrical outlet. If you purchased a Briggs & Stratton engine any authorized Lawnmower service center will be able to service most repair or maintenance work. If you purchased a Honda brand then you should take it to an authorized Honda service center.

You must use a grounded outlet when plugging in your electric Pressure Washer. Electrical requirements for the machine are typically 115 volts, 20 amps, single phase, 60 Hz. You could experience problems if the machine is plugged into anything less than a 20 amp circuit breaker. The pressure washer may not turn on due to a weak outlet or circuit breaker. We recommend you plug the unit into a *25* amp circuit breaker outlet if possible, similarly found with washer and dryer outlets. Check your manual for electrical hook up requirements.

We strongly recommend you use a Ground Fault Interrupter (GFI) to prevent possible electric shock. The GFI should be used whenever you operate all other electrical equipment as well. As with any piece of equipment always follow manufacturer's safety and warning instructions.

Care Of Your Equipment

1. Ensure you follow recommended service instructions in the Owner's Manual.

2. After the first 50 hours (break-in period) and 200 working hours thereafter of operation, change oil in Pump. For gas and electric powered Pressure Washers, be sure to use recommended motor oil.

3. In freezing conditions, flush pump with 1 to 1 mixture of automobile anti-freeze and water to PREVENT PUMP FROM FREEZING. Anti-freeze is a great lubricant.

4. After the engine has cooled, wipe down the washer with a clean damp cloth. We recommend you do this after each use.

* * * * * * * * **WARNINGS** * * * * * * * *

High Pressure Sprayers can Cause Serious Injury so ensure you observe all warnings! For Professional Use Only!

Before operating equipment, read and understand all instructions manuals!

WINTERIZING (ANTI-FREEZING) YOUR PRESSURE WASHER & WATER SUPPLY

In order to protect your machine from severe damage, due to exposed freezing temperatures, causing the water to freeze inside the pump, heating coil, and other components, follow the below procedure:

NOTE: IF COMPRESSED AIR IS AVAILABLE, BLOW OUT THE MACHINE USING THE AIR VALVE ON THE PRESSURE PUMP OUTLET.

1. Fill a *5* gallon container with anti-freeze.

2. Remove nozzle from wand and lay out the hose and wand flat on the floor so water can drain out completely.

3. If equipped with a Float Tank - remove the water supply hose and drain the tank. Then fill the float tank with anti-freeze, holding the trigger gun open, if equipped. Turn the pump

on, continuously pour anti-freeze in, and start and stop the pump. If there is NO Float Tank - remove the supply hose and place a suction hose from the pump inlet into the anti-freeze. Hold the trigger gun open, if equipped. Turn the pump on drawing anti-freeze into the system.

4. Turn off the pump when anti-freeze squirts out the end of the gun.

5. You can re-use the anti-freeze when you are ready to operate the washer again. Reconnect the water supply and have the anti-freeze container ready. Turn the pump on to get direct flow of anti-freeze back into its container. Anti-freeze, if kept relatively undiluted, can be reused again and again. Be sure to turn off the pump at this point.

Setting Up

1. Refer to your Owner's Manual for complete instructions on proper engine operation and maintenance.

2. Ensure you check the oil in the pump by removing the dipstick on top of the pump. We recommend you use only high grade 20W or 30W motor oil for the Gas Powered Pressure Washers.

3. Now attach any garden hose to the inlet swivel fitting on the washer. We recommend you use a minimum 1/2" hose size up to 75' length (3/4" over 75' length).

4. Turn on water supply through any standard garden hose.

* * * * * * * * *CAUTION* * * * * * * * *

RUNNING THE PRESSURE WASHER DRY CAN CAUSE SEVERE DAMAGE TO MOVING PARTS. ALWAYS TURN ON THE WATER SUPPLY BEFORE STARTING THE MOTOR.

5. Grip the handgun firmly and point away from anything you do not want to spray. Water will spray from the tip once you squeeze the handgun trigger. Be sure to continue spraying until the air in the line stops coming out of the tip.

6. Start the engine and follow the Owner's Manual for complete instructions.

7. Grip handgun firmly and point away from anything you don't want sprayed. Squeeze the trigger so that high pressure spray will come out of the tip.

* * * * * * * * **CAUTION** * * * * * * * * *

HIGH PRESSURE SPRAY IS VERY DANGEROUS SO WE HIGHLY RECOMMEND YOU NEVER SPRAY PARTS OF THE BODY.

8. If equipped with a Soap Knob, pressure will increase or decrease by turning the nozzle at the end of the handgun. The cleaning solution will be drawn into the sprayer as the pressure is decreased.

9. DO NOT LET MACHINE RUN MORE THAN THREE MINUTES WITH THE TRIGGER GUN CLOSED. This will cause the pump to overheat. We recommend you let some of the water run through every few minutes, or turn off the machine when not in use.

How To Clean

1. In order to save cleaning solution, use rinse water (high pressure) to remove as much dirt, mud, and grease as possible. For best results, stay about 16" to 22" away from the surface. You will achieve the best cleaning action by holding the nozzle at an angle to the surface. Use the water stream like a chisel to get under the dirt and lift from the surface. Move closer for tough spots that require more force and be sure to use overlapping strokes to rinse from the top down.

2. Before applying the cleaning solution, thoroughly wet down the surface with water.

3. The cleaning solution will be drawn into the water spray by turning the nozzle at the end of the handgun to low pressure. Ensure you first place the solution pick up tube into your bucket of pre-mixed soap. Hold the nozzle 12" to 16" from the surface being cleaned.

4. Work from the bottom to the top using a sweeping motion with the handgun.

5. Now turn the nozzle to high pressure to completely rinse the surface until all traces of soap and dirt are gone.

MAINTENANCE OF YOUR VEHICLES EQUIPMENT

Water Tank

It's essential you do periodic cleaning, especially during the hot summer months.

- For those water tanks that are *55* gallons or smaller - Dilute one-half gallon of bleach into a full tank of water and let stand overnight.

- For those water tanks that are *55* gallons or larger - Dilute one full gallon of bleach into a full tank of water and let stand overnight.

The bleach will keep the water clear and prevent algae from growing. Be sure to thoroughly flush out, drain, and refill with fresh clean water tank before each use.

To clean the outside of the tank spray surface with ALL PURPOSE CLEANER and a towel or if badly stained, clean with steel wool.

Safeguards And General Safety Instructions

BASIC SAFETY PRECAUTIONS SHOULD ALWAYS BE FOLLOWED WHEN USING ELECTRIC TOOLS OR EQUIPMENT. FOLLOW THE BELOW RECOMMENDATIONS TO REDUCE THE RISK OF FIRE, ELECTRIC SHOCK, AND PERSONAL INJURY:

For All Tools and Equipment:

- Keep your work area clean

- Prevent accidents by keeping area clear of clutter.

- Keep power tools out of rain and bad weather.

- Avoid using power tools in damp or wet locations.

For all Grounded Tools:

   Grounding Instructions:

- In order to protect the operator from electric shock, all tools should be grounded when in use.

- Ensure you have the proper grounding outlet when using tools that are equipped with approved three conductor cords and three prong plugs.

MAINTENANCE SHEET (This is just a recommended guide) Use manufacturer's product and instructions for your particular model.

GAS POWERED PRESSURE WASHER

- Briggs & Stratton or Honda Engine

- Break in Period: (Motors)   20 hours

- Recommended Oil: 10-40 Detergent Oil

After 20 hours of use the oil change interval will be every 100 hours. There are two (2) dipsticks located on the engine. Use either one to check the oil level. The oil should read at least half (1/2) full on the dipstick. Be sure to screw all the way in to check the level.

NOTE: ALWAYS CHECK OIL LEVELS ON <u>LEVEL</u> <u>GROUND</u>.

Gear Reducer (if applicable). *Note: Not all Pressure Washers have a Gear Reducer

- Break in Period: 50 hours

- Recommended Oil: 90 Wt. Gear Oil

After 50 hours of use the oil change interval will be every 500 hours. Check Sight Window for oil level. The oil level should be no higher than the top of the notch of the dip stick, or no lower than where the RED DOT in the Sight Window is located.

Water Pump (Valve Area)

- Break in Period: 50 hours

- Recommended Oil: 30 Wt. <u>Non-detergent oil</u>

After 50 hours of use the oil change interval will be every 500 hours.

Electric Pressure Washers

- Break in Period: 40 hours

- Recommended Oil: 80/90 Wt. Gear Oil

After 40 hours of use the oil change interval will be every 250 hours or when the oil has a milky color.

TIPS: We recommend you maintain a LOG BOOK to record your operating hours.

Check all oil levels on level ground only!

Important Freeze Protection

Serious damage can occur if water is left in the machine after operating high pressure water cleaning in cold and freezing climates. It is essential that water is not left in the machine when storing in freezing conditions.

We recommend the following steps to guard against freeze damage:

1. Affix a short length of garden hose (2 to 3 feet long) to the inlet connection of pump.

2. Place the other end into the anti-freeze solution.

3. Connect the high pressure hose and gun.

4. Remove spray nozzle from gun wand to allow for free flow.

5. Follow the normal starting procedures.

6. Direct anti-freeze back into the clean container and store for reuse, once water is purged from high pressure hose.

7. Machine is ready for storage once you follow shut down procedure.

Special Notes Page

Section 6

Engine Cleaning

The Motor 73

Steps For Engine Cleaning 74

The Motor

Even though engine cleaning can seem like a dirty job, it can also be an extremely profitable and impressive portion of professional detailing. As the saying goes, it may be a dirty job, but someone has to do it.

Keep in mind that most buyers and car dealerships judge cars not just by the overall appearance, but the engine appearance as well. They look for oil leaks, worn hoses, and in general the feeling of a clean engine means a well maintained automobile.

Most car dealerships will even go to the extent of having the engine steam cleaned, or will repaint and touch-up the engine block and valve covers. They will even go to lengths to dress up all the hoses and rubber with a silicone based dressing or in some cases spraying a clear lacquer over the entire engine compartment to give it a new sheen. The drawback to this method is that after a short period of time the lacquer breaks down and takes on an unsightly cracked/peeled appearance. However, for a car dealership the most important thing is how the car looks at is drives off the lot. A clean engine shows better and will definitely contribute to pushing the price of a car up.

Private individuals who want to impress a buyer will have the engine professionally detailed to show that the automobile has been well maintained.

Your mechanic will also appreciate a clean engine. An engine removed of grease and dirt would certainly be a welcome sight.

Many of today's engines have changed and have become much more sophisticated with advanced computerized electronics and solid state printed circuits. Much of the heavier metal parts have been replaced with plastic housings and paper cardboard shields. Even though they don't build them like they use to there are advantages of the newer designs. For example; the older style distributor caps had nothing more than a couple of clips to hold it in place, and has now been replaced with a new and improved waterproof sealed cap. Which means that the likelihood of fouling a plug or coil wire is substantially reduced.

Even with today's modern, nonflammable chemical engine degreasers, and pressure washers that are far safer and more user friendly, it still takes a professional detailer to do a proper job without risking damaging the engine compartment. Thus the reason a professional detailer can demand a good fee for their services.

There is a misconception that a steam machine is a safer method of cleaning the engine. In reality, the fact is that steam is far lighter and less dense than cold water causing a greater chance of penetrating into the distributor cap or plug wires and could potentially soften and remove the paint off the engine block or valve covers. That's why we recommend you use a cold water pressure washer. You will achieve a safer and more effective engine cleaning in the long run with less risk of fouling electronics and other components of the vehicle.

If you plan on including engine cleaning with your detailing job, we suggest you do this first before any other detailing process. When operating on a mobile basis be sure you consider the work area and park the vehicle away from a storm drain or away from any areas that do not allow proper drainage. If you provide this service at someone's house, ensure you have proper drainage so that you can rinse away any grease or oil residue that may contaminate the ground. A good engine cleaning will show no signs of grease or dirt anywhere, especially on the ground. Should you decide to do an engine cleaning at a business park or public place, we recommend you get permission from the property manager beforehand. You may also be required by your local city ordinance to recapture any water runoff from cleaning the engine compartment as it contains heavy metal solids and oily substances.

Another alternative for cleaning your customer's engine could be at a self-service car wash or local garage shop. Most of these facilities have pressure washers set up to do the job and approved compliant drainage wash racks set up for this type of cleaning.

Steps For Engine Cleaning

A warm engine helps to loosen grease and oil, so we recommend you run the engine for about 5 minutes before you start cleaning the engine. Much of the initial grease and dirt will be rinsed off in your first step of pressure rinsing. Below are the basic 7 steps for engine cleaning:

1. Ensure you cover the distributor, electronics, computer, alarm systems and other sensitive electrical components with plastic bags.

2. Pre-rinse the engine compartment sides and hood of the car.

3. Liberally apply the degreaser around the entire engine compartment and if requested the underside or undercarriage of the vehicle.

4. Hand scrub using brush work.

5. Power wash and rinse.

6. Condition the engine compartment hoses and plastics with a nonflammable silicone dressing.

7. Complete the final touches and check/start the engine.

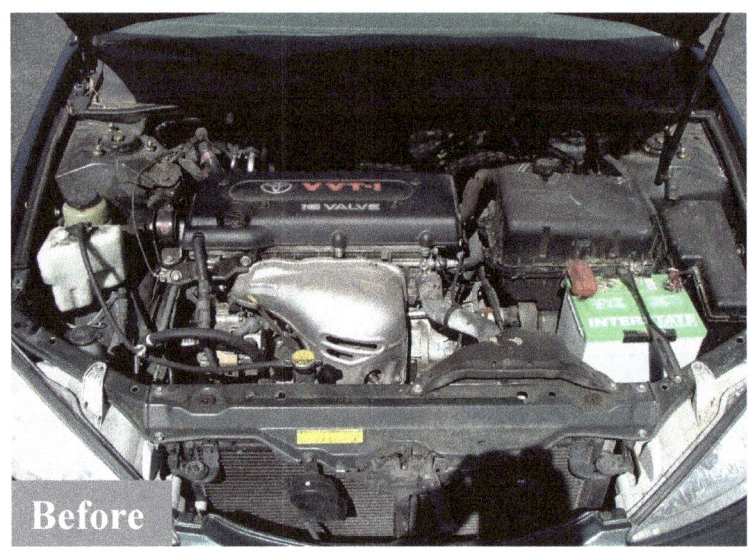

Directions:

STEP 1: It is NOT absolutely necessary but recommended to cover the distributor cap, carburetor, and electrical components especially when working on a very expensive automobile such as a Porsche or Lamborghini, which poses a much greater risk of problems. However, you can skip this step and simply do the best in avoiding a direct spray at these areas. With your pressure washer, we suggest you turn down the pressure to approximately 150 psi and use what we call the flutter wash method. This is simply a low volume of pressure spray that will lightly pass over sensitive areas. For stubborn, heavy grease or hard to reach areas, you will want to use the full force of the pressure washer. The end of the pressure wand acts as a peeling tool to remove grease from stubborn areas.

STEP 2: I also recommend you thoroughly wet down the exterior of the vehicle before attempting cleaning the engine, especially the front hood, windshield, front sides, and grill areas. By spraying these areas with water first, it will help suspend the cleaners and any contamination from the grease or dirt, keeping it from sticking and marring the paint during the engine cleaning process.

Since engine cleaning is a very dirty job chances are you will probably get wet, so we recommend you wear protective eye goggles, a protective work apron and even latex gloves to prevent staining and contact with harsh cleaners.

The engine compartment is a compact area, so get close to the engine and spray the water at an angle whenever possible. By doing so it will help to avoid any back-splash and keep the dirt and grease from ricocheting in your face.

Face the engine and use the full force of the spray to remove as much of the initial dirt and globs of grease as possible. By pre-spraying with water only, will save you time and give the cleaner a better chance in the following sequential step #5 to work on the actual metal and plastic components of the engine. We recommend you start at the fire wall and move the pressure wand systematically across the engine. Try to avoid spraying water directly on the distributor or spark plug areas. Be sure to use caution when cleaning around computers and other electrical components. Today's automobile's electronic mechanisms are sealed quite well, but some of the older car years may be more sensitive to water leakage and not designed to handle excessive high pressure washing. By using the variable pressure control on the pressure washer and flutter method you can keep the direct blast of water away from these areas.

NOTE: **At this time, DO NOT attempt to clean the upper hood or insulator area we will come back to this later within the manual.**

Move to the air cleaner and carburetor areas after pressure cleaning the firewall and top area of the car. Avoid any direct spraying on the spark plugs and now work closely on the manifold and rocker cover area. Now move down and across the engine block area. You may have to move to the side of the engine to get a better angle when cleaning these areas. Be sure to position yourself at different angles to ensure you are looking closely at your work at all times.

Look for hidden pockets of grease and dirt as you are pressure washing, as grease can usually be found under the rocker cover, around the power steering unit, battery box, air conditioning housing, and behind the alternator. Generally speaking, any moving component found in the engine compartment leaks lubricating grease.

Ensure you pressure wash the lower position of the engine, the wheel wells, engine mounts, and supporting frame areas since these are commonly overlooked areas. The engine block should be cleaned last, however avoid using too strong a spray on the any of painted areas. Remember to respect the power of the pressure washer.

Be sure to take one last look at the engine compartment after the initial cleaning to see if there were any missed areas.

In order to avoid water dripping on your head during the pressure washing of the engine block we suggest you wash the underside of the hood last.

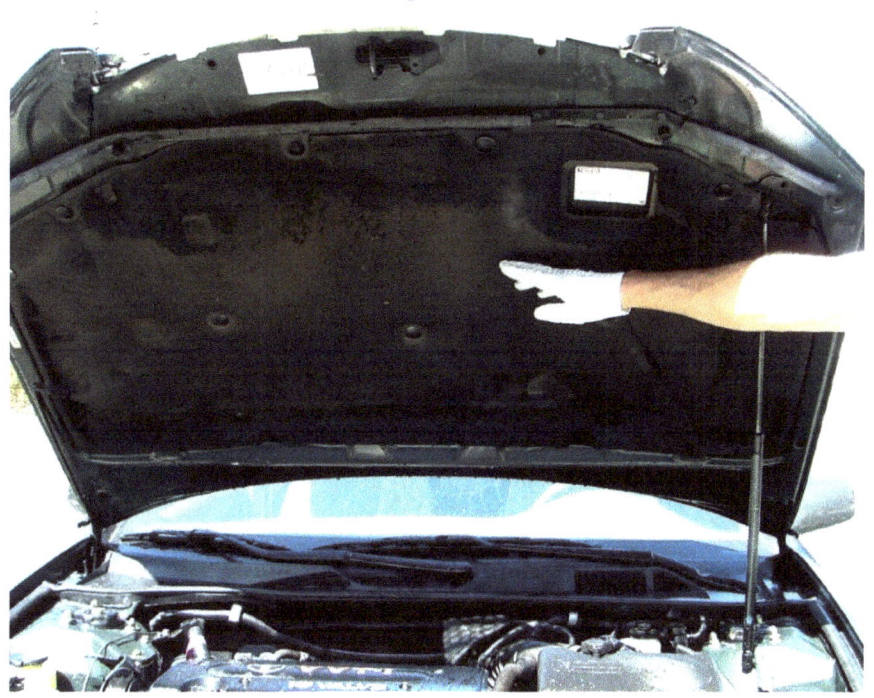

Next, work around the outside lip area of the hood with the full force of the spray. **NOTE:** Certain vehicles have a foam rubber type of material attached to the center of the hood. This is called a hood insulator and **should not get wet**. This hood insulator is used to protect any transfer of direct heat from the engine to the hood, as well as absorbing engine noise. If over wet, the weight of the water will weaken the adhesive and cause it to pull away from the hood.

STEP 3: Once the initial pressure wash is completed it's time to saturate the engine with the Engine Degreaser. Apply the Engine Degreaser with a spray bottle liberally to all sections of the engine compartment. Ensure to apply more degreaser to areas with heavier oil and allow to sit for approximately 5 minutes.

STEP 4: Now pre-scrub all the dirty areas of the engine compartment with your tool brushes including the hood area. Mix a bucket of soap solution using your car wash shampoo to help break down the dirt and with your fender brush scrub the inside track of the engine compartment where the hood closes. You can scrub this area with either your fender brush or bug sponge. The fender brush works best to clean large areas more quickly. This will also help to reduce the risk of cutting your fingers or hands around all sharp edges and ridges. The true color of the painted portion will really stand out nicely, once it's been cleaned thoroughly.

Now it's time to remove grease and corrosion from the battery box, cables, and terminals. Ensure to clean the brake fluid reservoir, rocker covers, power steering unit, oil filter, and all other hard to reach areas. Use your parts brush for tight areas. With your soap solution work the brush to clean in all hard to reach corners. Stop occasionally to get a real close up look at your work to ensure you've missed nothing. Many of the most commonly missed areas are the power steering units, alternator housings, and small pockets of grease on the engine block underneath the valve covers and spark plug areas. We recommend you use your parts brush to get to these hard to reach areas.

Most automobiles have an undercoating to prevent rust from destroying the painted portion of the engine and should not be removed. Be sure to explain the function of this undercoating material to your customer so they don't think you have overlooked this area. They will appreciate your concern and knowledge about detailing the engine.

When working on a lifted 4 x 4 truck, I suggest you use a ladder or simply turn a wash bucket upside down and stand on it to get closer to your work.

I suggest that you use an acid based wheel and mag cleaner for all the aluminum or chrome parts, should they become dull or rusty. This acid based cleaner will quickly brighten and clean these areas. Rinse these areas off immediately once you have used the cleaner as the acid in the Wheel and Mag cleaner could spot sensitive aluminum parts if left on too long. You can polish these parts later with a good Aluminum Chrome Polish.

Normally the under carriage is not included with engine cleanings; however some of your customers may request that the underside of the engine be cleaned. In this case, I suggest you loop your pressure hose on the ground in front of your work and kneel on the hose to prevent your clothes from getting wet and dirty. Clean only what is visible from the kneeling position. You could also use a back creeper if available.

STEP 5: Once you have completed the pre-scrubbing begin pressure washing and blasting away any remaining dirt and grease. Using caution around sensitive electronic car components and painted areas, systematically work back and forth across the engine compartment. Follow the same cleaning procedure as mentioned above. Work methodically and use the power of the sprayer to concentrate on and peel away any remaining pockets of dirt and grease.

Be sure to use caution around stickers and emblems. Most of these contain pertinent vehicle information and should not be removed. You can use the flutter wash method, whenever necessary, to reduce the amount of pressure. Now rinse the inside of the hood area above. You will notice that soap and degreaser will fall onto the engine compartment area, lightly rinse this area again until all residue is completely removed.

STEP 6: While the engine is still wet, leave the hood up and apply a nonflammable silicone Vinyl Dressing over the entire engine compartment with your spray bottle. This will really enhance the engine's appearance! Even though this step takes extra time the results will be worth the time spent. The whole idea of cleaning this area is to make your customer feel good about having a clean engine and they will appreciate the extra effort.

Before stepping into the automobile place a towel on the floor to prevent contaminating the carpet with grease.

Now start up the engine. Should the engine not start up chances are that water got into the distributor cap. If this happens, we suggest you take off the distributor cap and check it for moisture. You can remove the moisture either by using a towel or a common hair dryer or an air compressor. Once again, start the engine and close the hood. Now take a moment to move the automobile a few feet away from the work area, and power rinse the remaining residue of dirt and grease off the driveway and away from any storm drains. This is common sense and shows courtesy to your customer and/or property manager.

STEP 7: Allow the engine to run for approximately 10 or 15 minutes for the engine to completely dry. Use your time wisely, and start washing and prepping the automobile for detailing.

During this process you may experience a slight odor. This is due to the evaporation and burn-off of the engine degreaser residue. During the drying time, periodically check the temperature gauge.

Note: When the entire engine cleaning has been completed, with the hood closed, re-rinse the outer body of the vehicle to remove any remaining degreaser or contaminates that could stain the paint.

Pop open the hood and wipe or blow off any puddles of residual water or Vinyl Dressing at the end of your overall detailing. Have the hood of the vehicle open for the customer and ready for inspection. Congratulations! You've just completed your first professional detailed engine cleaning!

Once the engine is completed, be sure to rinse and thoroughly flush out your cleaning tools and wash mitt. I suggest you keep a separate complement of tools for engine work only.

In order to be on the safe and compliant side, I suggest you check with your city regarding acceptable cleaning procedures and disposal of contaminated rinse waters. Dependent upon local city ordinances, engine cleaning in public or private property may not be permitted without some sort of a recovery system that collects dirty water runoff.

Alternatives would be to either:

1) Take the vehicle to a self-service car wash.

2) Set up a portable water catch of your own by using a small vinyl blow-up pool or plastic catch basin. The collected water can be drawn out using your wet and dry vacuum or a sump pump. Professional recovery systems are available however with a little ingenuity you can make a system yourself rather inexpensively.

Special Notes Page

Section 7

Basics Of Prep Work

- Prep Work 87
- Washing The Car 88
- Washing The Paint 89
- Automatic Car Washing Facilities 90
- What Is Acid Rain And How Does It Affect An Automobile? 93
- What Causes Acid Rain Spots? 94
- Prepping For The Car Wash 94
- Prep Work Includes: 96
- The Initial Pressure Washing Sequence For: 99
- Wheels, Tires, And Undercarriage 99
- Rubber Tires And White Walls 103
- Grill Body And Undercarriage 105
- Road Tar And Sap Removal 107
- The Pressure Washing Sequence 109
- Vinyl Tops 110
- Convertible Tops 112
- Power Up The Suds! 113
- Hand Body Wash 114
- Power Rinsing 116
- Drying The Car 117
- Detailing The Interior 122
- Interior 122

Prep Work

We find that most people do not take care of their vehicles properly. Which could mean that either the paint finish was sadly ignored or the purchase of cheap over-the-counter polishes, cleaners, and waxes. Although many of these products promise amazing results, the owners do not do their vehicle justice by using the wrong type of cleaning and polishing products.

In fact a recent study done by the DuPont Company discovered that most typical over-the-counter commercial grade waxes melt down at a rate of 1 - 1/2% a day! This means that the average life cycle of this wax job on their car will only last an average of twenty days. Unlike PROFESSIONAL results which can last for six months to a year. By using these cheap grades of waxes and polishes the foundation has been laid for premature paint oxidation, and poor protection from the Earth's harmful elements.

In the old days, when Grandpa would spend hours rubbing his Model A with his Carnauba Wax paste, at a back breaking rate, he had much pride seeing his face reflected back. Today we have many options to get that same sheen only with a lot less effort.

Today we have much more sophisticated equipment and chemicals that are far easier to use than in the old days of Grandpa's Model A. As a professional detailer, you will appreciate today's advances in automotive detailing and restoration. The differences a professional detail can make will result from four basic elements:

1. Correct Washing and Cleaning Procedures

2. Polishing and Compounding Techniques

3. Proper Application for Glazes and Waxes

4. Set up Procedures for Prep/Work

In order to start off correctly for the basics of car care, these are some of the necessary ingredients you will be learning for the exterior of the vehicle.

Later in your Detailing Manual, we will look at the four individual points. These will teach you how to apply these methods in order to make the vehicle look its best and increase its value by extending the life of the vehicle.

Washing The Car

Understanding PH

Many retail soaps and detergents are very high in alkalinity, which can cause corrosion and pit the paint since Alkalinity is much like acid.

So what are the differences of an acid and an alkali?

An acid is a compound and when mixed with water creates a positive electrical charge. The stronger the acid, the stronger the positive charge.

On the other hand, an alkali has a negative electrical charge.

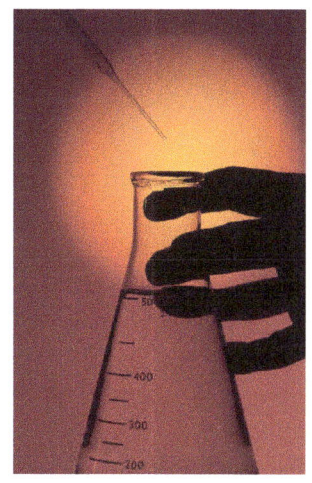

I'm sure you've heard of the term "Balanced". To further clarify this term, a pH scale is used to determine the measurement of positive and negative degrees for both acids and alkalis. A products pH scale is determined by actually measuring the temperature of the solution.

In order to break this down for better understanding think of the pH Scale as a thermometer. A normal thermometer takes the temperature reading of either water or fluids; however a pH Scale takes a temperature reading of the chemical heat of any given solution. Going a step further; a chemical solution that is loaded with alkali is considered to be "hot". Also, if an acid is loaded (Reads High) in a solution it is also considered to be "hot". Since there is no "cold" mark on the pH scale, a desirable low pH solution will read ideally around the middle of the scale. The pH Scale ranges from 0 to 14. Zero being the point of the highest acid or highest positive electrical charge. A middle number, such as 7 would be more of a neutral position void of both positive and negative charges. On the other spectrum, if the pH

Scale gets to the highest point of 14 then the negative electrical charge is much higher. By using properly balanced acid or alkali washing products you can avoid paint damage.

Washing The Paint

Keep in mind that most household detergents and soaps are not pH balanced. In order to have good pH balanced soap it must have a near neutral pH Formula as explained previously. Equally, it is important that it contains no harsh abrasives.

Throughout this Manual we will frequently refer to a term called "oxidation". Paint itself has a certain amount of oil content. Oxidation or starvation occurs when paint uses up its natural oil content. Oxidation is evident when the surface becomes dry or dull looking. Even mild detergents, such as "Joy" and other commercial products, can deplete the natural oil content and accelerate the starvation or drying of the painted surface. Thus the reasons why many professional body shops recommend you wash your car with only plain water whenever possible.

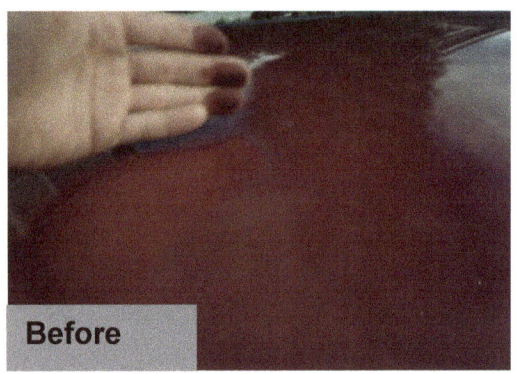

Any good car wash solution should contain a small amount of essential oils, as well as a blend of surfactants. Surfactants will react by lowering the surface tension and increase the natural solvency of the displaced water. The essential oils found in a good Car Wash Shampoo will dissolve into micron size droplets and fill the paint pores on the surface for additional protection.

We recommend you also use Car Wash Shampoos that contain water softening agents, which will help counteract any harsh chemicals found in water. These softening agents will also cause a sheeting reaction to help the rinse water to bead and roll off the vehicle surface, helping to reduce water spotting issues.

How do water spots form? Most of our drinking water is treated and full of calcium and alkaline type chemicals. You may have experienced seeing a chalky white residue on your car when you washed it from a regular garden hose after the water dried. Many of these chemicals in the water will leave a residue or spot the surface. These spots are actually dried compound chemicals. These can actually scratch the surface of a car during the waxing stage of detailing an automobile. Thus the importance of using the right type of car wash solution in order to prevent water and chemical compounds from sticking to the surface.

When operating a mobile or fixed location, we recommend contracting with a soft water bottling service. They provide more purified filtered water, free of chemical deposits. This service is inexpensive and will save you the time and effort it would take to remove stubborn deposits from a simple car wash.

Automatic Car Washing Facilities

Many of the Pros and Cons of automatic car washes have changed over the years. There are now more advanced and safer technologies used in these large washing stations. The old fixed car washes use to use large nylon roller brushes for washing the automobile and rotating drop cloths to dry them.

Over a period of time these types of facilities caused damage to the car's finish. Now-a-days, newer paint finishes are more sensitive to scratching and marring especially the new clear and base coat finishes of today.

Now-a-days, more advanced car washing facilities are using a "touchless" car wash method using pressure soap sprayers and powerful air blowers for drying the vehicle. Even with these advancements there is still one major drawback to the fixed car wash operators. All of these facilities use an average of 30 gallons of reclaimed or recycled water to wash a car. Because it is recycled water it is highly contaminated with millions of particles of dirt, oil, soaps, and other harmful elements. Not exactly the best option for someone that is conscious about what goes on their car.

This gives you and your detailing service an advantage over these types of car wash facilities, by providing your customers with a top quality wash using far less water. Plus you can offer an on-the-spot hand washing service these facilities cannot. Be prepared to be approached quite often when you're out in the field by interested on-lookers. Many of the advantages of starting a mobile hand washing are:

1. It will provide you with a regular weekly guaranteed income.

2. It will encourage more detailing work as drivers pass by.

3. A regular route would increase your exposure to potential customers.

4. Your regular wash customers will be your steady repeat customers and easier to clean since they are regularly maintained.

5. This service will also help to fill voids in your schedule should you not be booked up with detail appointments.

Okay…I might pass up on this one.

When you first start your new business it is important to try not to turn any work down. Regardless of the condition of the vehicle and as scary as it may sometimes look, everything you do will be good experience and will increase your bottom line in your business. You can be more selective later as your business continues to grow and you're consistently making big…. **$$$$$**.

The Deluxe Hand Car wash procedure includes:

- Prep wheels, tires and wheel-well areas.

- Thoroughly wash the exterior with soap and a wash mitt.

- Removal of road tar, bugs, and sap on the exterior.

- Drying the exterior with a chamois or air compressor.

- Thoroughly clean and dry the door jambs.

- Dressing the tires and dash areas.

- Glass polishing the windows inside and out.

- Vacuuming the interior including the seats, floor boards, ashtrays, console, rear deck, carpets, and trunk area.

- Last spritz Air Freshener to finish off for a clean scent.

Once you master the vehicle wash you should be able to complete any wash job in about 30 to 45 minutes. With an average charge of *$25* to *$40* a wash that averages out to approximately **$50** to **$75** an hour just washing cars!

What Is Acid Rain And How Does It Affect An Automobile?

You should now have an understanding of what improper cleaners and the effect of chemicals and the environment can do to the finish of any vehicle.

Today our car's painted surface is exposed to calcium salts, sulfur compounds, smog secretions, and acid rain. The difference between new and old paint finishes is the amount of paint automotive manufacturer's use. With today's paints only measuring an average of *5* to *7* mils of thickness, two stage (2 step) clear coat paints are designed to use less pigmented (color coat) paint with a top layer of clear urethane enamel, which is similar to a hard plastic casing over the painted surface. Unfortunately, these clear coat finishes which measure approximately 2 out of the 7 mils thickness, (about the same thickness of a piece of Saran wrap) are more susceptible to staining, scratching, and marring.

Stains due to acid rain are the most prevalent problem, other than paint oxidation.

When removing acid rain spots, non-clear coat finishes are easier to deal with because an abrasive compound may be used to remove these quickly, by abrading or scouring the paint. However, clear coat finishes must be handled carefully, which we will cover later in this manual.

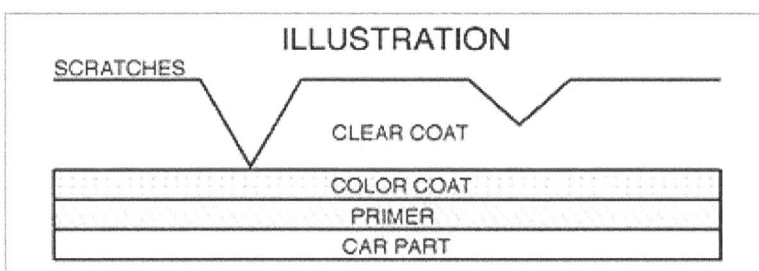

What Causes Acid Rain Spots?

An acid rain study and the effects it has on automobile finishes was conducted by Dr. Edward Edney, a U.S. Environmental Protection Agency Scientist. Dr. Edney simulated acid rain conditions in his own EPA lab using test panels from his own car. Also, he examined thousands of cars in the Virginia area finding that this area was more susceptible to acid rain damage. Subsequently, he found that an acid fog cloud, because of its penetrating nature, is the most damaging of all even more so than acid rain. His findings also found that acid rain causes more damage to an automobile than acidic lemonade or vinegar, which were relatively harmless. Dr. Edney found that acid rain contains a variety of acids including carbonic, nitric, and sulfur. When the rain water dries the nitric and carbonic acids evaporate, however sulfuric acid does not. This remaining acid will actually etch both the clear and non-clear coat of an automobile's finish. However, the non-clear coat has a more curable symptom that appears as dull white spots on the vehicles surface.

Prepping For The Car Wash

Be conscious of where you wash the vehicle in order to avoid over spraying adjacent cars. Once the vehicle is in place and ready to be washed, be sure that all windows are rolled up and the car keys are placed outside of the vehicle, preferably in your pant or work apron pocket.

When washing the vehicle at the customer's home or location, we recommend you park the car at an angle with the front end higher than the back. All automobiles are designed with drain tracks made to run off from front to rear. You can use a shop vac equipped with a blower attachment or grass blower, and use the force of the air to blow any remaining water out of the hard to reach areas.

After you have filled your bucket with water and a mixture of car wash shampoo, ensure you have your other detailing tools at a hand, such as your fender, parts, spoke, and wire wheel brush, bug sponge, wash mitt, and Pressure Washer. We will refer to the use of a pressure washer throughout the manual, however if you are equipped with only a standard garden hose and nozzle that is perfectly fine. We recommend a pressure washer as one of your best equipment investments as soon as you are able as this unit will save you valuable time and will clean much more efficiently.

The primary wash is actually the second step, after the engine cleaning sequence, to prepare the automobile for a thorough detailing. In other words, you are trying to clean as much of the vehicle as possible with your Pressure Washer and detailing tools during the washing sequence. This will help to save time and energy. This step is more commonly known as Prep Work.

Detailing Brushes and Tools You Will Need For This Section.

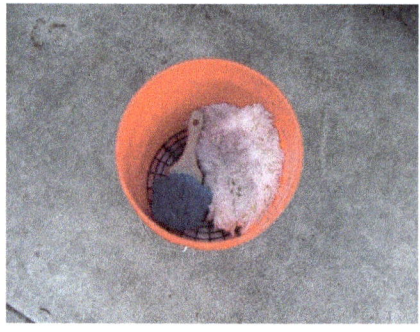

From left to right:

Wire Wheel White Wall Brush, Parts and Spoke Brush, Extended Fender and Tire Brush, Spoke Brush, and Short Scrub Brush.

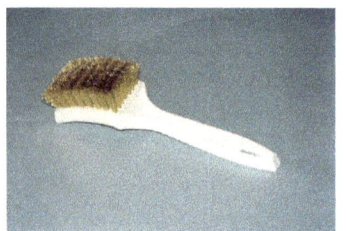
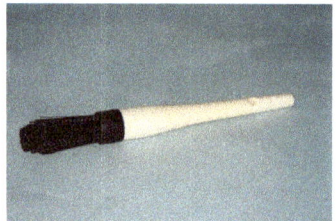

Prep Work Includes:

• Pressure Washing	• Road Tar Removal
• Hand Washing	• Tree Sap Removal
• Wheel Cleaning	• Rocker Panels
• Tire Cleaning	• Valance Debugged
• Wheel Well Area	• Vinyl Floor Mats
• Fender Well Lip Area	• Ash Trays
• Front Grill Area	• Old Decals and Stickers
• License Plate Cleaned	• Side Moldings Cleaned
• Door & Trunk Jambs Degreased	

We suggest you follow the diagrams indicating specific areas of the vehicle in order to use the "divide and conquer" method to understand the important cleaning areas. It is important to be consistent and systematic during your cleaning process.

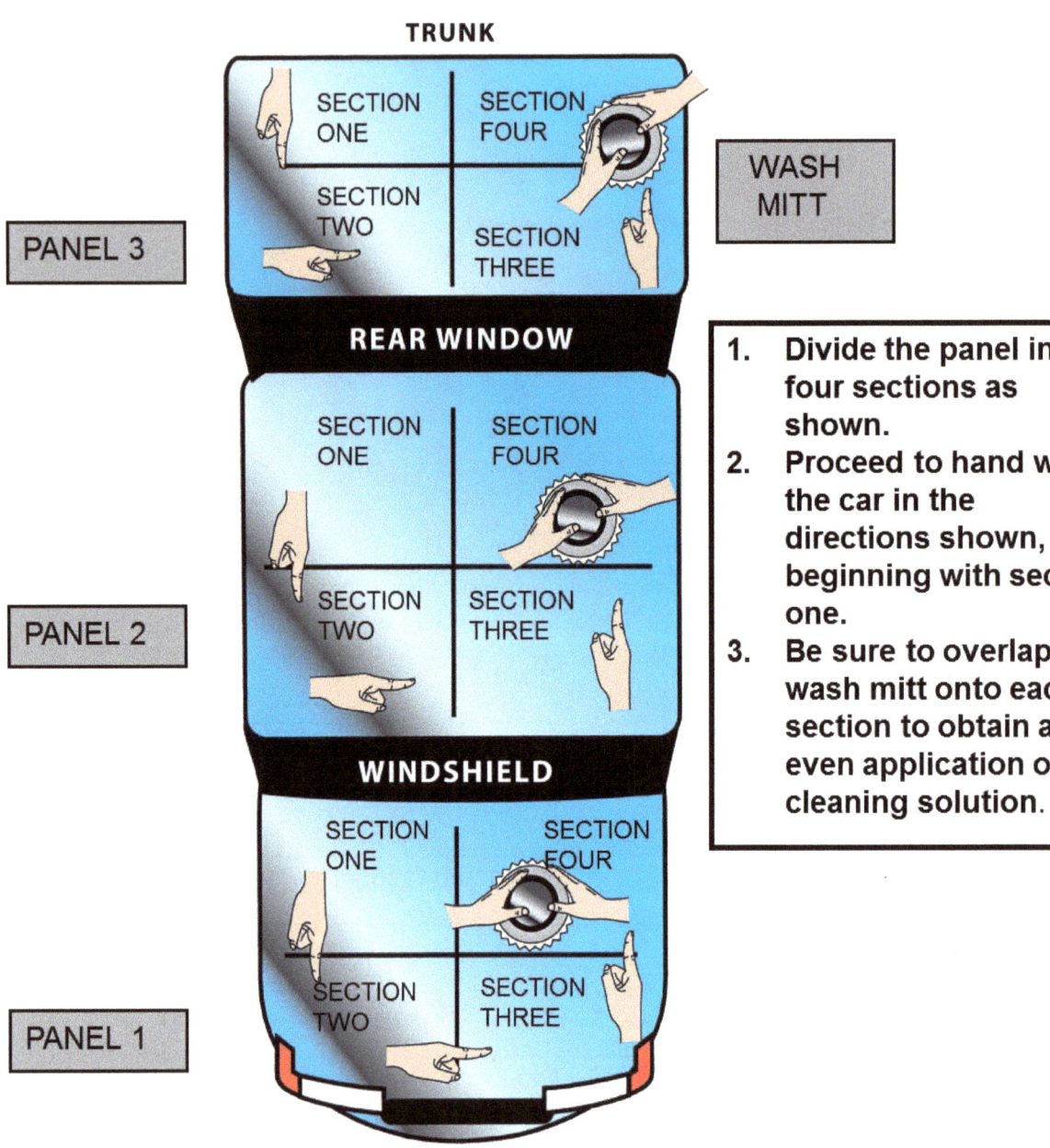

Divide and conquer procedure – section each panel into four areas for washing. Always start at the top of the vehicle completing panels 1, 2 and 3. Lastly wash the sides and bumper areas of the vehicle.

During your washing sequence, we suggest you start at the top of the vehicle and work down to the side, ending at the sides and bottom of the car. Since most of the dirt and sludge is located towards the bottom of the vehicle, these areas should always be approached last. Using lots of water, always pre-rinse your wash mitt from any dirt or grit to help prevent scratching the car's paint surfaces.

Rinse and scrub the car thoroughly by starting with the top.

Note: **The one exception will be if the surface of the vehicle is too hot or you are working in direct sunlight you will want to clean the wheels and wheel well areas as well as the front grill first** to avoid water spotting from the water or soap sitting too long on the surface of the vehicle. Use plenty of water, you can never rinse too often. Be sure to work systematically around the entire car until you've reached the last section. Being consistent will help to ensure nothing is missed.

It's best to wash an automobile with a cool surface. In order to best describe the importance for working on a cool surface, especially during the washing sequence, imagine the feeling you have when your body temperature becomes too hot from being out in the sun and you jump into a pool of cool water, your body essentially goes into a mild shock. Well the same holds true for an automobile. If the ambient temperature of the vehicle is too hot and cold water is applied, the paint can go into what's called "thermostatic shock". Over a period of time, these shock waves will create tiny cracks in the paint called Crazing.

Simply test the surface with the palm of your hand to the surface of the automobile. Also, you can control the surface temperature by placing the vehicle in the shade for a few minutes or use a Detailer's Portable Shade Canopy whenever possible. It's not only better for the vehicle but helps you keep cool while you are doing the hard work.

The Initial Pressure Washing Sequence For:

Wheels, Tires, And Undercarriage

The Prep Work will be relatively simple if the vehicle has been reasonably maintained. However, you will appreciate the importance of your Pressure Washer should the automobile have months or years of neglect accumulating a layer of dirt, grease, and road grime.

By developing a method of cleaning systematically will allow you and your employees to stay consistent in your washing techniques and save you time.

We suggest you start washing and prepping the non-painted areas first in order to avoid water spotting caused by soapy water settling on the automobiles painted surface. Cleaning these areas first will reduce the chance of picking up dirt/grit from the bottom area and avoid possibly scratching the painted surfaces.

The dirtiest and most time consuming areas are the wheels and tires. Most automobiles are equipped with front disc brakes, when applied through normal every day driving, expel a powdery residue called "brake-dust". This dust adheres to the spokes and holes found on every type of wheel. The constant accumulation of brake dust, road oil, and brake heat can bake this material into the hardest to reach areas of the wheel, particularly spoke type wheels. On a normal summer day the average temperature that a wheel will reach can be up to 190° F. As the wheel spins a small negative static charge starts to develop and collects the brake dust and adhesive bonding material. This process simulates baking the brake dust to the wheel.

You will find during the course of experiencing different wheels and cars you will find which products work best in cleaning them. Some automobiles accumulate more brake dust than others such as the BMW, Volvo, and Mercedes Benz.

The brake dust can permanently damage the finish of the wheel, since most brake pads are composed of asbestos, mono filament, carbon fiber, metal filings, and adhesives. Coincidently, the asbestos, fiber, and filings are not the problem with damaging the wheel, but instead the adhesive chemical used to mold the brake pads, which can etch and pit the surface of the wheel, as it makes contact with the very hot surface.

One important thing to note is to never wash or rinse a wheel if the automobile has just been driven. With this said, two problems can occur.

First: Damage to the wheel or rotors can be caused from sudden extreme temperature changes of thermostatic shock.

Second: A chemical reaction of the heat and your wheel cleaners can cause a cloud of toxic vapor to enter your nose and eyes.

If the vehicle has just been dropped off, we suggest you continue to prep the rest of the car until the wheels have had time to cool down.

Carefully examine the wheels prior to cleaning them as there are many different types and some can only be cleaned with certain types of cleaners. So it is important that you distinguish what type of wheels you are cleaning beforehand.

Wheels made of a coated alloy, aluminum, steel, plastic or paint can be severely damaged if the improper cleaner is used. We suggest you clean these types of wheels with your wash pad and soapy water with a good Car Wash Shampoo.

Note: You may sometimes notice the appearance of rust on the brake drum after treating the wheel with an acid based wheel cleaner. This is a perfectly **normal reaction**. Once you or the customer applies the brakes and the brake shoes come on contact with the drum the friction of the shoes will remove it.

Directions: Should the wheels be greasy and dirty, we suggest you pre-spray these with All Purpose Cleaner and scrub with your Bug Sponge or Fender Brush. For hard to reach and tight areas use your parts brush to clean in between the spokes and slots of the wheels. Now rinse this area thoroughly. Be sure to only **clean one wheel at a time**, because if you allow your cleaning solution to be left on the wheel too long, both the cleaner and dirt will dry and stick to the surface and cleaning will become less effective.

The easiest type of wheel to clean is a chrome wheel. If the chrome is dirty and full of brake dust, spray a liberal amount of Wheel/Mag Cleaner over the entire wheel and allow the acid based product to sit for approximately one minute. Now blast the wheel clean with your Pressure Washer. Repeat this step should the first application of cleaner not entirely remove the brake dust. Be sure to use your parts brush to accelerate cleaning, especially in the hard to reach spoke wire types, commonly found on Cadillac's.

NOTE: Since many of your cleaning products contain mild acids or solvents, we suggest you consider the area in which you are cleaning the wheels and tires. These products can permanently stain expensive concrete or custom tile work, **so we suggest you bring the car to the asphalt pavement in the street rather than using the driveway**. Be sure to rinse and clean up your area after the detail of any remaining residue caused by cleaning such things as wheels and dressing runoff on the tires.

ALWAYS WEAR PROTECTIVE GOGGLES, RUBBER GLOVES, AND CAREFULLY FOLLOW THE MANUFACTURERS INSTRUCTIONS WHEN APPLYING THESE PRODUCTS.

NOTE: If you choose to use an acid based wheel cleaner **apply to CHROME WHEELS ONLY!** Non-Chrome Wheels such as uncoated Aluminum types are sensitive and susceptible to blushing or permanent staining.

TEST TIP: If you are unsure if you are cleaning a wheel that is compatible with an acid based Wheel/Mag Cleaner, have running water in one hand and a spray bottle of acid based Wheel/Mag Cleaner in the other hand. Spray a small amount on a tiny section of the wheel. **If the wheel begins to foam, RINSE IMMEDIATELY!** This is a sign that the wheel is NOT compatible with this type of cleaner and permanent damage could occur if not rinsed off quickly!

Be sure to follow this same procedure on all other wheels that are not made of chrome.

Rubber Tires And White Walls

Now let's proceed to the proper care of the tire and white wall areas. Remember, this is one of the dirtiest areas of the vehicle so it's important that you continually rinse your brushes, bug sponges, wash mitt and even periodically change your bucket of soapy water. You will help to prevent contamination and prevent scratching the paint when it's time to wash the surface of the car.

Directions: Now that the mag wheel has been cleaned, it's time to clean the rubber and if applicable the white wall portion of the tire. Be sure to spray a liberal amount of All Purpose Cleaner or a water based degreaser over the entire rubber portion of the tire. Be sure to spray the complete tire, because if the cleaner is not applied evenly it could leave uneven spots or streaks on the tire where the chemical made contact.

A good All Purpose Cleaner contains a powerful cleaner called butyl, which will strip away dirt and oils from previously applied dressings. Now dip your fender wheel brush into your bucket of soap solution and scrub the entire circumference of the wheel. Should the tire have a white wall or lettering, spray an additional amount of All Purpose Cleaner or a White Wall Cleaner especially if you find rust or black scuff mark deposits. A White Wall Cleaner should contain a bleaching agent which will bring the white walls back to a snowy white look. Vigorously scrub this area with a white wall wire brush until clean.

For stubborn white walls you can pre-spray the white walls with a tar remover and use a wire brush to clean off any hard to clean black curb scuff marks. Rinse the entire wheel and tire one more time. You will find that a clean, snow white wall really sets off the tire, and you can bet your customer will notice this special touch to detail as well.

Now, the last section of the wheel is the wheel well area behind the tire. Keep in mind that this area can make or break the appearance of your detail. Should the vehicle have a black undercoating in the wheel well area you will have a nice contrast background for your wheel and tires to stand out. However, if the wheel well has only body paint exposed this will not look as nice since the paint will probably be stained, chipped or pitted.

As an add-on service many professional detailers will resolve this problem by spraying an undercoating in the wheel well area for a fee. This easy to apply undercoating can be purchased in most automotive retail stores and is sold in aerosol cans. If you decide to offer this undercoating service to your customer, we recommend you charge an extra $15 to $25 per wheel. Be sure to apply this at the very end of the detail, this way any overspray can be removed easily by using your tar and grease remover.

Before adding any undercoating pre-spray the wheel well area with your All Purpose Cleaner or you can use a water based Engine Degreaser for heavy accumulation of road oil. Allow the chemical to dwell for about 30 seconds to ensure the cleaner has time to really do its work and cut through the grease. By using your fender wheel brush you can pre-scrub the wheel well area to loosen dirt, leaves, mud, road salt, and other debris. Now blast the wheel well area with the full force of the Pressure Washer to completely rinse the soap away. Should the vehicle have mud flaps, be sure to scrub these as well including any white lettering on the back side of the flaps. For some of your fancier mud flaps, be sure to polish any chrome or aluminum plating as well.

You have just completed cleaning the wheel area, with the exception of the dressing, which will be covered later in the manual.

TIP: To ensure you have not missed any areas, back up the car to ensure the wheel rotates approximately ½ turn from top to bottom (180) degrees. Rotating the wheel with the top portion of the wheel now on the bottom, will allow you to see if any brake dust or grease was missed.

Grill Body And Undercarriage

Let's now take a look at cleaning the front grill, front and rear underbody, and the side or rocker panel areas.

We'll start with the front underbody. This area is below the license plate or the valance/spoiler area. Often this area is missed by many detailers, however if you stand back far enough the underside areas of the vehicle will be quite evident. Therefore, we highly suggest you pay close attention to these areas.

Directions: Using the Pressure Washer, blast away any accumulated dirt and bugs. Ensure you pressure wash the front grill area as well, removing as many bugs and dirt as possible. Pre-spray the front underbody and grill areas with the All Purpose Cleaner and with your bug sponge start working systematically across the top area working the bug sponge into the headlights, grill area, front bumper, and reflector lights. Be sure to work the sponge in all the nooks and crevices of the grill area. Now scrub the harder to clean areas with your wheel and fender brush. Ensure you remove stubborn bugs on the license plate and in between the grill fins. After you dip your fender brush into your bucket of soapy solution, scrub the valance area underneath the bumper.

Rinse the area thoroughly with clean water, once all these areas have been cleaned.

On the rear tail light section of the car and under the bumper area where the exhaust and road tar accumulate, follow the same cleaning sequence. Be sure to pre-rinse these areas first with the Pressure Washer in order to remove caked on mud as well as other debris. Also, pre-spray these areas with the All Purpose Cleaner. Start with the underbody and then around the license plates, lens light covers, and rear emblems. Should the vehicle have a chrome rear bumper, it may be stained from carbon exhaust and should be pre-sprayed with the All Purpose Cleaner as well. Using your bug sponge hand scrub these areas clean.

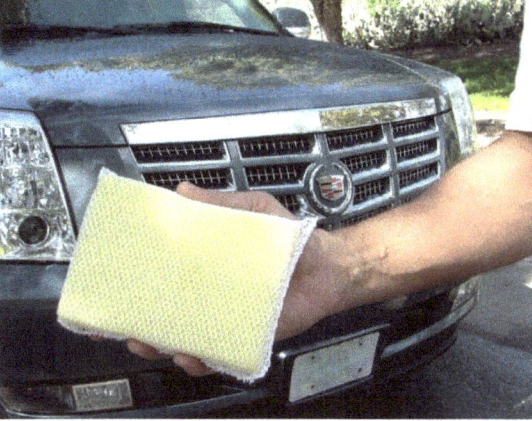

There are detailers who will go to extreme efforts and take off license plates and emblems during the detailing process. Since this method can be extremely time consuming and risky of breaking something, we highly suggest you don't practice this method. Instead, we have found that by simply spraying an amount of All Purpose Cleaner directly on the emblem and rinsing will clean this area just as well. However, be sure to power rinse the area with water before spraying the All Purpose Cleaner. This cleaner contains butyl and as it strips away dirt it also strips away wax and will leave streak marks on the paint. Remember to always pre-rinse the paint with water to help dilute the cleaner and prevent it from sticking to the paint.

The three areas you will most likely apply All Purpose Cleaner directly to the paint are the front and rear bumpers, side door guards or moldings, and the body emblems.

Directions: In order to clean the emblems, we suggest you take out your toothbrush, bug sponge, and Q-Tips. By using these tools work the dirt and exhaust build-up loose in between and around the letters, until the area is clean. To do a proper job, you may have to clean and rinse 2 or 3 times. You can also apply this same technique to the light lens and license plate areas.

Road Tar And Sap Removal

Since Tree Sap and Road Tar can be another time consuming project, we suggest you do this work prior to washing and soaping the vehicle.

Road tar is a sticky black residue and appears as small dark spots on chrome or paint. It can be found on the underside of the vehicle, around the lip areas of the fender wells, and directly behind the wheels on the bottom of the rocker panel area.

Another culprit is tree sap and is found on the roof, hood, trunk or top side of the vehicle. It can have a characteristic of a clear sticky soft glue or sometimes little hard specks from tree fall out. It may also have a pine scent odor for the softer of the two types of tree sap.

Road tar or tree sap can be treated with a Gum and Tar remover that is safe to use on clear coats, non-clear coats, enamels, lacquers and can be sprayed directly onto the paint. After spraying the Gum and Tar remover you may notice a slight white haze - DO NOT WORRY - this wipes and polishes right off. We recommend cleaning these areas before the soap wash, because it's easier to find your target. If the vehicle is extremely dirty then this process would be best done during the soap and rinse sequence of the car wash.

Directions: **To remove road tar**; spray some of your Gum and Tar remover directly on the tar found on the rocker panels. Rub briskly, agitating the tar material loose by using a soft towel or bug sponge. The tar will start to dissolve quickly. To get the best results it's best to spray, rub, and rinse the affected tar areas in small sections. If you don't rinse the area off quickly the dissolving tar will dry and stick once again to the surface. Thus the reason we suggest you address these areas prior to the hand wash. You can remove the remaining residue by using the wool wash mitt and soap.

Directions: **To remove tree sap**; spray some of the Gum and Tar remover directly onto the clear sap and let the cleaner sit for approximately one minute in order to loosen the sap. Use either your fingernail or a thin plastic razor blade, designed for removing tree sap, to avoid scratching the surface. You can also use your bug sponge, however be sure to not rub too hard especially on darker colored vehicles. Scratches will appear much easier on these dark colored surfaces.

The Pressure Washing Sequence

Now it's time to move on to the power rinsing and washing of the vehicle.

Directions: Ensure you begin by thoroughly rinsing and removing any grit and dirt from your detail brushes and wash mitts before proceeding.

The goal is to remove as much dirt and debris as possible using the Pressure Washer.

Using the force of the spray start at the top of the vehicle and work your way down. Mud and dirt are much heavier than water and will flow to the bottom of the automobile. Remove all bird droppings, tree sap, and bugs by starting at the top with the pressure washer. Move across to the rain gutters, hood, and trunk area using the force of the Pressure Washer to clean all the hard to reach areas. Now work your way to the windows and then down the sides of the car. With your pressure washer, get up close to the door edge protectors or side moldings. Be sure to use, with your pressure washer, a concentrated force to work lose any trapped dirt. Lastly, work your way down to the front grill, underside of the car, and the back underside area.

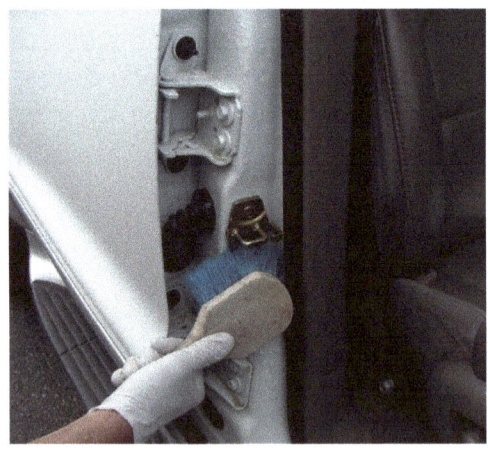

This would be a good time to clean the door jamb areas as well, due to the heavy grease and dirt that accumulates in this area. We suggest you, once again, use the Pressure Washer to cut down on your time making it that much easier to clean when it's time to go back in and hand clean this area later on.

Keep in mind that cleaning door jambs is a lot like cleaning the engine. There are many hard to reach areas especially around the door hinges. Also, due to the grease that builds up in  this area it will require the same cleaning tools. After you rinse the car, open all of the car doors and spray a liberal amount of All Purpose Cleaner on the door jambs. Around the greasier parts of the door hinges, you may want to spray a Water Based Engine Degreaser or Tar remover in order to dissolve the grease. At this point, don't worry about getting any chemical on the paint, as the remaining water on the vehicle will help suspend the product from staining the paint.

 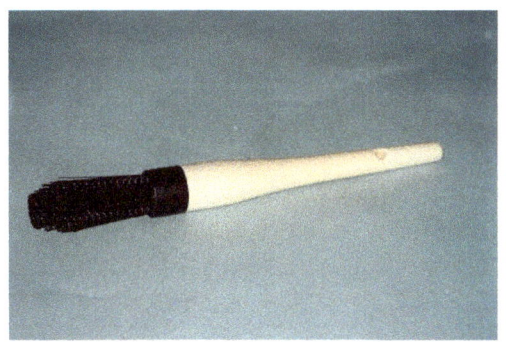

By using your parts or fender brush, work them into the hinge area in order to break loose the old grease as well as the door latches or any other hard to reach areas. Move to the inside curves and lip areas by using your bug sponge. Clean all flat painted surfaces as well with your sponge. Now dip your fender brush into your soap and scrub the underside of the door area. Prepare to get dirty, because this is an area commonly forgotten. Note: Some Mercedes models have a plastic lip edge on the bottom of the door. We suggest you clean this area with an All Purpose Cleaner and your fender brush. Be sure to blast these areas clean with the force of the Pressure Washer. Be sure to avoid getting chemicals or water back splash inside the vehicle. Some of these strong chemicals can spot or discolor the interior of the car. In order to keep water and chemicals from ricocheting inside the car, reduce the amount of pressure spray. Be sure to always get close to your work to help prevent any overspray and if necessary wipe off the interior upholstery immediately with a damp towel or chamois.

Vinyl Tops

Should the vehicle have a vinyl top now would be the best time to clean this area. Keep in mind that there are many types of vinyl, some are harder than others. Be conscious of the difference in the feel and touch of a vinyl top, dash board or vinyl seat. These pieces of vinyl are a resin thermoplastic material and are created in much the same way, and share a common technical name known as Naugahyde vinyl. However, in order to keep it simple we will refer to it as a vinyl top.

Cleaning a vinyl top is just as important as cleaning any other surface. Due to dirt and environmental excretions becoming deeply embedded into the texture of the grain, as well as direct sunlight, you should pay special attention to these areas to both clean and preserve the pliability and sheen of the vinyl top.

Directions: Remember to work from the top to bottom of the vehicle in order to save you time from having to rinse an area more than once.

Should the surface of the vinyl top become dry, rinse again with pure water and spray an amount of All Purpose Cleaner directly onto the top - one quarter panel at a time. Hand scrub this area vigorously with an iron shaped carpet brush or horse hair brush using circular motions, and then working back and forth in straight lines. Only clean 1/4 of a panel at a time. Use plenty of rinse water should the surface of the top become too hot, as the dirty cleaning solution will stick to the vinyl. Rinse thoroughly, each time you complete scrubbing a ¼ panel and then move to the next section until the entire top is completely clean. Be sure to miss no areas by overlapping as you go.

After completely cleaning the vinyl top, we recommend you rinse the entire vehicle one more time. Due to the fact, that if the All Purpose Cleaner is left on the paint surface it could leave unsightly streak marks. Should you feel the vinyl top is in pretty good shape and not in need of much cleaning, then we suggest you only need to hand wash this area using your bucket of Car Wash Shampoo and your wash mitt.

Should there be rips or tears in the vinyl, then precede carefully using lower pressure from the Pressure Washer. We also suggest you step back a few steps while using your pressure washer to get the same results. Be sure to use caution when applying direct spray at the seams as these are held together by nylon vinyl thread.

Use good judgment before cleaning any vinyl tops; especially if the top is damaged or discolored beyond normal appearance. Should this be the case, you may be better off avoiding this area all together. We will be covering the last step in treating the vinyl top, (proper vinyl conditioning, using the right softening silicone conditioners) later on in this manual.

Convertible Tops

When it comes to convertible tops, there is really no special treatment. Most convertible tops are made of different material than vinyl. Usually these are made of a canvas type of fabric. Thus where the term "Rag Top" came from! These are normally cleaned by simply using mild soap and a wash mitt. We suggest you use your carpet or horse hair brush should the top be really dirty. Keep in mind that convertible tops are not like vinyl tops and are not always watertight, so we highly suggest you avoid spraying water directly at the top portion of the windows where the canvas top meets. A great ad-on service would be to offer a Scotch Guard treatment once the top is cleaned and dried. Ideally a Rag Top should be resealed once a year.

Should you use your carpet brush to clean the top, be careful to avoid the sensitive plastic windows, usually found with most convertible tops. This area can be scratched very easily, so we suggest you use your wash mitt only in this area.

Use caution not to scratch plastic convertible windows.

Power Up The Suds!

Now that you have gone through most of the Prep stage and have periodically power rinsed the overall vehicle to remove most of the dirt, mud, and leaves it's time to activate the automatic soap cleaning system. Displacing soap through the Pressure Washer will save time and steps as it is a fast way of blanketing soap over the entire area, which is accomplished through the use of the soap injection system located on the Pressure Washer. This will help cut through the bulk of the dirt before starting the hand body wash sequence.

Directions: First, take a separate empty gallon container and fill it about ¼ full with concentrated car wash soap. Then fill the container with water. Now simply use your soap injector system by placing the clear chemical hose with the pickup strainer into the premixed solution of Car Wash Shampoo.

TIP: Should your tap water have harsh chemicals or you find calcium deposits and water spots after washing, we recommend you invest in purchasing a soft water system tied into your tap water line.

If you have a pressure washer with a soap injection system hold the trigger gun firmly in one hand and with the other hand turn the downstream injector knob all the way to the left side. This will cause an air passage suction to pull through the hose, and automatically dispense the soapy suds out of the end of the wand. As the soap is being pulled through the hose it also being diluted with water and will provide you with mild foaming suds.

Note: **If you are using a garden hose you can use a Soap Bottle Foam Gun** like this one to accomplish the same thing. By squeezing the trigger gun, move slowly across the entire car from top to sides to bottom, dispensing the soap over the entire vehicle. Allow the car shampoo to sit on the surface for roughly 2 minutes in order to break down all the dirt and bugs in order to make your hand body wash more efficient.

The Foam Gun provides a quick and easy way to distribute the foamy soap solution on the vehicle. Just coat the entire surface and follow up with your wash mitt.

Hand Body Wash

Now it's time to hand wash the vehicle. It is impossible to remove all the dirt without agitating or hand washing the surface, even though the soap cuts through the initial bulk of the dirt.

Directions: Use your wool wash pad and dip it into a bucket of premixed soap solution, usually about 2 ounces per gallon of water. Work the pad in a circular motion across the surface starting with the top and working down. A good quality wash pad is made of safe synthetic wool that is extremely absorbent and yet soft enough not to scratch the surface of the vehicle. The deep wool pile encapsulates dirt and carries it deep down inside the fibers to keep the abrasive contaminants away from the surface of the paint.

Over a period of time dirt and grit can get trapped and scratch the surface, so we suggest you rinse your wool wash pad thoroughly with the Pressure Washer to remove all the dirt.

Start with the roof of the car, wash in a systematic fashion using the divide, and conquer method. We suggest you work on one half of the car at a time to ensure the soap does not dry too quickly before you have a chance to clean the area. As before, start at the top and work your way to the bottom by starting with the roof, then the trunk, and the hood of the car. Ensure to overlap your hand washing to help avoid missing any areas. Keep in mind that when water sheets onto paint it gives an appearance of a very shiny surface and can be deceiving. Missed dirt areas can easily be seen on dark colors such as black and dark blue.

Now continue washing the second half of the car. On hot days the soap may dry too quickly and leave a film on the paint, so be sure to rinse more frequently with clean water or you may want to work in smaller sections at a time.

Concentrate on thoroughly washing the body of the car, and move down and across the windows and window frame. Be sure to lift the windshield wipers off the glass to the up position and wash these as well. Now move to the sides of the car by starting with the front side and fender area, then the driver or passenger door, side moldings, rocker panels, exhaust pipes, side mirrors, and any outside body vents, like those found on the older Corvette models. Should the car have flip-up head lights, be sure to activate them and wash them as well. In order to activate the pop-up headlight, simply turn the key to the "On" position and turn the headlight switch on. Since many pop-up lenses are activated through an air pressure system, you may need to physically start the car in order to open or close the head light mechanism.

Go over the front grill and rear end bumper areas one more time. Ensure you check to see if all areas of the car have been completely soaped down. At this point, any missed areas should be re-cleaned as well.

Power Rinsing

The next step is to purge the soap from the hose and power rinse the entire car. Simply turn the soap injector knob all the way back to the right, and squeeze the trigger gun until the remaining soap is cleared out of the hose. Usually takes no more than about 20 seconds to fully clear the hose.

By angling the spray away from you, start working systematically to power rinse the dirt and water down away from the car and towards the ground. When rinsing, don't forget to work from top to bottom.

Always respect the power of the Pressure Washer by using common sense and not pointing the powerful spray too close to the vehicle you are washing.

Be sure to rinse the windows and window tracks thoroughly as these areas tend to hold water and soap. To avoid damaging vinyl tops, decals, simulated vinyl wood grain sidings, emblems, and stickers, take advantage of the variable pressure control and use caution when power rinsing these items. Should you notice any paint chipping, be sure to use caution around these areas as the powerful spray can actually do further damage by lifting the paint loose causing an unsightly dilemma. Now power rinse the remaining bugs on the side view mirrors, license plates, and grill areas. Power rinse under the front and rear bumper, valance, spoiler, tail pipe, wheel well, and tire areas to ensure the car is thoroughly clean and ready for the last step of prep work.

Drying The Car

We recommend you use a synthetic chamois (Water Sprite) or a Waffle Weave microfiber highly absorbent towel for the drying process. This soft and absorbent material is unlike any ordinary towel and one of the key tools to your detailing business. A store bought chamois cloth is processed using a softening and conditioning product made from animal oil, which actually tends to draw wax off the painted surface reducing the life expectancy of the wax job. However, by using the synthetic chamois, which contains no animal oil, it reduces the likelihood of pulling the wax off the painted surface thus extending the life of the wax job.

Once again, by starting at the top of the vehicle carefully wipe off all puddles of water. By paying particular attention to the window frames, side moldings, grill, between the bumper guards, headlights, tail lights, body vents as well as any other hard to reach area, work the chamois into each nook and cranny. Remove as much water as possible. One trick to safely and quickly remove excess water is to use a Silicone Water Blade like this one shown. Remove as much of the water first with the blade and then follow up with the synthetic chamois or waffle weave towel.

Open all of the doors, hood, and trunk area and allow jambs to be exposed in order to wipe these areas dry using the chamois cloth. By ensuring these areas are cleaned thoroughly will help to save time later on.

> **NOTE:** Be sure to use a detailer's towel instead of the chamois cloth, should there be any grease or oil present in these areas.

Caution: If your chamois gets contaminated with grease or oil it will become difficult to do any further cleaning without smearing the grease on painted surfaces or windows while drying the vehicle. If you accidently pick-up grease or oil in your chamois cloth, you can clean it with mild laundry detergent. Always air dry your chamois, never put it into a dryer!

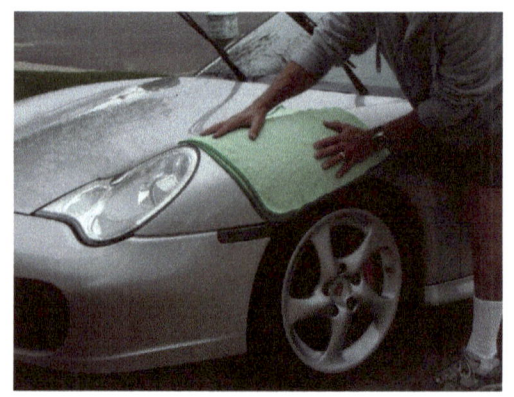

In order to do a thorough job ensure you remove as much water as possible from the chamois by wringing it out frequently. Water spotting can occur if the water is not wiped off quickly, especially during the hot summer months. You may notice drying lines in the paint once you've completely dried the car, especially with darker colors.

To remedy this, take a slightly damp chamois in one hand and a clean dry micro fiber towel in the other hand and quickly wipe a 3 x 3 foot area with the chamois cloth following up with a wipe down using a micro fiber towel immediately thereafter until all the lines have disappeared.

Should you plan on compounding and waxing the vehicle next, it is very important that you remove every bit of water. Just as water and oil are not compatible with each other, the same thing holds true with mixing sealants and waxes with water. If this occurs you will end up with streaks in the paint. There are 4 things you can do to completely eliminate excess water in order to avoid this annoying situation:

1. You can use an air compressor or if you have a wet/dry shop vacuum with a blower attachment, use the force of the air along with your crevice tool to blow out any hidden water in the cracks and seals of the vehicle.

2. You can start the car and take it around the block, carefully stopping and lurching forward as you go, to help run off excess water.

3. You can remove the excess water on the surface first by using a water blade before towel drying.

4 The best method of removing water is to simply allow the water to air dry and evaporate, once the main chamois drying has been completed.

We recommend you proceed to the interior to allow the car ample time to dry by itself in order to be ready to accept glazing and compounding.

Directions: Once the car has completely been wiped dry, spray a liberal amount of Vinyl Dressing on the rubber portion of the tires, soaking every square inch of the rubber. At this point, do not wipe off excess dressing. This will allow better saturation and penetration of conditioning silicones. This would also be a good time to dress the vinyl roof, should the car be equipped with one. Since the roof is such a large area apply the dressing in even strokes and more than one coat may be necessary. The dressing protects the vinyl from sun and rain similar to what a sealant does to the paint. Work well into the vinyl top by spraying the dressing on a palm sized towel or wax pad applicator. Be sure to avoid spraying any dressing on surrounding painted areas as well as the back window. We also suggest you avoid spraying or misting Vinyl Dressing near the car, unless you are planning to compound and wax the car later. Towel dry the residue from these areas, should the dressing come in contact with the painted surface of the car.

TIP: For those old faded bumpers often found on VW Jettas, Rabbits, and some Toyota Sedans we suggest you follow these steps in order to clean and condition them to a deep glossy look:

Scrub vigorously by using your All Purpose Cleaner and a brush to remove any of the old Vinyl Dressing on the bumpers. The rubber will accept a fresh coat of long lasting silicone by using the Vinyl Dressing and working it in thoroughly.

NOTE: New rubber and vinyl will get an excellent even sheen by saturating these areas with either a clean towel or wax pad applicator.

For old faded or dry looking rubber, particularly on rubber bumpers and tires, it may be necessary to use a Solvent Based type of Tire Dressing in order bring back the life of these parts. Don't forget to wipe off any excess residue on any painted surfaces. Allow the dressing to sit and penetrate these areas and then buff off the excess residue in the final Touch Up Section.

Caution: Many Solvent based dressings are flammable and should not be used for treating engine compartments or vehicle interiors.

Now the car looks clean and is thoroughly prepped for our next phase of detailing the interior.

Special Notes Page

Section 8

Detailing The Interior

Interior	123
Vacuuming	125
Animal Hair	131
Shampooing The Interior	133
Headliner - Shampooing	134
Cloth Upholstery Seats	137
Sun Rot	138
Carpets And Mats	138
Removing Carpet Stains	141
Extreme Circumstances	142
Shampooing/Extraction Method	143
Operating Instructions For The Carpet And Upholstery Cleaner Solution	144
Cleaning Vinyl Headliners	145
Sunroof	146
General Area Cleaning	146
Dashboard And Gauges	147
Vents And Recessed Areas	148
Steering Wheel	149
Ashtrays	149
Seat Belts	150
Floor Mats	151
Fabric Guard	152
Cleaning Interior Vinyl	153
Door Jambs	155
Vinyl Upholstery And Trim	156
Vinyl Dressing	157
Leather Upholstery And Trim	158

Interior

Since it is the interior of the car your customer will spend most of their time in, it is crucial to strive for absolute perfection in this area of detailing. After all, a perfectly detailed interior is the essence of what really brings together the overall success of detailing a vehicle.

It is a must to have complete knowledge of your cleaning compounds, be disciplined, and follow a strict format of cleaning procedures. The general rule of thumb is to **treat your customer's car as if it where your very own**. By following this principle you will always do an outstanding job that both you and your customer can be proud of.

Keep in mind that when you put great emphasis on detailing the interior you create a driving environment like no other for your customer. They will be pleased with your work when they are able to see the luster, feel the clean surface, and enjoy the clean smells of a well detailed vehicle. This is what will keep your customer coming back again and again.

By maintaining your customer's vehicle you will be able to extend the life and value of their car. You can revitalize the interior carpets through shampooing and extraction of dirt and grit, which can cause premature wear and tear. Using vinyl and leather cleaners will recondition the interior to its original soft sheen and luster.

Some of the basic areas we will cover in revitalizing the interior are:

1. Thorough Vacuuming
2. Shampooing and Extraction
3. Vinyl and Leather Cleaning & Conditioning
4. Dressing the Interior
5. *Removing* Stubborn Spots
6. Cleaning Those Hard to Reach Access Areas
7. Special Sensitive Cleaning Procedures

There is so much more to detailing a vehicle than a barrage of cleaning every speck of dust, dirt, and grease on the car. There are a variety of surfaces, angles, contours and other unusual areas that must be paid attention to. Including the dashboard, console, steering wheel, foot pedals, seat pleats, trunk, ashtrays, carpets, upholstery, and other small but important details.

In order to set up and prep, the equipment you'll need is:

1. Wet/Dry Vacuum

2. Carpet & Upholstery Extractor

3. Fabric Guard Applicator

4. Detail Brushes and Towels

For the cleaners you'll need:

1. All Purpose Cleaner
2. Carpet & Upholstery Shampoo
3. Pre Traffic Lane Cleaner
4. Tar and Gum Remover
5. Spot and Fabric Cleaner
6. Vinyl Dressing
7. Leather Dressing

It is very important that you remember "there are at least two sides to everything" and each side must be cleaned. As you will experience during the detailing process there are various angles and an enormous amount of components on each vehicle. So we highly recommend you both clean and pay attention to every item on the car as well as every angle or side of the section you are cleaning.

Before starting get yourself acquainted with the car and make a mental note of all the difficult areas to clean. Note how the seats operate, are they manual or electric, and is the upholstery cloth, fabric or leather. By making a mental note of these things up front, will help you determine your course of action in how you plan to systematic clean the interior.

At this time we suggest you open up all of the doors, trunk or hatch-back. Note: Should you feel that the interior detailing will take longer than one hour we suggest you turn the overhead dome light off to ensure you don't run down the battery life of the car.

Vacuuming

By thoroughly cleaning the interior of a car it rejuvenates the whole vehicle. Carpets and fabric will look plusher and smell fresher once cleaned. Remember, it's the interior of a car that produces the feeling of newness that your customers will appreciate. In the business of detailing, this is what we call the "playing on a customer's ego" factor. In a sense the customer's car is an extension of their personality, so pay special attention to all of the details.

The interior of a car is what detailing is all about, so be careful to systematic plan how you will proceed with the cleaning process. This will save you a lot of time in the long run. Since there are many nooks and crannies, including different materials to polish and clean, be aware of the interior with an intense thoroughness. With a glance you will get a first-hand look at how either a customer is meticulous or messy based on the interior of the car. However, you will find that most vehicles are in desperate need of cleaning, thus the reason they have come to you. With this in mind, try not to become overwhelmed when a customer hands you their vehicle that's 3 feet deep in newspapers, dirt, and who knows what else!

Just take each car one step at a time, and admire your work from taking a dirty car to a master piece of shine and cleanliness.

By vacuuming the upholstery and carpeting, it will actually extend the life expectancy of these fabrics. As you know, every time shoes or clothes come in contact with the upholstery and carpets this can cause these fibers/material to lose their ability to respond or plush up and can become dull and flat. So the main purpose for a thorough vacuum is to remove all dirt and grit that becomes embedded in the fabric/material.

Using your crevice and floor tools, you will be able to remove all embedded dirt and grit and bring the fabrics back to life. You can loosen the dirt by agitating the fabrics using a brush and brisk back and forth movements.

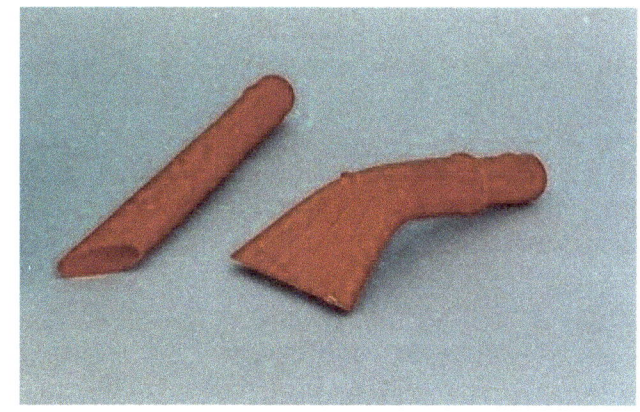

As mentioned before in this manual we suggest you start at the top and work your way down. In other words, start vacuuming the ceiling, work your way down to the dash, the seats, and lastly the floor area. You should always finish up your vacuuming on the carpet sections of the car.

Directions: Be sure to remove any large pieces of paper, pencils or any other objects too large to fit through your vacuum tools before you begin vacuuming. Now move both the front and passenger seats all the way back in order to get up close to your work area. Be sure to get at eye level of the floor to ensue nothing is missed. By using your crevice tool you will be able to get into those hard-to-reach areas. This crevice tool will also help to provide a stronger suction in order to pull stubborn gum wrappers and pencils caught way down deep in between the side of the seat and console area. By using the floor tool, which has a broader base like a hand claw, will allow you to vacuum larger areas quickly. With the combination of these two tools you will be able to vacuum everything including in between and underneath the seats and trunk area, the headliner, dashboard, console, ashtrays, seat pleats, piping, vinyl and leather, doors, door compartments, foot pedals, knobs, and rear window sill.

Ensure you concentrate on vacuuming up as much as possible; however remember you will be shampooing and extracting the seats and upholstery later. This will allow you to remove the last of any remaining sand or dirt.

For ease of operating your vacuum, be sure to place it at the back door behind the drivers' seat. Most vacuum hoses are long enough to reach from one side to the other, saving you time from having to pick up the vacuum each time you clean a section. Ensure the hose is free of dirt before you drape it across the carpet or upholstery. With the crevice tool use brisk back and forth movements to dislodge ground in dirt. You can use the large floor tool to pass over and pick up any of the dislodged dirt. Since the floor and crevice tool is made of a hard durable plastic it could possibly tear more sensitive materials, so use good judgment when cleaning these areas by using a lighter touch.

Directions: Use the crevice tool and gently vacuum the headliner first. You will find that many headliners are made of a perforated vinyl material with tiny holes which tend to accumulate dust. However, other headliners are made of a soft velour or cotton type of material. Ensure you vacuum these types of materials slowly as you will find that by using too much suction it can cause the fabric to pull away. Most of these types of headliners use a suspended wire frame formed into the ceiling of the roof, and then covered with a fabric. In order to check whether or not the car has a suspended ceiling, gently push on the fabric with the flat palm of your hand. Should the ceiling feel hollow, this is a strong indication of a suspended wire ceiling. Ensure you use extra caution when running the crevice tool across a suspended ceiling. By using too much pressure, at the sharp pointed part of the tool, you could rip or puncture this area.

Now, slowly guide the edge of your crevice tool in between the front windshield and dash area, picking up any foreign materials too hard to reach by hand. Ensure you vacuum out all air vents, knobs, and the console area. By taking your paint style toothbrush you can loosen any stubborn embedded dirt in those tough to reach areas. The paint style toothbrush also works well for loosening dirt in air vents, gauges, grooves, foot pedals, interior handles, and armrests. In order to clean other stubborn areas, too tough for the soft bristle paint brush, use the standard detail brush. Work the brush back and forth along the seams and buttons and then follow right behind with the suction of the vacuum, as this will pick up the dirt as you go along. Another personal favorite cleaning tool for these areas is a dusting brush which looks very similar to a basting brush you'll find many times in the kitchen. The long soft bristles get in the hard to reach deep pockets and crevices.

Now slide the front seats completely forward and start vacuuming at the rear of the vehicle. Using your crevice tool, vacuum the rear dash area above the back seat and in between the window.

Before moving down towards the seat portion of the car, first vacuum the back side, working the crevice tool around the button areas and pleats of the upholstery. You can use one hand to spread apart hard to reach areas and to separate the cushion portion of the fabric resting against the seat itself. This area is where you will find the heaviest accumulation of dirt and debris. Using the crevice tool, move along the pleats that run up and down or across the center of the seat as well as along the outer piping found on the edge of the seat. Work lose any sand or dirt by using the paint style toothbrush and follow right behind with the vacuum to pick up the loosened dirt.

You will find when cleaning cloth or velour type seats that tiny fibers, hair, and lint tend to cling and get woven into the fabric making it difficult to remove with just the vacuum. We suggest you take a soft full bodied hair brush and start working the brush sideways across the sets. Follow up with the vacuum nozzle to pick up the

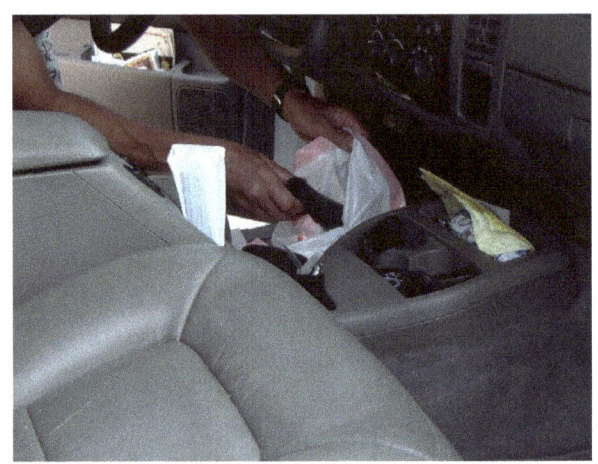

dirt and lint. Use this procedure towards the bottom of the seat until the seats are completely clean of dirt and lint. Should you not have a hair brush handy, a good quality lint brush will also work well.

Before moving to the door panel area, be sure to empty both the panels and compartments of any papers, maps, pens, etc. Thoroughly vacuum this area by using the crevice tool.

In order to save a few steps, we suggest you do half of the back portion of the

vehicle at a time. Using the crevice tool, vacuum underneath the front seat area being sure to reach as far under as possible to ensure nothing is missed. Since the front seat is in a forward position, it should be far easier for you to reach under this area. Ensure to vacuum out as much dirt inside and around the metal seat tracks as well. Should you find the vacuum doesn't do a thorough job, then we suggest you take a treated cloth using a good All Purpose

Cleaner, and remove the dirt.

Ensure you vacuum along the side corners and along all the crevices between the seat and the console. Retrace your steps by removing the crevice tool and replacing it with the large claw floor tool, and begin vacuuming the upholstery seats. By using the wide angle suction you will quickly pick up any remaining dirt previously dislodged and left behind. Most vehicles will be pretty much the same when going through the vacuum procedure. However, there are always exceptions to the rule, such as hatchbacks, Jeeps, and station wagons, which are different in regards to additional storage compartments and extra seating.

Since many detailers often overlook these areas, we suggest you pay close attention to the positions of seats, especially those that collapse forward or fold down. Most fold down seats are not adjustable from the floor so find the release catch, which is usually located on the side panel or on the upper back seat. In order to move these forward you must lift the bench seat up and then move it forward towards the back side of the driver and passenger seat. Once the bench seat has been lifted and moved forward, thoroughly vacuum the area. After this is completed, release the catch and lay the seat down in the forward position and vacuum all of the crevice in the folded area, which is normally hidden when in the up position.

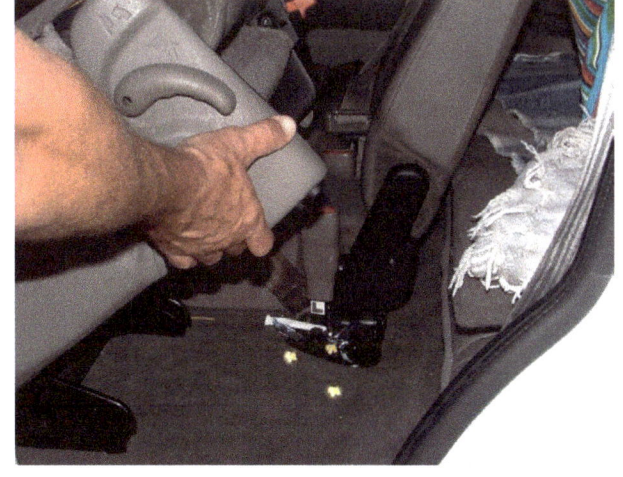

Now move to the carpet area and briskly agitate the carpet with a back and forth movement. Generally, these floor carpets have more dirt and sand embedded in them than any other area of the vehicle. With the flat of you palm tap the carpet firmly in order to speed up the vacuuming process. This will allow all the trapped sand to pop up to the surface making vacuuming that much easier. Another technique is to take a 5" wire brush or an old hair brush, and agitate the carpet while following up with the vacuum. Whenever you are faced with removing clumps of dirt, sand, straw, pine needles, fox tails or animal hair, the brush works best.

Be sure to remove all rubber or carpeted floor mats prior to vacuuming. Place the floor mats outside of the vehicle in order to brush and vacuum after you complete vacuuming the interior. For the front section, clean all of the seat pleats, piping, in between the seat siding and console areas, as well as underneath the floor of the seat and all the metal slide areas. Ensure you don't miss

vacuuming underneath the foot pedals and along the floor board located to the side of the seats.

Remove all ashtrays and vacuum them out. Should the customer be a smoker, you'll often times find ashes underneath the ashtray as well, so be sure to vacuum this once you've pulled the ashtray out.

Once the interior is thoroughly vacuumed, start on the trunk area by bringing the vacuum over to this section. Be sure to remove any obstructions, such as the spare tire, emergency road kits, and any other miscellaneous objects before you start vacuuming. By using the same procedure as before, vacuum the carpet and go over every square inch of trunk. Most hatchbacks and station wagons have pull up carpeting and should be lifted and vacuumed as well as those areas located beneath the carpeting. Usually the carpet is left unattached for the purpose of accessing the spare tire located in this area.

Should the trunk have a removable carpet mat, take it out of the car and set it on the ground for easier access to the area underneath. Keep in mind that trunks are generally the dirtiest areas of all.

Animal Hair

Even though we all love our animals, they are the least considerate when it comes to keeping the interior clean. Nose prints on the windows, animal odors, and worst of all animal hair found everywhere in the car can make vacuuming that much more challenging. Even after vacuuming you still find animal hair, there are several things that you can do to alleviate this problem. By using a stiff full hair brush, with tightly lined bristles, you can loosen all of the animal hair and vacuum it up. However, hair tends to usually weave itself inside of velour and cotton types of upholstery and will need to be pulled out, not just brushed. Another trick is to use a piece of duct tape or masking tape and by using the sticky side up you can lift the hair out. You can also use a lint brush or clothing sticky roller, usually available at most dry cleaners. Also, the lint brush works great for picking up particles of lint left from your Micro Fiber Towels. You can also purchase a rubber dog hair removal brush at most pet stores. Should you experience static during your brushing, take a moment to go over this area with a damp towel or chamois.

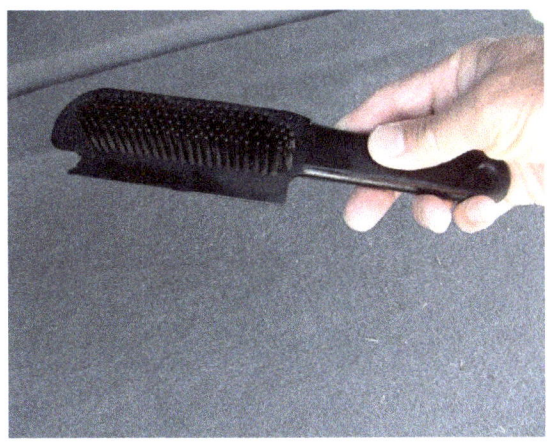 

There's nothing like a good vacuuming for pulling out the bulk of dirt and hair from the upholstery. Brush in a downward motion to help pull up loose hair in order to collect the hair in one specific area, so that you can pick it up easily with either the tape or a brush. Keep in mind, that most of the remaining animal hair will be picked up during the shampooing and extracting procedure, so don't worry about vacuuming up every little bit of hair at this time.

Tip: Another popular tool is this Animal Hair Removal Stone.

Caution: This tool should only be used on carpet never on hard surfaces such as Vinyl or leather upholstery.

Dog hair removal is one of the most difficult and time consuming procedures. Because of this you should explain to the customer that removing the dog hair will take a substantial amount of time in addition to the normal detail. For this reason explain to the customer that excessive dog hair removal is above and beyond what is included in a normal detail and therefore an additional procedure charge must be met. How do you determine the charge for this or for that matter any other detailing procedure that is above and beyond what is normally included in your standard detailing rate? I always look at it as an hourly rate. If you are not sure of just how long something could take you to correct then adjust your pricing based on an hourly rate rather than a job rate. How much you charge will be based on what you think your skills are worth per hour.

Greg Dumond – Success Training Manual

Shampooing The Interior

The process of shampooing and brushing the foaming cleaning solution with the iron brush will help break free any dirt or contaminants lodged into the fibers.

This step should follow the vacuuming sequence so be sure to decide whether or not the car will need a complete shampooing or not. Should the carpets and fabric upholstery be fairly new or extremely clean, spot cleaning may be all that is necessary. A combination of the shampoo cleaner and brushing with the Carpet Iron Brush will increase the full plush feel of the fabric. After the shampooing process is completed, you can remove the embedded dirt with either the wet/dry vacuum or the Carpet and Upholstery Extractor. Be mindful that shampooing is usually done before cleaning and dressing the interior. Be sure to wipe off any splatters of water and shampoo from any vinyl or leather surface during the shampooing process. After shampooing and extraction we recommend you apply fabric guard prior to detailing the exterior of the car. Usually the interior can take approximately 1 to 2 hours to fully dry, so by doing the interior first, you can be sure that the upholstery and carpets will be dry before you deliver the vehicle to the customer. Should you only be detailing the interior of the vehicle, and the cloth seats are still damp, we recommend you take the time to place a plastic seat protector over the driver and passenger seats to prevent your customers' clothes from getting wet. Once again, your customer will appreciate your thoughtfulness.

Directions: With a freshly mixed solution of Carpet and Upholstery Shampoo and your Iron Brush in hand, begin working the brush and solution on any cloth or velour upholstery first. For heavily soiled seats, pre-spray them with a light solution of a good Traffic Lane Cleaner and pre-scrub these areas before using the shampoo. A good standard Traffic Lane Cleaner like FOLEX is found in most hardware stores. It is best for spot removal and is generally spray applied and scrubbed into dirty carpets prior to shampooing. FOLEX does not foam up like a Carpet Shampoo.

NOTE: In order to help keep the seats and carpets dryer, we suggest you use the foam portion of the Carpet and Upholstery Shampoo when scrubbing. Should the foam dissolve in your bucket, be sure to blast the concentrated shampoo with water to make more suds. To avoid getting the seats too wet spread the cleaning solution lightly over the seats and avoid over saturating the fabric with carpet shampoo. Use back and forth movements to do most of the cleaning. Also, to avoid any mildew problems later on, use just enough shampoo to completely blanket the fabric with a thick foam, but not too much to ensure you don't over saturate the material. Ensure you avoid scrubbing too hard over cigarette burns, rips, holes or tears. The stiff bristles on the brush may be too harsh for certain sensitive areas and could cause further damage. If this is the case, we suggest you try cleaning with a terry towel.

Headliner - Shampooing

As before, always start at the top and work your way down. The vehicle's uppermost area of the interior is the material attached to the roof of the car and is called the headliner. Many headliners are made up of different types of fabric such as vinyl, cloth, or velour. At this point, we will cover the method for cleaning both the cloth and velour types of headliners. However, farther in the manual we will cover the proper method of cleaning the vinyl headliner.

Directions: As mentioned earlier in this manual, fabric headliners can be very sensitive to tearing. However, headliners made of vinyl are more durable and can handle more aggressive cleaning.

Headliners made of cloth or velour are more absorbent and can permanently stain due to smoking, dust, and vapors. Many times you can tell whether the customer is or was a smoker by the yellowing appearance of the fabric. We suggest you ask your customer before cleaning any fabric headliners. Some of the pitfalls of cleaning fabric headliners are:

1. It's possible that you may not be able to completely remove all of the smoke stains from the fabric.

2. There may be water rings left on the fabric especially if you only spot clean particular areas.

3. Should the fabric become too wet, the adhesives underneath the fabric could dissolve and cause the fabric to pull away and droop.

Many of these pitfalls can be minimized through your knowledge and expertise of cleaning. However, due to the possibilities of further damaging or staining the material, we suggest you don't take any unnecessary chances. Ensure you make the customer aware of this potential cleaning problem. However, if they insist you clean the fabric headliner then we suggest you proceed as follows:

Directions: It is a good idea to first test the ceiling to determine if the headliner is suspended from a wire frame. Carefully push the fabric with the palm of your hand. Should the ceiling feel hollow when you push upward, then it's a suspended wire frame. Be careful not to apply too much pressure, as the wire frame could push through the material. In order to safely clean the fabric headliner we suggest you use a terry cloth towel and a hand full of Carpet & Upholstery Shampoo. Now, gently rub with a light, brisk movement across the material cleaning small sections at a time. Continue this method until the ceiling is completely clean. For stubborn stains or spots we suggest you spray an amount of Traffic Lane Cleaner directly onto the terry cloth towel and lightly rub the spot clean.

We suggest you clean any sensitive fabric material and velour headliners with a dry powdered Spot and Fabric Cleaner. This product is available at most janitorial supply stores. The many pitfalls of cleaning weak fabrics are that they are easily stained when they become over wet. We recommend you tell your customer, that even though you agree to clean their headliner you can't guarantee the outcome look of the fabric. You can shampoo this area with your Carpet and Upholstery Shampoo; however you should make it clear to your customer the possibility of staining. Should you decide to shampoo the headliner we suggest you shampoo the entire area - not just spot clean. Remember, spot cleaning can at times leave water rings. However, for best results when spot cleaning, should you decide to attempt it, is to spray a small amount of either the All Purpose Cleaner or Traffic Lane Cleaner directly to your towel. Then lightly wipe the towel on the spot until clean, but avoid rubbing too hard due to the materials sensitivity. Immediately dry the spot thoroughly with a separate dry towel.

You can use a more aggressive approach when cleaning velour type headliners, commonly found with American cars. After mixing up a batch of high foam shampoo, dip the Carpet/Upholstery Brush in the suds and gently scrub the fabric. Use short straight directional movements and only clean a 3 x 3 foot section at a time. Blot any excess moisture by using a dry towel after scrubbing each section. Should the customer be a heavy smoker, you may have to repeat this process 2 or 3 times. You will notice that your towel will become heavily coated with the yellow nicotine being pulled from the ceiling. Eventually most of the nicotine will be removed after continuous blotting. Continue this method until the entire ceiling is completely clean. You will find that you will achieve better cleaning results if you inspect that every square inch of the fabric is shampooed uniformly. Note: You can cause water spot stains by applying too much moisture in one section. Should you only need to touch up areas, we suggest use a terry cloth towel and spray a small amount of Traffic Lane Cleaner on the area and briskly agitate this section. You can even try a diluted Citrus Based Engine Degreaser for those hard to remove stains. It is also possible to clean the fabric headliner using a Carpet & Upholstery Extractor; however this should only be used as a last resort because you will be applying a lot of moisture with the machine.

Cloth Upholstery Seats

Keep in mind that cleaning cloth or velour fabrics can be trickier than cleaning seats made of non-absorbent vinyl or leather. If you took apart a car seat you would see how the materials surround a structural steel frame attached by springs, which hook into a wire mesh. Over this material is a thin mesh skin made of tear resistant cotton stretched over a foam cushion and sewn into the wire mesh. The last layer and outer portion is made of a thick layered material of rayon/cotton cloth or velour. It is this outer portion of the seat that you will be cleaning. There will be some cases where you will not be able to remove every stain. The cloth material can become permanently stained from sodas, coffee, and heavy body oil. You can still clean this material, even though you may not be able to remove permanent stains. Keep in mind that a stain is a discoloration of the material and dirt is just dirt. However, you can do the best job possible in shampooing and extracting the dirt from the cloth seats, but some stains may not be removable.

Directions: By using your Carpet and Upholstery Brush with a good mixture of dry foam Carpet and Upholstery Shampoo, follow the same procedure of order as you did during the vacuuming sequence. Using up/down and side to side motions, scrub the upholstery on both the upper and bottom portion of the seat. Agitate the cloth fibers so that the nap of the fabric turns in both directions and starts to fluff up. This process will help to loosen any embedded dirt and bring it to the surface. Start on the front driver's seat, then the passenger seat, and lastly followed up with the rear or cargo seats. Ensure you move the front seats in the back position and start shampooing the top of the headrest, then the backrest to the bench portion of the seat. Ensure you shampoo any unseen areas in both the front and in between the side of the seat and console areas. Since the area between the seat and console area can be hard to reach, we suggest you scoop up some foam and scrub this section with either your hand or try using a tooth brush or angle brush.

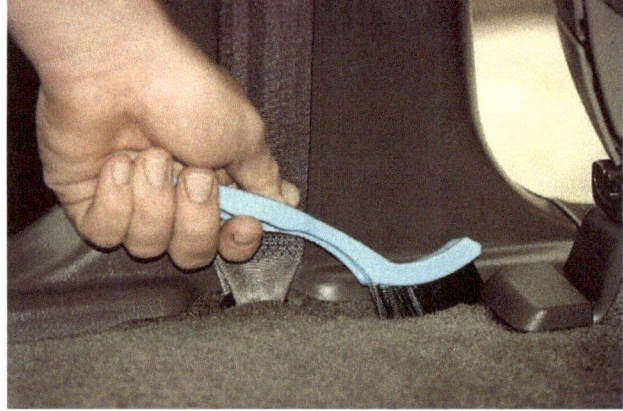

Move to the backside of the headrest and lower portion of the back of the seat. Once completed, move to the opposite side of the car and clean the passenger's seat using the same method. Lastly, clean the back seat and any cargo or extra bench seats, similar to those found in SUV's. Prior to scrubbing with the Carpet/Upholstery Shampoo, pre-clean all problem areas using the concentrated pre-cleaners, such as Traffic Lane Cleaner or Spot and Fabric Cleaner. As a rule, the driver's seat gets the most wear and tear and is susceptible to heavy body oil, clothing and suit dye transfers, pen marks, and food stains.

Sun Rot

Sun Rot is caused by ultra violet rays and the sun's heat beating down on the cloth or velour materials. This long term exposure can eventually weaken and disintegrate the fabric. The most apparent areas of sun rot is on the upper portion of the back bench seat closest to the rear window.

We highly suggest you carefully examine any cloth or velour seats before shampooing or brushing. Some symptoms of Sun Rot are as follows:

1. Fabric color fading in exposed areas

2. A dry, almost crispy feeling to the fabric when touched

3. Weakening or fraying of the fabric most exposed to the direct sun

Ensure you use a towel when cleaning these problem materials - **NOT A BRUSH**. If you aren't careful you can either remove patches of sun rotted fibers or split the seats open, so carefully inspect the material and proceed with caution.

Carpets And Mats

Remove all floor mats and shampoo them after you have shampooed the floor of the vehicle. Start cleaning the floor area around the seats and console. Be sure to add more water to your bucket of shampoo, should the suds be getting low.

Directions: Prep the floor carpets by pre-spraying grease spots with a gum and tar remover found at most detail supply companies or at your local janitorial supply store to loosen grease or any gummy substance. You can also use a Spot/Fabric Cleaner for pen marks or heavy stains. Scrub vigorously with the Carpet and Upholstery Brush or fender brush using enough shampoo to wet the carpet without saturating it.

Over saturating the carpet could cause a mildew issue. By using the palm of your hand, ensure you test the dampness of the carpet as you move along. There should be no visible foam or heavy moisture on your hand, if you are shampooing it correctly. Start with the center console area and work your way to the side and towards the underneath portion of the driver's seat. Then work your way towards the foot pedals, dash area, and the area along the side of the seat. Use either your fingers or a small tooth brush to scrub hard to reach areas. Now move your way to the door and scrub this area should it have any carpeted material. Once you are done with this area move the seat to the forward position and start cleaning the underneath portion of the rear seats and rear carpet area. Follow the same cleaning procedure as the front area, regarding stubborn stains, before shampooing the rear portion of the car.

In order to save time, always start in the center area and work your way out towards the side of each section. Work the lather into all the nooks and crannies underneath the seat and in between the seat railings. Now shampoo the wide carpeted area ensuring you pre-spray with the Traffic Lane Cleaner first.

Should you be detailing an SUV or Hatchback, ensure you shampoo the cargo floor as you did with rest of the carpeting. Open up the tailgate or hatchback and fold down back seats that are attached with floor carpeting. Be sure to prep the carpet with either a Traffic Lane Cleaner or Spot and Fabric Cleaner, dependent upon the stain, before shampooing. Heavier and more aggressive brushing may be necessary due to this being a high traffic area. Use back and forth strokes and then side to side to agitate the fabric as much as possible to bring the small particles of dirt and grit to the surface. The wide angle fender brush or carpet brush is perfect for this type or area. Now work your way to the trunk area and shampoo it thoroughly.

Keep in mind that the farther you go down the more dirt you will find. With this said, always rinse your carpet brushes frequently as they can accumulate dirt and grit, which can be ground back into the carpet if they are not rinsed frequently.

The last sections to shampoo are the floor mats. Since this is where the heaviest accumulation of grease, dirt, gum, and grit are embedded. Before you begin, ensure you have enough time to allow them to dry. You can speed up the process by using a wet/dry vacuum to draw out any remaining moisture. After thoroughly cleaning and shampooing the mats, use your high powered pressure washer to rinse them clean. This process will help flush out any remaining dirt and grit too stubborn to remove through normal vacuuming. We recommend you use this method for extreme cases only. Hang the floor mats somewhere to allow them to drain and dry completely. Once again, be sure to vacuum the mats after shampooing to remove any loosened dirt and excess moisture if you don't use the pressure washer.

Removing Carpet Stains

You will find that many of the carpet stains and spills you encounter would be difficult to clean, should you have not had the proper cleaning knowledge. Thus the reason you should have a clear understanding of the different types of stains and how to properly clean each one. By using the correct procedures and proper chemicals you can achieve miraculous results.

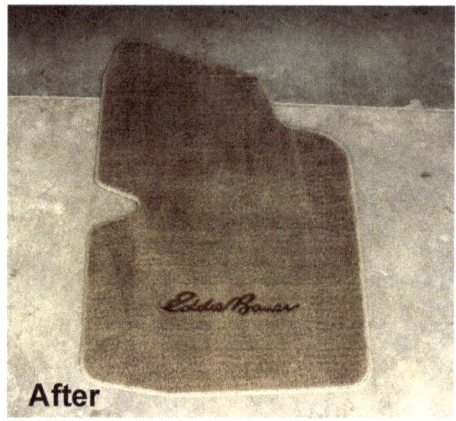

Keep in mind that most automobile carpeting is made from a synthetic nylon which is susceptible to staining from dyes found in sodas and fruit juices. Most of these substances will leave a purplish color when they come in contact with the carpet. However, spilled caffeine takes on a pale yellowish look as it comes in contact with carpet or fabric. In most cases, these stains can become permanent especially if they have dried and been present for some time. Many of the dyes found in these products are very similar to those found in hair color dyes, which simply cannot be washed out with soap and water. Over time these stains may fade away but not completely.

Extreme Circumstances

Paint spilled like this on the inside of carpet or upholstery could seem impossible to remove. However, we recommend you first try to determine, by checking with the customer, what type of paint are you dealing with? Is it water based or oil based? Once this is determined, you will need to make a trip to your local hardware store to find out what product would work best to remove the specific paint. In most cases, you can use either mineral spirits or enamel reducer to remove the bulk of the paint. However, these products contain volatile solvents, so use extreme caution by wearing protective gloves, goggles, and a respirator. Be sure to test a small area first before proceeding. Be careful, because too much aggressive rubbing may strip or discolor the fabric or carpeting. In these images we were able to extract the paint out before it completely dried. If the paint was allowed too much time to dry, removing all of the stain may have been impossible.

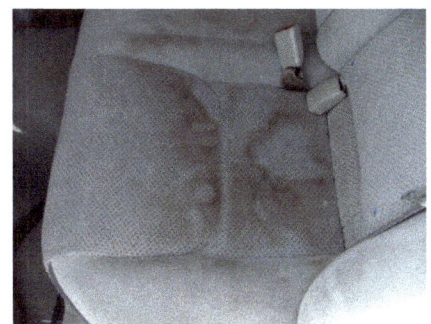  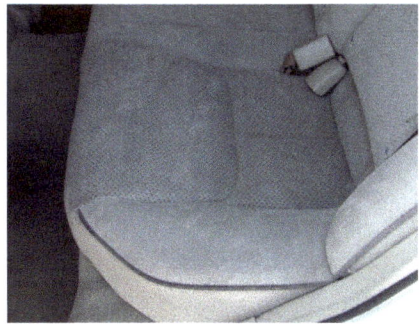

Don't worry if you can't remove every stain under normal circumstances. Over 95 percent of the stains you encounter will be successfully eliminated. You will be using three basic chemicals when dealing with most stains:

Gum and Tar Remover -- dissolves gum & greasy foods.

Spot & Fabric Cleaner -- breaks down ink and cosmetics.

Traffic Lane Cleaner -- is an excellent general cleaner for all other types of spills and stains.

Start off with your general cleaner first and clean from the outer portion of the stain inward so as not to let it spread.

Should you come across either a melted crayon, piece of lipstick or any other cosmetics follow the special procedure for cleaning this problem. Many of these materials are made of a wax like base and can smear and spread incredibly fast. In order to contain the material from spreading lift the bulk of the material with either a putty knife or screw driver and then spray a heavy solution of Spot & Fabric Cleaner directly onto the spot. **IMPORTANT NOTE: DO NOT RUB BACK AND FORTH!** Instead use a blotting approach by taking a thick terry cloth towel and pressing down lightly with your fingertips. Start pressing down a couple of times and then lift the towel off the spot. Now turn your towel over to a clean side and continue with the same procedure. Don't forget to first spray the Spot & Fabric Cleaner and then start blotting. Continue until the spot disappears. Unless you plan to extract the carpets, you may not be able to completely remove the stain by just using cold water, shampoo, and the Spot & Fabric Cleaner. You should, however be able to achieve good results by using this method. We recommend you use a hot water Steam Extractor and pre-spray the spot with Spot & Fabric Cleaner. Ensure you pick up as much of the stain as possible using the blotting method, and then use the hot water extraction method to remove any remaining stains.

* * * * * * * * * * **CAUTION** * * * * * * * * * * *

Be sure to not over saturate the material when applying Spot & Fabric Cleaner. It is important to go back over the area with a damp cloth to remove any excess cleaner. Check that the Spot Cleaner is colorfast and safe for upholstery as well.

Shampooing/Extraction Method

The final process will be extracting to eliminate remaining odors, grease, dirt or sand that can't be removed with your wet/dry vacuum. This is the best method to eliminate any remaining contaminants, leaving a completely antiseptic environment.

Now set up your Carpet & Upholstery Extractor and attachments, and fill your clean wash bucket half (1/2) full with fresh clean water. It's very important to keep dirt and grit out of your initial mixing steps in order to not contaminate or clog the interior parts of your Carpet & Upholstery Extractor.

Note…If you have purchased an extractor with a built in heater then skip this section. Now set up your Immersion Heater inside the bucket, standing straight up to ensure the cord loops over and out of the top of the bucket. Connect a properly grounded extension wire to the end of the Immersion Heater plug. Now plug this into the proper household outlet or your generator outlet.

NOTE: The water level should be approximately ¾ of the way up on the black insulation portion of the heater shaft in order to set the Immersion Heater in the proper position.

* * * * * * * * * * **CAUTION** * * * * * * * * * * *

Never allow the cord/plug to enter into the bucket of water.

The water in the bucket should be sufficiently warm in roughly 7 to 10 minutes. You are now ready to begin operating your Carpet & Upholstery Extractor. Be sure to follow the same cleaning sequence as those you followed in the previous section of Interior Cleaning and Shampooing.

Operating Instructions For The Carpet And Upholstery Cleaner Solution

Into a wash bucket, mix 4 ounces of Machine Extractor Cleaner with one gallon of water. I have found the best Machine Extractor Cleaners at my local janitorial supply store. Now pour the solution from your preheated water bucket into the tank holder. As much as possible, be sure to use lukewarm water (max *75* degrees F).

> **NOTE:** Only use an approved low sudsing extractor cleaner in this machine. Since the Carpet & Upholstery Shampoo is a high foaming shampoo it's only meant for manual scrubbing, and should **never** be used in the Extractor Machine.

Now connect the vacuum suction hose to the suction outlet and ensure that the quick disconnect coupling of the spray pressure hose is engaged properly. Plug it in and switch the water suction cycle on by simultaneously pushing both the "Suction" and "Spray" buttons. Simply turn the water button off to use the machine as a vacuum.

> **TIP:** Pour a few ounces of water based Interior Car Fragrance along with the detergent into the Carpet Extractor for an extra fresh smell. This will last for hours and leave a clean fresh scent.

After Use:

1. Be sure to remove all of the cleaning solution from the tank and partly re-fill the tank with clean water to flush the machine out thoroughly, including the spray nozzles.

2. Now switch the water cycle off by pushing the button and removing the plug from the main power outlet.

3. Disconnect the spray suction hose. Empty the water and clean the unit with an All Purpose Cleaner.

4. Refer to the Manufacturer's Operating Manual for more detailed instructions.

> **NOTE:** Should you not have the use of a Carpet & Upholstery Extractor good results can still be obtained by spending an extra time manually shampooing with the Carpet Brush, Shampoo, and the use of a heavy duty Vacuum Cleaner. Just remember to be very thorough!

Cleaning Vinyl Headliners

Shampooing will not be necessary regarding vinyl headliners. You will instead use a Carpet Brush, All Purpose Cleaner, and a dry towel. Ensure you examine the headliner before your proceed cleaning. Should it appear to be clean with no apparent marks, then a simple dusting will suffice. Even though we don't suggest you take shortcuts, some areas may already be clean and no further cleaning may be necessary saving you time. In order to clean a dirty vinyl headliner, spray a small amount of All Purpose Cleaner onto a terry cloth or micro fiber towel and wipe it into the surface area. Continue until the surface is completely clean. To get out stubborn marks, use your Spot and fabric Cleaner or a diluted form of Citrus Based Engine Degreaser to loosen the dirt by agitating these areas with a wipe down using a clean dry towel. Ensure you **avoid spraying your cleaners directly onto the vinyl** above your head, because three problems can occur:

1. Spray mist can get into your eyes.

2. Mildew can form due to the many perforated holes found in most vinyl headliners.

3. You need to avoid getting any overspray onto the windows, as the cleaners can sometimes be difficult to remove from glass.

Ensure you separate your dirty towels from the clean ones after you are done cleaning the headliner. Be sure to inspect the headliner and check for any missed areas especially around the center dome light and clothes hanger hook area. Should the car have a sunroof, we suggest you start cleaning this now.

Sunroof

For those vehicles equipped with a sunroof it is best to pay close attention to the most difficult areas to clean such as the grease around the edges of the sunroof closure.

During the cleaning or shampooing sequence determine the type of material you are cleaning. Should the sunroof be made of vinyl, clean any visible grease by rubbing in a small amount of Gum and Tar Remover with a terry cloth towel or you can use a Carpet Brush or bug sponge. If the sunroof is made of a fabric material such as velour, spray a small amount of Gum and Tar Remover onto a terry cloth towel and briskly rub the grease spot out by hand or you can use a Carpet Brush. We suggest you follow up by wiping this area with a Traffic Lane Cleaner. This cleaner will help dissolve any remaining grease and residue absorbed into the fabric. Retract the roof to the open position, once the interior surface is cleaned. Now wipe the open track and edges around both the roof and car opening with the All Purpose Cleaner and a clean terry cloth towel. Many sunroofs are made of either a tinted glass or a painted hard top. However, you would clean the tracks and edges the same way for both. Don't clean the glass area at this point. We will discuss the proper method for cleaning clear glass and tinted windows in the window cleaning section. Also, we suggest you don't clean the sunroof should it be made of the same painted material as that found on the car. We will discuss the proper procedure for polishing and compounding paint later in the manual.

General Area Cleaning

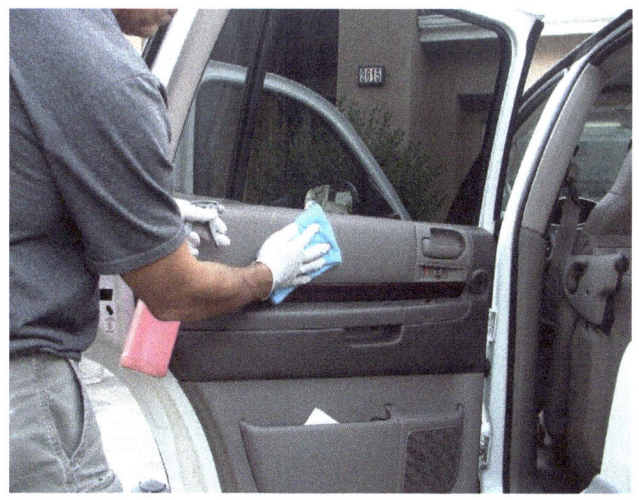

In general, a good practical approach to detailing is to take a process of elimination. With this said, we suggest you take care of all the small details first before approaching the bigger and more time consuming areas. This could also be considering another approach to prepping the car. The most time consuming and tedious chore of the interior detailing is cleaning the vinyl or leather seats. We will cover this last, since there is so much to clean. Let's first look at cleaning the smaller details of the interior. This would include the dashboard, ashtrays, air vents, gauges, console area, steering wheel, door handles, door panels, arm rests, sun visors, door jambs, seat belts, floor mats, stick shifts, foot pedals, and seat brackets.

Dashboard And Gauges

The vehicles dashboard area or instrument panel is a complex array of buttons, gauges, glass, polished chrome, vents, and covered with either vinyl or leather. You must take your time when approaching the cleaning process in this area and work in a very systematic order. Be sure to pay attention to every little nook and cranny. Remember, this is the area that the customer sees first when they sit in the car. As you know, most of the time spent in a car is behind the wheel.

Directions: We recommend you start cleaning by sitting in the Driver's seat first. This will give you a better vantage point to start cleaning. Be sure to place a couple of clean dry towels nearby in the passenger's seat. Spray a small amount of All Purpose Cleaner directly onto a clean towel and start wiping down the dash board. Ensure you avoid spraying any cleaner directly onto the

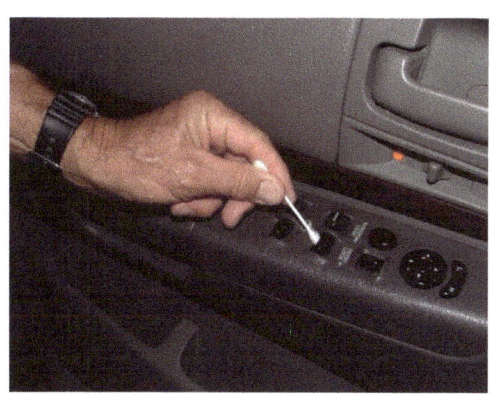

dash, because you can end up with chemical spotting and a possible film from over-spraying on the windshield glass. So we suggest you avoid spraying and use a wipe down approach. Ensure you change towels frequently as necessary. The dashboard tends to absorb deeply embedded dirt and oils and gets particularly dirty. Also, air vent dust and settling dirt can leave a thick layer of grime. Should the dash feel gummy, this is usually caused by your customer using an inferior vinyl protectant made of oily petroleum based products. These inferior products can cause premature aging and cracking of the dash especially

when it makes contact with the sun's rays. Be sure to carefully remove as much of the gummy oil as possible. We will discuss how to treat it with the proper dressing later. Now move your way down to the gauges, using your paint style tooth brush or long soft bristle brush. Work any dust or dirt loose by agitating the grooves in the glass rings in and around the gauges. Also be sure to work the brush along contours and lip edges of the dashboard and along the console area. Be sure to use the soft paint style tooth brush to clean in between radio knobs and channel setting buttons.

Spray a small amount of All Purpose Cleaner onto directly onto the surface or on your brush for those gummy and extra dirty buttons. Brush briskly until all the dirt is worked free and follow up with a wipe down using a clean towel. Be sure to use the stiffer toothbrush to clean slots and the grooves in both the knobs and buttons. This brush works well for loosening dirt and old gummy residue. Avoid using excessive pressure so as not to scratch sensitive plastics. Use cotton swabs to clean in between console buttons and grooves. These work best if you clean with one that is slightly damp. This will help to absorb more dust and dirt. Now follow up by drying the area with a separate clean dry cotton swab.

Vents And Recessed Areas

Since many air vents can accumulate dust and become gummy, we suggest you pay close attention to these areas. Should the vents be fairly clean, a simple dusting with the soft bristles of the paint style toothbrush should be sufficient.

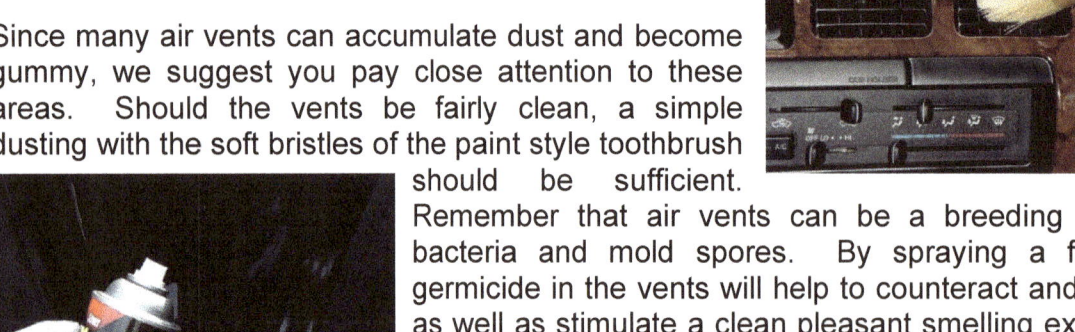

Remember that air vents can be a breeding ground for both bacteria and mold spores. By spraying a fragrance with a germicide in the vents will help to counteract and destroy bacteria as well as stimulate a clean pleasant smelling experience for your customer. You can also use your soft paint brush or a long bristle dusting brush to remove dust that collects in the grooves on the face plate of the car speakers or vents.

Cotton swabs work best for cleaning dirty air vents, however for especially dirty or gummy air vents we suggest you pre-spray a cotton swab with the All Purpose Cleaner and work it back and forth into each slot. Ensure you turn the slots in both directions when cleaning them. Once you have cleaned both sides of the slots, clean the top, bottom, and sides of the area where the vents set in. Follow up wiping the vents with a dry separate cotton swab. Ensure you reposition the air vents in their original position.

Only in extreme cases – when the air vents won't come clean, spray a light mist of Vinyl Dressing or an interior spray silicone into the slots and wipe dry with a separate clean cotton swab. This will help give unsightly or worn out air vents a little extra shine.

Steering Wheel

One of the grimiest parts of the car is the steering wheel due to the dirt, makeup and oil from hands that can cause a layer of sticky film. Smoker's nicotine and vinyl vapors as well as food stains can be a real contributor to one of the dirtiest areas in the vehicle. You will need your cotton swabs, paint detail brush, and a stiff toothbrush and bug sponge to clean the steering wheel correctly. Begin by spraying a small amount of All Purpose Cleaner onto a clean towel and wipe the entire wheel. Now concentrate on cleaning the face of the wheel and backside of the wheel. Since the backside of the wheel can be difficult to see, we suggest you get as close to the working area as possible in order to do a thorough job. For those steering wheels that have a grainy texture to them, use your stiff toothbrush or bug sponge and All Purpose Cleaner to loosen the dirt and follow up by wiping it clean with a separate towel. Be sure to change to a clean side of the towel each time you move along to ensure you don't spread the dirt and oil to other sections. Now clean the wheel column area. We suggest you use a toothbrush to loosen the dirt from the grooves in the knobs and handles of the shifter and turn signal arms. Drape the flat portion of the towel over the column and apply a shoe shine cleaning motion (moving the towel in a back and forth motion) to clean and polish the area. The towel edge should be able to slide far enough down the column and up against the dash to do an excellent cleaning job. All hard to reach areas can be cleaned using your Q-tips, paint detail brush or dusting brush. Ensure you turn the wheel side-to-side in order to expose any hidden dust or grime found where the wheel and column meet. Use your stiff toothbrush to loosen the dirt from the front cap of the steering wheel and dust it clean with a soft brush and towel.

Now put a light coat of Vinyl Dressing on the wheel and allow the protector to penetrate the vinyl for several minutes. Buff the wheel with a clean towel until most of the protectant is gone. Keep in mind that your customer will be happier with a soft sheen and non-oily surface when they come in contact with the steering wheel. The objective is to simply apply a finishing product, not to cover the surface with a filmy residue.

Ashtrays

Since ashtrays are removable it would be best to remove them and set them outside of the car for cleaning. Ensure you remove all of the ashtrays. Many larger vehicles have ashtrays located in the dash or front console, door panels - both front and back, rear console area and rear hatch areas. Most of the ashtrays should have been emptied during the vacuuming process. For those ashtrays only needing to be cleaned and dusted, spray a small amount of All Purpose Cleaner into the cavity of the tray and wipe it clean with a dry clean towel. Use your bug sponge or toothbrush to remove stubborn dirt by agitating and loosening the dirt, followed up with a towel wipe. You can remove stuck on gum by spraying a generous amount of Gum and Tar remover directly onto the gum, and letting it stand for 2 minutes. Now you can pry it loose with the tip of a screwdriver. Be careful to not scratch the plastic when using this method. In those cases of extremely messy and gummy ashtrays, we suggest you pre-spray the cavity with All Purpose Cleaner and submerge the ashtray into warm water for about 30 minutes. Now pressure rinse the ashtray to remove any remaining stubborn materials. Note that any towels used for cleaning ashtrays should be put away and not used for cleaning anything else. Also be sure to thoroughly rinse all brushes or bug sponge as well.

TIP: Some detailers will use the technique of restoring old, pitted, and rusty ashtrays by repainting or lacquering them. Should you decide to do this as well, we suggest you ensure the ashtray is completely clean and dry beforehand. Now tape the outside edges and external area with masking tape. Use a bright aluminum spray paint for metal type ashtrays, which can be found in most hardware stores. Now spray a coat in the entire cavity. You can use a clear lacquer for plastic type ashtrays to restore them to a nice sheen. Be sure to carefully follow the manufacturer's directions.

Seat Belts

Begin by pulling the belt as far out as possible and spray a small amount of All Purpose Cleaner directly onto the belt. Be careful not to overspray onto any surrounding vinyl or glass. Now scrub  the belt with your Carpet Iron Brush or Bug Sponge in an up and down motion. With a clean dry towel, wrap it around the belt and pull it down while holding the belt in place with the other hand. Seat belts can be susceptible to staining due the nylon type of material they are made of. Don't get discouraged if you can't remove all of the stains, as Nylon is a highly porous fabric that does not release soil and stain easily. Just do the best you can in removing all the dirt and moisture from the fabric. Rubber Boots And Foot Pedals

Those vehicles that are manually driven have a stick shift covered with a pleated rubber boot. This accordion type boot hides trapped dirt and particles in between the pleats. In order to clean the boot area, grab the top of the boot and pull it up by stretching the rubber so that the pleats flatten out. Now spray a small amount of All Purpose Cleaner onto the rubber and wipe it clean with a dry towel. You can clean the metal mounting ring, located at the base of the boot and floor area, with a towel or toothbrush. Use the same method to condition the rubber later by extending the pleated area.

In order to clean the foot pedals, drape a towel underneath the pedals to catch any loosened dirt. Spray a small amount of All Purpose Cleaner directly onto the foot pedal. Scrub the rubber to loosen any dirt particles with your Carpet Iron Brush. When brushing, ensure you follow the grain in order to pop out lodged in dirt. Follow up with a towel wipe once cleaned and brushed. Next, fold the towel you previously draped under the pedals in half and spray a small amount of All Purpose Cleaner directly onto the rubber floor mat located just below the pedals. Scrub this area with your Carpet Iron Brush and follow up with a towel wipe. If applicable clean the rubber foot wear guard located to the right of the accelerator pedal.

Floor Mats

As you can imagine, floor mats tend to be one of the dirtiest areas of the car. These ultimately protect the carpeting underneath from wear and tear. It's much cheaper to replace floor mats than to replace an entire floor carpet.

As mentioned in the vacuuming section, it is important to thoroughly extract all dirt, animal hair, lint, and other contaminates. Remember clean floor mats can set the interior floor area apart from the rest of the car, which your customer will surely appreciate. Most floor mats are made of either carpet or rubber, or in some cases, a combination of both.

Directions: Before you clean the floor mats, place them away from the vehicle on a clean flat surface, free of dirt, to ensure you don't contaminate the underside area. The tailgate makes a nice cleaning platform, should you be operating out of a pick-up. For both rubber or combination of rubber/carpet, pre-spray the mat with the All Purpose Cleaner and vigorously scrub the entire surface with your Carpet Iron Brush. Now pressure wash the mats. Don't worry about getting the small area of carpet wet should you be working on a combination mat of rubber and carpet. This type of carpet is made of an indoor/outdoor synthetic nylon (Short fiber Mat) and dries very quickly. Now hold the mat up with one hand and pressure rinse the reverse side of the mat. Hang all the mats or lay them at a sharp angle to allow the water to run off. Ensure you always check the back of the floor mats for dirt before replacing them into the vehicle. You can use the same technique when cleaning fully carpeted mats. Before you begin, hold up the carpet mat with one hand and with the other slap the back side to bring remaining dirt and grit to the surface. Now lay the carpet mat on a clean surface, spray the entire mat with the Traffic Lane Cleaner, and scrub vigorously with the Carpet Iron Brush. Pre-spray any

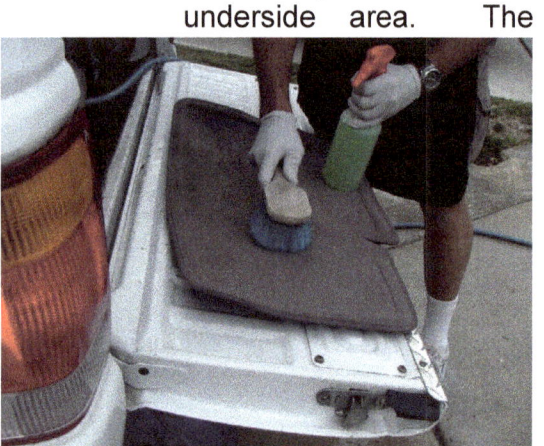

apparent grease spots with a Tar and Gum Remover to dissolve the grease. With a premixed solution of your Carpet & Upholstery Shampoo, scrub the entire carpet mat in opposite directions. By using a crisscross method you will be able to lift the nap of the carpet in two directions for a deep cleaning. You can also use your Carpet & Upholstery Extractor as previously discussed in the extracting the carpets section. Should you be using only a Wet/Dry Vacuum, attach the wide angle floor tool and thoroughly vacuum any remaining moisture, grit, and dirt from the carpet mat. Once clean, set them aside to dry as you will be replacing them in the car later.

Any mats made of rubber or vinyl should be dressed at this time. By applying the dressing now will give them enough time to both penetrate and condition the vinyl or rubber. Now apply a small amount of Vinyl Dressing to any uncarpeted portion of the mat including the emblems and trim edges. You many need to use more than one coat especially if the rubber or vinyl is dry. For really dry areas you can spray the vinyl or rubber with the Vinyl Dressing and let it penetrate for at least 30 minutes before wiping it off with a separate towel. Next dress the shoe guard vinyl floor piece on the mat located near the foot pedal area and to the wear guard located to the right of the accelerator pedal. Be sure to not apply too much as it can become slippery when a shoe comes in contact with the vinyl piece.

* * * * * * * * * * * **CAUTION** * * * * * * * * * * * *

You must never apply any dressing directly onto the foot pedals as this could cause your customers foot to slip off and cause an accident. Always use good common sense and judgment whenever applying the dressing.

Fabric Guard

"Scotch Guarding" can be an optional service you can provide to your customers. Fabric Guard provides a barrier of protection between the elements of soiled clothing, pets, food stains, grease, tar, and liquid spills such as; coffee, sodas, milk, fruit juice, and hot chocolate. Fabric Guard retards these elements, extends the life of the fabric, enhances the beauty, and resists fading due to ultra violet rays.

Directions: Be sure all the carpets and upholstery have been thoroughly shampooed, cleaned, and vacuumed before applying Fabric Guard. Spray your Fabric Guard with the Pressurized Spray Applicator while the fabric is still damp from the initial shampooing and extracting. Use slow methodical back and forth strokes when spraying, by starting with the car seats, both front and rear, move down to the floor carpets, and lastly the floor mats. Ensure you lay the mats outside of the car to spray them to allow enough time for the underlying carpet to dry before replacing the mats back into the car.

NOTE: Should you experience overspray when spraying Fabric Guard, take a damp towel and wipe off all excess overspray from any of the vinyl, leather or wood grain areas. Avoid spraying any Fabric Guard onto any window areas as this product tends to resist water and other liquid cleaners.

Cleaning Interior Vinyl

You will need the All Purpose Cleaner, Carpet Iron Brush, Detail Tooth Paint Brush, Q-tips, Interior Dusting Brush and plenty of towels to clean the interior vinyl. Ensure you always use good judgment when cleaning vinyl. Should the surfaces already be fairly clean then they may only require a light dusting followed up with your vinyl dressing. Normally we don't recommend taking shortcuts; however it's not necessary to overdo areas that are already perfect to begin with.

Directions: Start by placing yourself in the front seat so that you are facing the dashboard. Now take a moment to look around and find all the miscellaneous vinyl portions of the car that have not yet been cleaned. Spray a small amount of All Purpose Cleaner onto a towel and start cleaning the sun visors front and back as well as the arms and hooks. Now clean the vinyl frame around the top of the windshield glass, and down along the sides where it meets with the dash area. Ensure you clean the rear view mirror as well as the unseen area behind the mirror.

Clean all areas in between the seats, along the sides of the console area, and inside the seat belt locking mechanism. Move towards the door panel and clean all the vinyl with the All Purpose Cleaner and the Carpet Iron Brush. Scrub the arm rest area and work lose any deeply embedded dirt with the brush wiping as you move along with a dry clean towel. Once the majority of the door has been cleaned, spray a small amount of All Purpose Cleaner into the well area of the arm rest. Use the paint style tooth brush to clean any trapped dirt lodged into door screws and grooves. Blot up as much of the surfaced dirt as you can with a clean towel or Q-Tip for those hard to reach areas. Clean the door handle or strap with the All Purpose Cleaner and a towel. Be sure to clean behind the strap and in between the door handle levers. We suggest you use your stiff tooth brush to loosen stubborn dirt lodged into the grooves. Since many cars have door panels equipped with chrome buttons, we suggest you clean these buttons with a light spray of the All Purpose Cleaner, following up with a clean towel or cotton swab. You can use the soft Q-Tip to both dry and polish these chrome buttons. Be sure to push the buttons from side-to-side so that you polish the entire button with the Q-Tip.

Door Jambs

We've already done most of the dirty work during the washing sequence; however it's impossible to clean every section of the door jamb area without a certain amount of hand detailing. Using your All Purpose Cleaner and a towel wipe down the entire window railing and any other visible areas not previously cleaned with the pressure washer. Clean any residual dirt or grease around locking mechanisms, door latches, and in between the closure areas of the door. Use a water based Engine Degreaser or a Gum and Road Tar removal product to remove any remaining grease that the All Purpose Cleaner can't remove. On the upper portion of the door you will notice a black ring located on the car body side just inside and below the rain track. This is caused by the rubber seal located on the upper door side surrounding the window frame. Since doors are continuously opening and closing a small mark from the rubber may be present on the painted portion of the jamb area, which can be removed with a towel saturated with a Tar and Gum Remover. You can remove scuff marks and dirt found on the floor running boards along the opening of the door area, by spraying a small amount of All Purpose Cleaner onto a towel and wiping it clean. It may be necessary to dislodge any dirt by scrubbing the running board grooves with the Carpet Iron Brush first. Rub off any heavy black scuff marks with a saturated towel of Water Based Engine Degreaser or Gum and Tar remover.

Tip: For black scuff marks try using a Mr. Clean Eraser pad.

 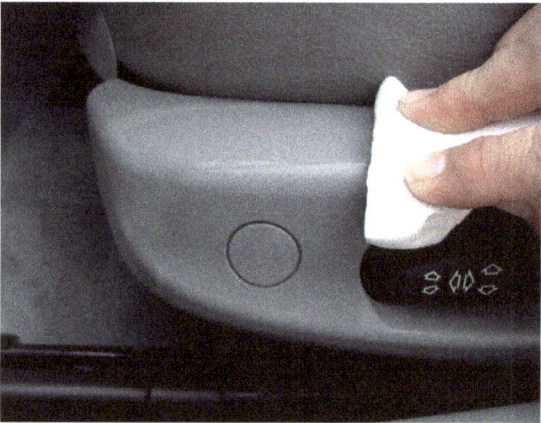

All of your general cleaning is now done. By simply using a process of elimination and working methodically you have achieved what we set out to do from the beginning, clean the many smaller details of the interior.

Now we will cover the largest section of the Interior Detailing, working with the vinyl or leather seats.

Vinyl Upholstery And Trim

It is essential to understand how chemicals and dressings react to fibers, vinyl or leather upholstery as well as matching the right equipment for the job. With modern day automotive interiors comes new technology in cleaning, dressing, and feeding these fabrics with conditioning nutrients.

Vinyl and rubber products absorb constant wear from exposure to heat, cold, and continuous washings with non Ph balanced liquid treatments. Some of the poor quality products sold for cleaning and dressing vinyl use a petroleum or Formaldehyde base which can accelerate the deterioration of rubber trim and vinyl. The concept for proper cleaning and dressing rubber and vinyl is to release trapped solvents by using a high end non-solvent cleaner like All Purpose Cleaner and to moisturize or feed with a high end silicone base nourisher as found in a good high quality Vinyl Dressing product.

A common problem found in many vehicles, is vinyl vapor residue. Evidence of this oily residue is more noticeably seen on the vehicles interior windows and has an appearance of a hazy foggy residue. Vinyl and rubber release a chemical gas as the fabrics are exposed to oxygen. Common Naugahyde and plastic vinyl, releases gaseous oily vaporous in the air and coats everything around it. Conversely leather interiors do not have as much of a problem with emitting these fogging residues since leather does not contain typical plasticides found in only vinyl materials. Some leather conditioners however could contribute to releasing an oily residue as they contain collagen oil.

Directions: For Cleaning Vinyl Seats

Clean the vinyl in the same manner, whether the seats are heavily textured or have a smooth surface. The most soiled areas are the head rests, arm rests, and seat cushions. Use your All Purpose Cleaner, Carpet Iron Brush, and clean towels to clean the vinyl. Your Bug Sponge used gently to clean stubborn embedded dirt is a great tool used for cleaning.

Be sure to bring the spray bottle up close to your work to avoid overspray. Start cleaning at the top of the seat at the headrest. Pull the headrest up as far as possible into the highest position to allow for a thoroughly cleaning. Now clean the back rest and in between the pleats and buttons, work your way down to the seat cushion area. Don't forget to clean the entire backside

of the seat as well. Ensure you move the seat forward or backward to get the best position for cleaning the side panels of the seats. Spray a small amount of All Purpose cleaner directly onto the vinyl and rub vigorously with your towel. Be sure to change the towel sides frequently as they become saturated with dirt and oil. Spray the cleaner directly onto the towel instead of misting over the area if you are cleaning small trim or portions of vinyl. This will help prevent unnecessary overspray. For larger surface areas, spray the cleaner over the entire section and scrub vigorously with the Carpet Brush followed up by a towel wipe. You may have to apply another coat of All Purpose Cleaner for heavily grained vinyl. Be sure to scrub with the brush in between the seams and pleats. By pulling the pleats apart with one hand you can get the bristles from the carpet brush down deep in between the creases to remove debris and dirt.

You can use the stiff bristle tooth brush to loosen any trapped dirt in between seat cushion buttons and around the piping of the seat. For the passenger seat, rear seat, and/or hatchback seats, follows the same cleaning procedure.

Vinyl Dressing

A good Vinyl Dressing contains high grade conditioning silicone oils which rejuvenates old, dried, and weather beaten vinyl. These oils rehydrate faded and neglected upholstery. Harmful effects of the sun can fade and bleach out the color of untreated materials like the dashboard. The Vinyl Dressing provides protection from Ultra Violet Rays and renews the luster of all vinyl and plastics.

Directions: For Applying Dressing

Start by heavily spraying a good amount of Vinyl Dressing onto a folded micro fiber towel. However, a wax pad applicator works extremely well for applying dressings. The applicator is about palm size and perfect for holding and spreading dressings evenly.

Start by heavily spraying a good amount of Vinyl Protector onto a folded micro fiber towel. However, a wax pad applicator works extremely well for applying dressings. The applicator is about palm size and perfect for holding and spreading dressings evenly. Start dressing all the interior vinyl and rubber, avoiding contact to any non-vinyl material such as glass, chrome or plastic. Dressing applied to these hard non-porous surfaces can cause the dressing to smear and is difficult to remove. As before, start from the top and work downward. Dress the headliner first if it's made of

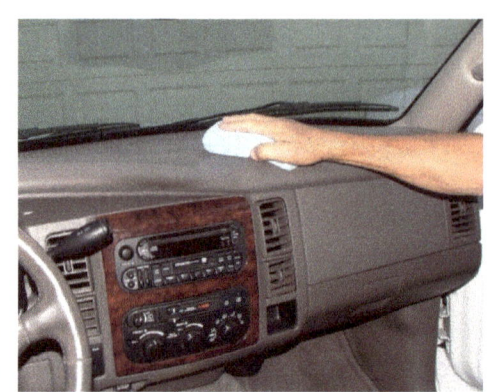

vinyl. Now dress the visors, dashboard, console, door panels, seats, side walls, and all rubber door edge trim.

NOTE: You will find that some console and dashboard areas have either genuine Burl wood or synthetic wood grain. You can add an extra rich shine by applying a light coat of silicone Shine Spray onto the wood. Buff the wood until all the streaks are gone with a clean towel.

A second coat may be needed for extremely dry vinyl. First apply one heavy coat, wait about 10 minutes, and then apply a lighter second coat of dressing. Ensure you apply the dressing evenly. With seats that have pleats, pull them apart with one hand and work a saturated micro fiber towel or wax applicator into the crevices and folds of the seat. Since the Vinyl Dressing is a cleaner as well as a conditioner, you may notice a light coat of dirt on your towel. If the interior vinyl is already pretty clean and no pre-cleaning was necessary, applying just a coat of Vinyl Dressing may be sufficient.

SPECIAL NOTE: Now that you have applied a dressing to the entire interior, take a clean dry micro fiber towel and re-wipe over all of the conditioned vinyl. This will absorb any heavy accumulation of excess dressing and will even out the finish of the vinyl by removing streaks made during the application of the dressing.

Stand back and admire your work, because there's nothing like the look of a beautiful piece of car furniture!

Leather Upholstery And Trim

Generally, a car buyer will pay substantially more for the luxury of a leather interior. The extra investment spent is well worth protecting. A well-kept and dressed leather interior will be luxurious and pliable. The concept of leather dressing is to hydrate, condition, and moisturize aged leather. Neglected leather loses moisture and becomes acidic. Using a good collagen product, such as high quality Leather Conditioner, can replace any loss of moisture. Remember, cleaning fine leather is as important as conditioning it. As before, a well-cared for interior may only need a dusting or wipe down with a damp cloth followed up with a light coat of Leather Conditioner. Should the interior leather be dirty then apply a good leather cleaner first, such as a PH balanced Traffic Lane Cleaner or compatible leather cleaner.

Be sure to use cautionary measures whenever cleaning raw leather. Keep in mind that too strong a cleaner can actually strip and remove leather dyes. Most of the more sensitive leathers are found in European cars. Should you experience difficulty with pulling out too much of the dye color, try using a mild non-alkaline saddle soap for cleaning the leather and follow-up with the Leather Conditioner. Most European leathers are raw with no protective coating, unlike the cotton and fabric type upholsteries, where the color dye is cooked into the fabric. Raw leather is color dyed on the exterior of the hide - not through and through. Ideally raw leather should be cleaned with a Ph balanced cleaner to maintain its natural lubricantcy and sheen.

Many of today's domestic leather, although sold as high grade leather, are in fact plastic coated. The leather is top coated with a product called "polyvinyl chloride plastic" or vinyl. This type of leather is protected by a clear layer of vinyl spray coating, very similar concept to the clear coat finishes found in the paint of a car. However, this type of treated leather is generally impervious to moisture. Since no moisture can penetrate the vinyl coating using the Leather Conditioner it serves no purpose, as it cannot penetrate the leather. The advantage of this type of leather is normally maintenance free, because of its vinyl coating. You would treat this type of leather the same way you clean and dress the interior vinyl upholstery. By cleaning with the All Purpose Cleaner and condition with the Vinyl Dressing.

Directions: **For Cleaning Raw Leather**

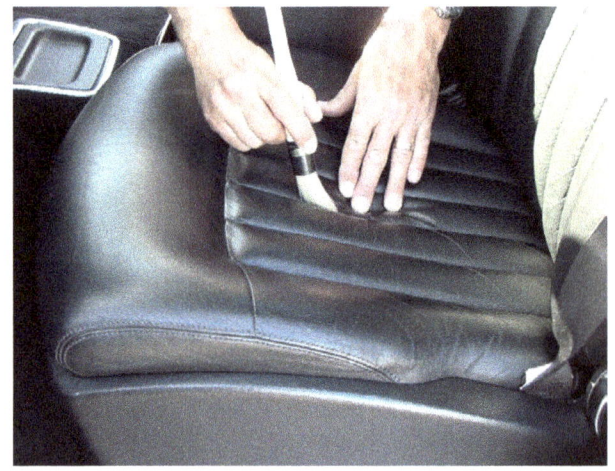

Be sure to test for colorfast reactiveness before applying any cleaner. We suggest you test an inconspicuous area near the bottom of the seat. Apply a small amount of All Purpose Cleaner onto a towel and gently rub a clean spot on the leather. Now check to see how much color dye bled onto the towel. Should the amount of color dye be light then proceed cleaning the leather with the All Purpose Cleaner or comparable leather cleaner. Should there be too much color dye on the towel using the All Purpose Cleaner then switch to using a mild Traffic Lane Cleaner. You can strip the outer layer of dye should you find the leather is not colorfast. However, always proceed with caution. Some customers may ask you to clean their expensive leather seats with Saddle Soap, which can be found at most western supply and feed stores, as well as some local drug stores. After you decide which cleaner to use, spray a small amount of cleaner onto a cloth and gently rub it into the upholstery. Never spray the cleaner directly onto the leather upholstery as this may cause chemical spotting. Never allow the liquid cleaner to puddle and always clean in a continuous motion when applying pressure with your hand. With stubborn dirt apply a small amount of cleaner directly to the Carpet Brush and **gently** agitate the affected area with the brush. As you work the dirt loose, immediately follow up with a clean towel to remove excess moisture. Clean around seat buttons and in between the seat pleats by using the small stiff toothbrush. Be sure to clean around the piping as well.

Now that the leather upholstery has been cleaned apply the Leather Conditioner. Use the Wax Applicator Pad to apply the Leather Conditioner since it's the perfect size for spreading the dressing evenly. Work the pad in between both the seat pleats and buttons. Remember a little dressing goes a long way, but only apply enough dressing to saturate the leather. Try using a Mink Oil Conditioner for badly worn, cracked and dried out leather. Mink Oil is an excellent natural conditioner for both vinyl and leather, and also repels moisture and seals leather better than any other type of conditioner. Ensure you apply the dressing onto the leather in even strokes and allow the dressing to penetrate the hide for about 30 minutes before removing excess conditioner. With a clean and dry towel, rub briskly and buff the upholstery. You will notice that at first the seats will feel sticky, however proceed buffing the seat while continuously turning the towel to a clean side. If done properly you should have a soft satin sheen affect without a heavy oily residue.

Many fine leathers like that found in BMW, Mercedes, Lexus, Rolls Royce, Jaguar, and Porsche's (particularly black interiors) require using only the finest leather dressing to achieve superior results. If you substitute using a vinyl dressing on these types of leathers, especially on dark interiors, it can produce a blotchy uneven look about them. Use only the best Leather conditioners that contain natural feeding Collagen in them.

Special Notes Page

Section 9

Exterior Polishing

- Polishing 163
- Automotive Paint Technology 164
- What Is A Natural Sealant? 164
- What Is A Synthetic Sealant? 165
- Silicones 165
- Waxing - Sealing - Glazing 165
- Saving Time With Combo Or One Step Products 166
- What Is POLISHING? 167
- Achieving Perfect Paint Is Possible 170
- Technical Glossary And Illustrations 171
- What Is Crazing 172
- What Are Fisheyes 172
- Cobweb Paint 172
- What Is Oxidation? 173
- Can Oxidation Be Cured? 174
- What Is Compounding? 175
- Consistent Paint Cleaning 175
- The Importance Of A Paint Thickness Gauge 177
- Paint Measuring Gauge 178
- Polish: Non-Abrasive And Abrasive 180
- Directions For Applying A Polish 180
- Compounding And Buffing Procedures 181
- Divide And Conquer Procedure 182
- Keeping Bonnets And Towels Clean 186
- Sealing 187
- Combination One Step Products 188
- Base Coat/Clear Coat Paint 190
- Paint Type Analysis 191
- Compounding Base Coat/Clear Coat 192
- Water Spots 194
- Treating Chemical Fallout, Acid Rain And Water Spots 195
- Industrial Fallout 195
- Paint Overspray Removal 196
- Paint Transfer 196
- Wood Grain And Aerodynamic Body Parts 197

Polishing

You will find this section to be the most challenging and rewarding part of the whole detailing experience. Up to this point you have spent a great deal of time in prepping, washing, and thoroughly cleaning the car. The car is now clean and ready for the paint conditioning and renewal process, otherwise known as "Polishing".

Keep in mind that a beautiful and clean, sharp looking exterior is just as important as a freshly detailed interior. In fact this is the first place your customer will notice the quality of your work. Achieving perfect mirror like paint is your end goal and the amount of time and effort you contribute to the vehicle will result in a customer's satisfaction beyond their expectations. The vehicle's iridescent beauty and new look will bring back your customer's "Pride of Ownership"

There are many reasons why your customer purchased their vehicle and the important features are different for everyone. Maybe it was the most economical or they just liked the style. Decisions like, what color do I like? There are many determining factors why people choose a certain type of car. No matter what your likes or reasons are, everyone's basic need is to drive a great looking car.

Your skills developed by following our training methods will really help to determine the course of action you will take in order to achieve the proper methods for cleaning and polishing the paint. Over time, you will develop the skill to recognize the proper products to use as well as the different types of paint. Having this skill will separate you from the amateurs and put you in a class of your own. Become a student of learning and will soon be a pro!

Over your detailing career you will come across a badly neglected vehicle where the paint is hazy or chalky and has lost its color due to oxidation. So it's important to understand that the outer layer of the vehicle is the basic defense against ultra violet rays, oxidation, and the destruction of the environmental elements. It will be important for you to understand the fundamentals of polishing and how this process protects the vehicles finish with prevention and maintenance. Take a look at what can happen with a poorly neglected car like this one. This is one car detailing job that you would probably want to pass on!

Automotive Paint Technology

At times, it will be difficult to determine what type of paint is actually on the car. Many of today's paints are made up of alkali, water or solvent based products. These types of paints cover acrylic enamels, lacquers, and urethanes (alkyd enamel is mostly found on foreign cars.) Even an experienced body shop man can have difficulties determining the types of paint used particularly on some of the older paint types used pre-1980's. Some of these included Imron, Glasurit, Laquers, and single stage paint.

The key ingredients to building a successful detailing operation is by educating yourself of the new product technology and expert training of automotive paint reconditioning.

What Is A Natural Sealant?

There are two types of sealants: 1) Natural Sealant and 2) Synthetic Sealant

The natural sealant is a standard wax type, made of either carnauba, bee's wax or monton wax (derived from coal) that tends to deteriorate at a rate much faster than its counter product Synthetics. Thus even more reason for detailing as periodic maintenance and reconditioning can actually add to the life of a vehicle. Professional detailers recommend that a car's paint finish be polished and waxed every 3 to 4 months or a minimum of twice a year depending on whether or not the car is kept garaged or is outside exposed to the elements. From a business standpoint auto detailing is a perpetual service that needs your expertise to maintain the life and beauty of the paint finish.

What Is A Synthetic Sealant?

Synthetic sealants are manmade products that create a longer lasting finish than that of the natural sealant products like carnauba paste wax. The physical appearance of either product, when applied, are almost identical, however the synthetic sealants contain little or no natural waxes. Synthetic sealants like those containing polymers are much harder and more durable and tend to break down at a much lower rate making the synthetic sealant a far superior product. Provided the vehicle has been well maintained, the life expectancy of a synthetic sealant will last between 6 months to a year whereas a natural sealant's life expectancy is between 3 and 4 months.

Knowing these facts, what products are best for the vehicle's finish? Regardless of what most say the debate of whether or not to use natural versus synthetic waxes or sealants will always be a topic of discussion between professionals. Many of today's sealants contain a blend of both creating a "marriage of mixtures". Even with modern science the best approach is knowing the types of paints you will be dealing with. Depending on the paint finish certain products will apply easier than others and are easier or more difficult to remove.

Silicones

Many of today's car sealants contain a small amount of silicone oil. First developed in Germany during World War II, silicone oil became a cheaper and more readily available artificial lubricant and was an excellent substitute for crude oil. Previous to the 1960's paraffin wax, also a derivative of crude oil was and still is used as a lubricant agent when blending carnauba based products. Scientists later discovered that silicone was an excellent substitute for paraffin wax. They found that Silicones proved to be far superior to paraffin wax because they resist higher temperatures and provide a higher gloss finish.

Professional detailers benefit from using sealants containing silicones since they enhance lubrication and gloss on all painted surfaces. However products containing silicone must have the right balance or paint damage could occur. Too high an amount of silicone can play havoc on a paint and body shop. Poor paint adhesion could result if there is presence of silicone oil on the surface prior to painting the car. A professional grade silicone sealant should contain no more than 3% silicone, because silicone is a lubricant. It repels moisture and is very difficult to wash off. This is the reason why most body shops sand the paint prior to repainting the vehicle for better paint adhesion.

Waxing - Sealing - Glazing

The final stages of buffing a car are waxing and sealing. Keep in mind that a good wax job gives the paint its final radiance as well as a hard protective seal against harmful environmental effects and other harmful chemicals. You can tell a good wax job by its lasting properties, a finish that retains a reflective depth of gloss, and the ability to bead when water contacts the paint surface.

When a film of sealant or wax helps in repelling water it is known to have hydrophobic properties. In fact you can bet that if the vehicle's surface does not bead up when water comes in contact chances are there is no longer a wax protection. Many commercially available products contain a high amount of water or cheap paste waxes can be loaded with soft beeswax and whipped with a high percentage of water. Most of these products look good once they are applied, but tend to dissipate after just a few short weeks. Liquid waxes of today are more sophisticated with a blend of high grade silicones, polymers, high grade hardening carnauba, and monton waxes. The monton wax, found in more expensive types of waxes and polishes, is a coal derivative wax. However, there have been no substantial advantages shown by using this product over the popular carnauba based products. Carnauba wax is the hardest natural wax known. It comes from a species of Palm that grows in Central and South America, and has a high melting point of 185°F. In its natural state it has a grey color and when extracted is very flaky before being processed for commercial use. It is then formed into blocks by mixing the flakes with lubricating agents such as paraffin, silicone or solvents, which are then shipped to manufacturers for processing and mixing. The raw carnauba wax remains flaky until cooked in order to blend the wax, which is then poured into retail containers taking on a banana gold color. Carnauba wax is one of the best in attaining the deepest, hardest and most dazzling finishes over all other wax products. Although this is a very expensive wax, one of the greatest qualities is that it spreads on easily and quickly. Due to its durability it requires less maintenance even after several vehicle washings.

GLAZING is a term used when a sealer containing a higher amount of silicone and synthetically manufactured oil base products is applied. This oily substance helps to produce a deep gloss found in darker colors and metallic type paint finishes. Glazing will also help to hide microscopic and hairline scratches in the finish. The glaze will also help to rejuvenate dry chalky paint surfaces with its nourishing oils. Most of today's products contain a certain amount of glaze.

SEALANT is the final stage of waxing the surface, once the pre-polishing and compounding have been done. Compounding strips out oxidation and other surface contaminants and exposes the paint finish to its barest and cleanest form prior to sealing. An unprotected finish will need to have a protective sealant applied to it. Once the sealant is applied it creates a barrier against the harsh environmental elements like alkalis, acid rain, ultra violet radiation and more. The sealant is also what gives the finish its final shine and gloss.

Saving Time With Combo Or One Step Products

With today's advanced automotive products, they are not only easy to apply, but also do everything from removing oxidation, scratches, and blemishes to sealing the paint with a hard durable finish. Better noted as the "combo" product, which is a common term used with detailers to describe a combination product that effectively cleans and seals, all in one application. Many combo products use a <u>non-abrasive</u> cleaning solvent additive combined with a wax product. Other products combine diatomaceous earth (clay - a mild cleaning product) and a wax. The clay acts as a mild compound to remove surface contaminants at the same time leaving a wax or sealer on the painted surface. In most cases, combo products will help you save time and energy and can produce excellent results. Here are some examples that would be good candidates for combo products:

- Brand new vehicles;

- Vehicles with only light oxidation;

- Vehicles in good condition with mild paint blemishes or scratches;

- Vehicles that are routinely maintained with a regular waxing programs.

Those vehicles that are oxidized and in poor shape should be pre-cleaned with a mild polish or compound prior to applying a combo product. Be sure to test whether or not a car can be cleaned and polished with a combo product, by rubbing a small circle on the hood of the car using a towel and a small amount of the combo product. If the towel becomes substantially stained with the color of the car, then this is a good indication that too much oxidation is in the paint and requires pre-cleaning with a polish or compound before applying a combo product. Should the towel only show a slight or pale color of the car color finish, then this is a good indication that the car has very little oxidation and would be an excellent candidate for a combo product. This is a good test for non clear coated vehicles.

What Is POLISHING?

Polishing and waxing have often times been misconceived as meaning the same thing. However, polishing the vehicle paint involves abrading or cleaning the paint surface by using either a mild abrasive cleaner or non-abrasive chemical cleaner. Whereas waxing a car's paint surface is simply to seal the paint with a top coat of non-abrasive sealer using a carnauba based wax product or synthetic sealant.

The polishing process is made up of pre-cleaning and is necessary for creating a good foundation. By polishing the surface first, it helps to create a better adhesion of wax or sealant. Many individuals never polish prior to waxing the surface. However, this is a key process in order to ensure a longer lasting wax job which will double the reflective abilities and create a mirror-like finish. An example would be if you were comparing this process to waxing a kitchen floor. After time, the floor has built up a dingy yellow appearance that can't be removed without having to strip the floor with a heavy duty stripper. This process then gives you a clean foundation for sealing the pores with a fresh coat of wax, leaving the floor with a high gloss look.

Without a good clean foundation to bind with, your wax job will break down quickly. In fact, most experts will agree that just waxing and buffing alone will not produce the same brilliancy as that of a surface that has been pre-polished. By polishing a vehicle prior to waxing will define the difference between "sharp" and "classic" detailing.

Polishing is similar to cleaning the vehicle by using the same method of divide and conquer we spoke of earlier in this book. I suggest you divide the automobile into sixths and work one section at a time. The key is to be consistent during the polishing application. It is important that each section matches the first and so on in order to attain a consistent shine.

When the entire vehicle has been properly polished it will be time to move on to the next phase. The concept of polishing is to remove all the imperfections that could diffuse the sun's rays. The brilliant shine comes from the ability to reflect as many light rays as possible.

Polishing the paint before applying the wax or sealer will help to clean out the pores and smooth out the surface as flat as a mirror. However, if you were to inspect the cars paint under a microscope it would look rough and have the appearance of deep crevices and high mountain tops. This is what we call high peaks and low valleys in the paint. When you think of high peaks, think of surface contaminants like paint overspray, bird droppings, tree sap, rail dust, surface calcium deposits, and dirt. Low valleys are pores containing dead oxidized material, sludge, oil and dirt. These are the contaminants under the surface. A good tool to use is a high powered 10X paint magnifier like this one to closely examine the surface of the vehicle.

By just looking at the surface with a naked eye will not give you the ability to really see the degrees of roughness. By simply running your hand across the paint surface, you will get a better feel of the condition of the paint. Remember to keep in mind that a well maintained car should feel very smooth and not dry. When you do find surfaces that are not smooth, hazy, dry, and you find the water does not bead, is more than likely a good candidate for polishing.

First you must cut the paint in stages by using different levels of aggressive compound followed by a lesser abrasive polishing product. Think of this process as being similar to sanding a piece of wood starting with a more aggressive sandpaper down to a fine grit sandpaper for an ultra-smooth finish. As with the wood, this process of abrading the wood with different levels of polishing will help to remove the high peaks and become one single flat piece of material. Low valleys will remain in the paint until enough abrading is done. These low valleys or pores hold the sludge, oxidation, and embedded dirt which can be pulled to the surface by chemical cleaners found in the polish. A perfectly polished paint finish will be optically flat and free from valleys and pores.

Achieving Perfect Paint Is Possible

The entire concept of polishing the paint is to first deep clean the pores of the paint and to smooth out the surface until it is optically flat like the surface of a glass mirror. To achieve this, you must cut or abrade the paint first. This is typically done in stages by applying different levels of aggressive compounds followed by the use of less abrasive polishing materials. Once achieved, the high peaks and low valleys are removed from the surface and it is now prepped for sealing or waxing.

ACHIEVING PERFECT PAINT IS POSSIBLE
When uniform light rays reflect off the surface (see Fig. 4)

PAINT SURFACE BEFORE COMPOUNDING (Fig. 1)
HIGH PEAKS
ROUGH SURFACE--VERY LITTLE OR NO SHINE
LOW VALLEYS

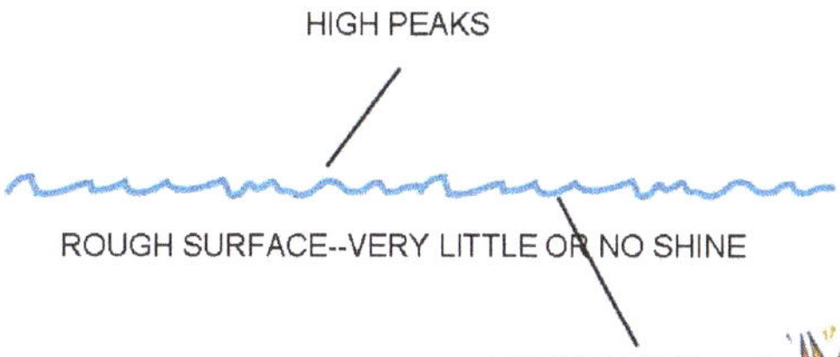

SIMULATED LOOK AT A SEVERELY OXIDIZED SURFACE BEFORE FIRST STAGE OF COMPOUNDING.

PAINT SURFACE AFTER COMPOUNDING (Fig. 2)
SMOOTHER SURFACE—STILL SCATTERED LIGHT RAYS

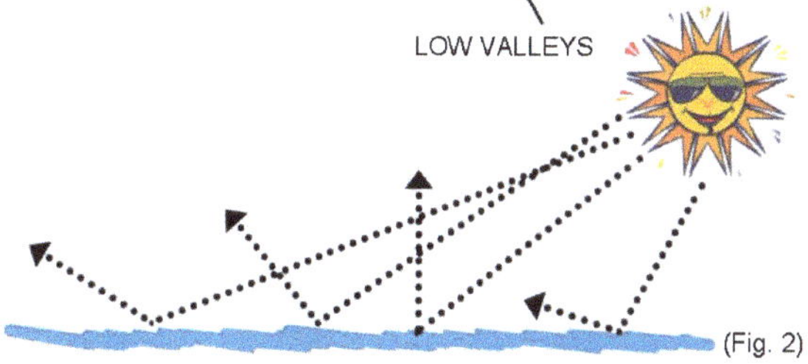

1ST STAGE

SIMULATED LOOK OF A SURFACE AFTER COMPOUNDING AND REMOVING INITIAL OXIDATION.

REQUIRES USE OF A COMPOUND EITHER:
PRODUCTS 1 — HEAVY RUBBING COMPOUND
          2 — MEDIUM RUBBING COMPOUND

A COMBINATION OF THESE PRODUCTS MAY BE USED

PAINT SURFACE AFTER POLISHING (Fig. 3)
SURFACE IS NOW PREPARED FOR SEALANT
SMOOTH FLAT SURFACE—NO PEAKS OR VALLEYS

2ND STAGE

SIMULATED LOOK OF A SURFACE AFTER POLISHING AND REMOVING REMAINING OXIDATION AND LEVELING THE PAINT.

REQUIRES USE OF A CLEANER POLISH
PRODUCTS 1 — MILD POLISH WITH DIMINISHING MICRO-ABRASIVES
          2 — MEDIUM POLISH....CLAY BASED

A COMBINATION OF THESE PRODUCTS MAY BE USED

PAINT SURFACE AFTER WAXING OR SEALING (FIG. 4)
OPTIMUM PAINT REFLECTION = PERFECT PAINT

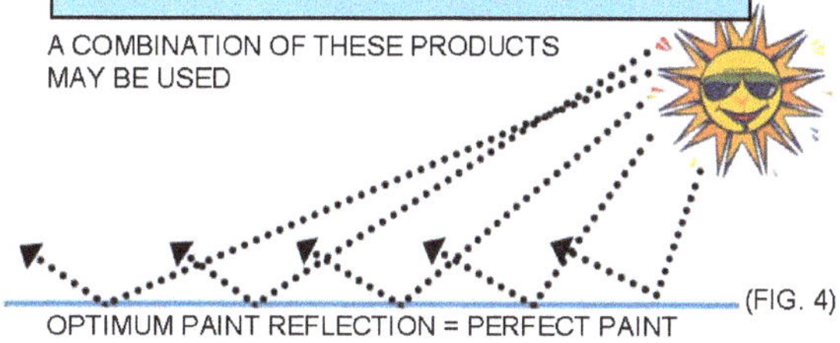

3RD STAGE

SIMULATED LOOK OF A SURFACE PROTECTED WITH A SEALER OR WAX. SURFACE FEELS SMOOTH AND GLOSSY. OPTICALLY CLARITY AND A FLAT SURFACE PROVIDES OPTIMUM REFLECTION AND DEPTH OF COLOR.

REQUIRES APPLICATION OF SEALER OR WAX
PRODUCTS 1 — HIGH GRADE LIQUID SEALER
          2 — COMBO ONE STEP WAX
          3 — POLYMER BASED
          4 — CARNUBA WAX

A COMBINATION OF THESE PRODUCTS MAY BE USED

Technical Glossary And Illustrations

TECHNICAL GLOSSARY AND ILLUSTRATIONS

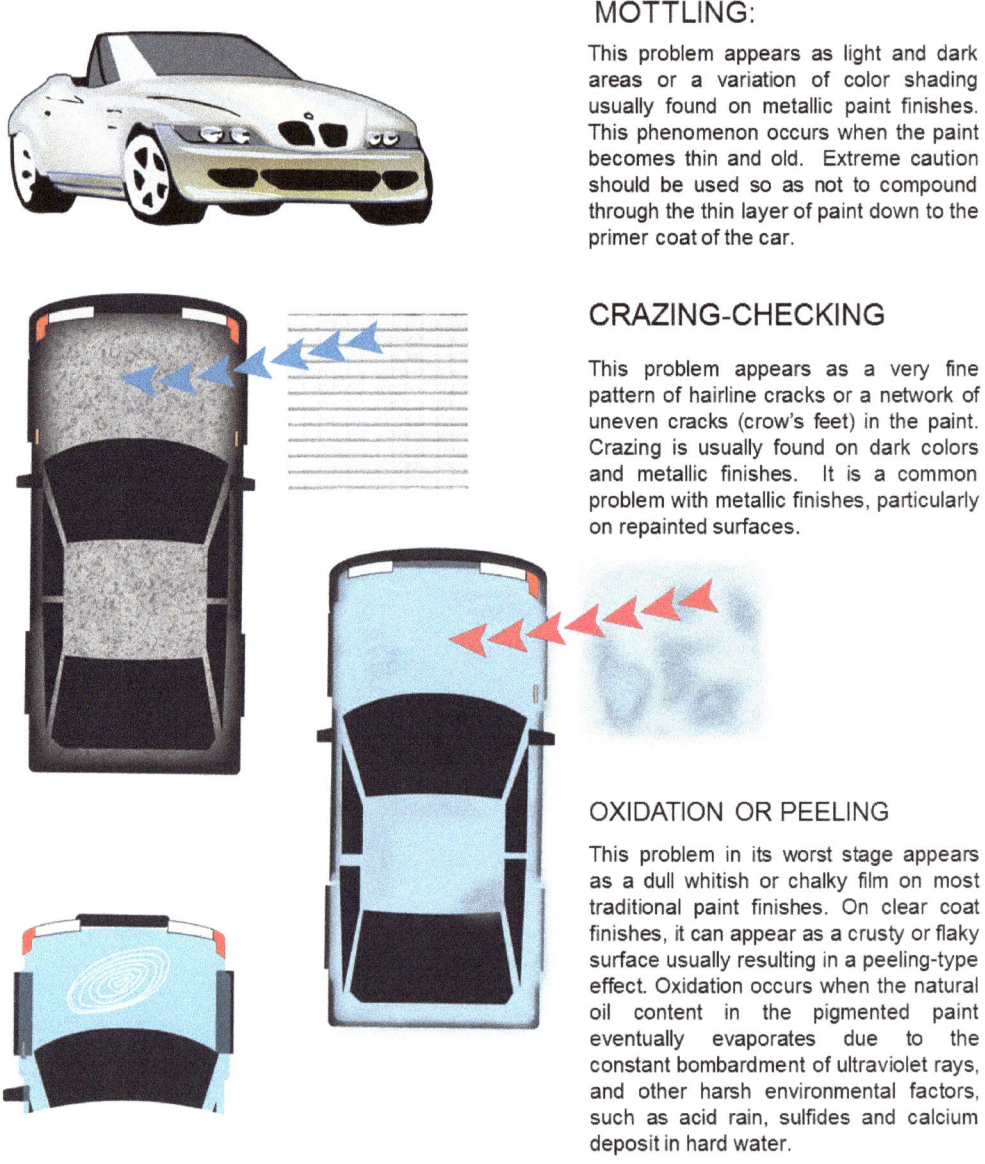

MOTTLING:

This problem appears as light and dark areas or a variation of color shading usually found on metallic paint finishes. This phenomenon occurs when the paint becomes thin and old. Extreme caution should be used so as not to compound through the thin layer of paint down to the primer coat of the car.

CRAZING-CHECKING

This problem appears as a very fine pattern of hairline cracks or a network of uneven cracks (crow's feet) in the paint. Crazing is usually found on dark colors and metallic finishes. It is a common problem with metallic finishes, particularly on repainted surfaces.

OXIDATION OR PEELING

This problem in its worst stage appears as a dull whitish or chalky film on most traditional paint finishes. On clear coat finishes, it can appear as a crusty or flaky surface usually resulting in a peeling-type effect. Oxidation occurs when the natural oil content in the pigmented paint eventually evaporates due to the constant bombardment of ultraviolet rays, and other harsh environmental factors, such as acid rain, sulfides and calcium deposit in hard water.

SPIDERING

Spidering usually resembles a cobweb effect in the paint. This phenomenon is found on new and old cars alike. This situation appears as perfectly formed circular lines spreading outward within each other. It is more noticeable on dark colored paint finishes, particularly under direct sunlight or florescent lighting.

What Is Crazing

Crazing is a very fine pattern of hairline cracks found in the paint finish especially in aftermarket or repainted cars. Unfortunately, these types of surfaces are usually impossible to completely restore. In most cases, these cracks usually extend all the way down from the top layer of clear coat to the primer coat. I recommend that you suggest to your customer to have the vehicle repainted properly. At all costs, avoid waxing or compounding over this type of paint as it usually worsens the appearance of the paint.

What Are Fisheyes

A fisheye is a defect in the paint finish which you can only recognize, but can do little to remedy it. Fisheyes are caused by poor body shop preparation prior to painting the car. If there is any remaining residue, wax, grease, cleaning solvents or oil on the surface prior to painting the car the paint will not adhere properly. Similar to the action when water and oil separate when mixed together. A fisheye appears as a small indented droplet, like a miniature crater or flaw in the paint. Thus where the term "Fisheye" comes from looking like a small sunken eye socket. In most cases this situation won't be noticed by an individual car owner and is commonly found on repainted cars with a clear coat finish. However, once again, this cannot be corrected through detailing.

Cobweb Paint

This type of paint surface appears and looks like a cobweb where there are thousands of scratches in the finish, especially under fluorescent light as well as in natural sunlight. These tend to be more apparent on darker finishes such as black, red or dark blue. Oddly enough, these are not seen as random scratches but rather a defined uniformed flow of lines in the paint, sometimes called Spidering. As you take a close look you will see thousands of perfectly formed lines within another circle of lines. This is usually caused when new paint dries on the surface of the car and takes on the natural grain of the metal below. The best way to explain this to a customer is to assure them that there is nothing wrong with the paint finish, but that it is the natural grain of the paint and cannot be completely hidden or polished out. I suggest you use a glaze type polish to temporarily help hide these fine lines. Even show cars cannot escape the natural occurrence of cobwebbed paint.

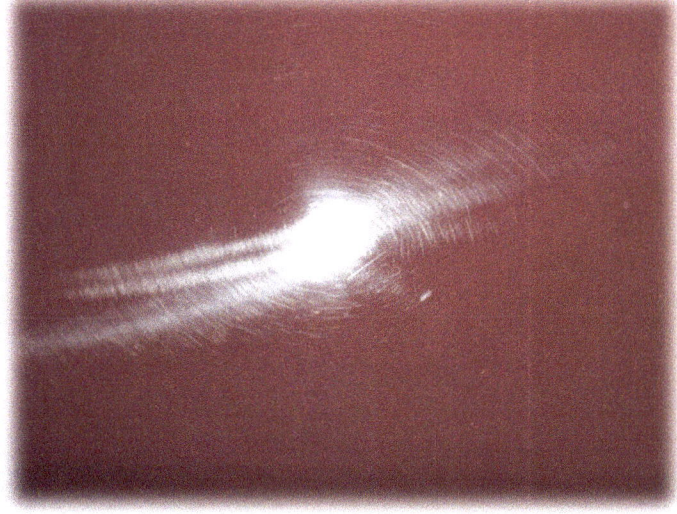

Orange Peel

Special skills are required!

This is usually caused when a paint or body shop operator sprays too heavy an amount of paint rather than using several light coats better known as the "Orange Peel" effect. By examining the paint surface closely you will see uniform dimples, much like the surface of an orange peel. At first glance you may mistake this as a problem resulting from high peaks in the paint. However, unless you are a skilled paint and body man the only way to eliminate this problem is to use a process called "color sanding". There are special sandpapers made specifically for color sanding paint and used to eliminate the orange peel effect in order to smooth out the surface.

There are generally three degrees of sandpaper used with the last being a super fine 3,000 grit paper. Once the surface has been sanded, you would need to perform several stages of polishing through the means of using a high speed buffer. Note: Color Sanding is an art for the ultra-sophisticated detail person who wants to offer it all!

* * * * * * * * * * CAUTION * * * * * * * * * * *

I HIGHLY RECOMMEND YOU DO NOT ATTEMPT TO COLOR SAND A CAR UNLESS YOU HAVE HAD PROPER TRAINING AND THE PROPER TOOLS TO DO THE JOB. COMPARED TO THE STANDARD ORBITAL POLISHING, COLOR SANDING IS AN EXTREMELY HIGH RISK PROCEDURE.

What Is Oxidation?

Oxidation is a natural and ongoing process involving paint deterioration from many contributing environmental elements that affects every type of paint finish. Oxidation occurs when heat, ultra violet light and oxygen combine, breaking down the molecular composition of the paint. You will be able to recognize this problem when the appearance of the paint looks dull, hazy or chalky. Most traditional automotive paints have a basic oil content which can evaporate over a period of time due to overexposure to the sun. Both sunlight and heat accelerates the drying of the painted surface leaving a whitish chalky residue. This type of surface is beyond any hope of repair unless the car undergoes an aggressive compounding and re-nourishment process of valuable conditioning oils. The majority of oxidized vehicles will be within the realm of repair through your expertise; however occasionally you will come across one or two that simply won't respond. In this type of situation it would be best to professionally and constructively suggest to your customer to have the vehicle repainted. Keep in mind that clear coat paint finishes are not immune to oxidation either. Underneath the layer of clear urethane is a thin sensitive layer of base coat color paint that is constantly bombarded with ultraviolet light, dulling the underlying paint. Even though the clear coat is an extremely hard material it is also exposed to the elements, which can break apart over a period of time and become thin and weak. Eventually this will cause a whitish snow flake or peeling effect to the surface of the car.

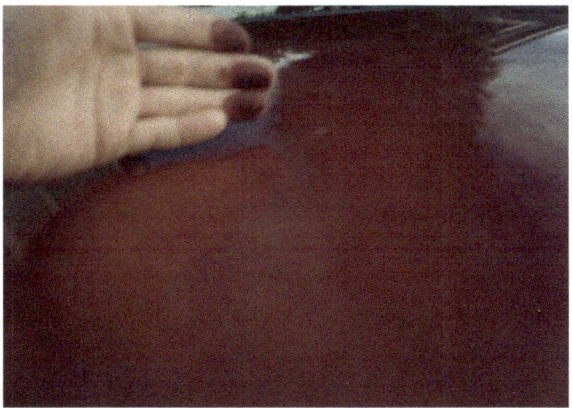 

Can Oxidation Be Cured?

As we discussed earlier, oxidation prevention is an ongoing process that requires routine maintenance. To better understand let's use the following analogy. Imagine the paint as a sponge. As you know, a wet sponge is full of moisture allowing the fibers to stay soft and resilient. However, once the sponge's moisture is gone the fibers become stiff and dry. Consider this to be in the same case with paint finishes, once the pores lose their oil content the surface becomes dry and chalky, and loses its ability to be resilient. A freshly painted car goes through a different process of steps known as a curing. This is when the paint hardens and sets its permanent color. The curing period is believed to be from a couple of days to a few months. Expert body shops agree that a freshly painted vehicle should be allowed to cure for approximately 4 to 6 weeks before any type of wax or sealer is placed onto the surface. While the paint is going through the curing process oxygen in the air combines with the hardener and catalyst in the paint to form a hard shell of protection. Even though paint does not actually breathe, if a sealer or coat of wax is placed over fresh paint before it has time to set and cure, it prevents the necessary oxygenation to combine with the paint hardeners and catalyst. This will cause the paint to look dull and hazy in just a few short months. When the paint has had time to cure, a protective sealant should be applied for the best method of protection against naturally occurring oxidation. By maintaining and re-waxing the paint surface you will help to extend the life of the paint. When proper care and routine maintenance is done on a good paint job, the life of the paint will last for many years!

What Is Compounding?

Compounding is taking polishing even a step further. For old dull and worn out paint, this process requires a more aggressive cleaner to revitalize the finish. Compounding restores the life to traditional paint finishes, such as single stage acrylics and enamels. Compounding is best used when paint becomes rough by either paint overspray, oxidation or build-up of environmental excretions. By using this process you can effectively smooth out the surface by removing the dull and oxidized paint. Compounding removes the layer of oxidized material by stripping or cutting the first layer of paint. You will be able to remove any hairline scratches by removing the upper most layer of paint in order to prepare it for its final polishing. You can judge the degree of grit to be used based on the severity of damage to the paint. Compounds have different levels of aggressiveness. More coarse compounds have a higher ratio of cleaning agents, where the particles are much larger. Silica is an abrasive product found in heavier compounds. By placing a dab of product in between your fingers and rubbing together you can judge the degree of abrasive ingredients. Over time you will be able to judge the appropriate grit of compound when cutting the paint. Ensure you always use caution when applying compound to any vehicle. Be sure to only use the mildest compound necessary to get the job done. Keep in mind that too harsh a compound will scratch the surface causing you to spend more time than necessary to remove all the fine scratches. The concept of compounding is to simply cut out the heavy contamination and level the paint to an equal plane. There may be times when you experience heavier scratches which seemingly go down to the primer coat. You may not be able to remove all of these deep scratches, but by compounding the surrounding area you will be able to level the paint around the scratch making it smoother and less noticeable.

Note: Compounding should be your last resort to cutting an old faded finish. Be sure to first test an area with a mild polish or chemical cleaner before you continue. You may not have to strip as much paint if good clarity is achieved. Should you have to use an aggressive compound be sure to re-nourish and seal the paint with a conditioner (Glaze) before waxing or sealing the surface. When I speak of chafing the paint, it is similar to chafing or drying out your skin after shaving your face using a razor blade. In order to get rid of the dry skin or surface, replenishing oils need to be re-applied. By re-nourishing the oils in the paint you help to restore and brighten the color pigmentation of the paint as well as slowing down further oxidation.

Consistent Paint Cleaning

Your major concern should be how even the finish looks after the compounding and sealing are done. Many detailers constantly battle with paint smearing or streaking, thus the importance of clean paint. Remember that paint is exposed to many elements that can be trapped making the paint look soiled and stained. These are oils, dirt, scuffs, scratches, and oxidized paint. Knowing this, you need to ensure that all of these elements are cleaned from the surface to reduce the likelihood of streaking. Improper surface preparation cannot produce an even high gloss reflection in the paint.

Not only will you need to learn how to use the correct cleansers and polishes, but you will also need to learn the proper pressure techniques when polishing and waxing. There's one common mistake most novice detailers make with their hand polishing technique, which is to press down with their fingertips instead of using the entire surface of the hand when applying a wax or sealer.

The Wrong Way

The Right Way

By using the whole surface of your hand when pressing down, you will produce a more even distribution of the product. Imagine your hand as an orbital polisher with the flat palm of your hand distributing even pressure as you apply your polish or wax. Be patient when learning this technique as you will need to develop hand strength and concentration. Streaking can occur when applying uneven pressure with your fingertips instead of using the flat palm of your hand and fingers together. There can be many reasons for streaking including when the pressure and the chemical cleaner is concentrated on the highest pressure points which will remove more oxidized paint on these areas. Since the surrounding area has only been lightly cleaned it will appear as shading or streaking in the finish. Another cause is the application of combining incompatible products. Product performance can be affected by cheap incompatible products that have been applied by your customer in the past. Keep in mind that many professional grade products may react unfavorably if used with many over-the-counter consumer products which is another reason why paint must be thoroughly cleaned prior to waxing or sealing.

Another cause is from applying too much product to the surface of the car. More is not always better which is a common misconception that you will better the protection. Since paint is porous and has a very thin skin, only a small amount of wax or sealer can be absorbed into the paint. It is not the amount of product applied, but the manner in which it is applied that is important. Even though a heavy coat of wax or sealer has been applied and appears to have cured on the surface, it may be that underneath the wax surface there are still layers of sealant curing. These uncured sealants may still be wet and will cause smearing if wiped off too soon.

The last and most common problem of paint streaking is insufficient or uneven removal

of old dirty and dull oxidized paint. Each vehicle should be polished or compounded before applying any wax or sealer to ensure you are dealing with clean paint. Be sure to strip and remove all old wax so that the compounding can do a proper job of removing dead paint. Keep in mind that some vehicles will be more oxidized than others. In order to save time upfront you will need to determine whether the entire vehicle will need to be polished or compounded. The topside portions of the car are more susceptible to oxidation which includes the trunk, hood, and engine compartment areas. These areas oxidize and dull out first since they are exposed to the direct sunlight. Since the sides of the car are exposed to far less ultra violet rays they are usually in better condition. Due to this fact, it's possible that some cars may only require compounding or polishing on the top surfaces, whereby the sides may only require a one-step combo type product. However, I recommend you polish or compound the entire car if you are not sure of the paint condition before applying any wax or sealant. Your customers will only expect perfection so you should do everything possible to produce nothing less than professional results.

The Importance Of A Paint Thickness Gauge

You will greatly reduce the risk of paint damage by knowing how much paint is on the surface of the vehicle prior to compounding. By using a paint thickness gauge you can instantly get an approximate reading of how thick the paint really is. Factory painted cars, including the primer, range between 4 to 5 mils thick. However, cars that have been repainted will indicate a thickness of up to 6 to 8 mils.

The paint thickness gauge measures by magnetic resistance or surface pull. The paint is a buffer between the upper most surface and the metal of the car. The thinner the paint the greater the magnetic pull. I suggest you acquire a thickness gauge that has a range from 1 to 15 mils (one thousandth of an inch thick). Keep in mind that the higher up on the indicator the thinner paint will be. However, if the paint on the surface is thicker, the magnet passes through more paint and weakens the pull of the magnet. You will see on the indicator a lower number as the magnet releases quicker due to less magnetic resistance. This is a very impressive tool when you discuss the condition of the paint with your customer.

Paint Measuring Gauge

PAINT MEASURING GAUGE™ #1099

EASY TO USE AS 1, 2, 3

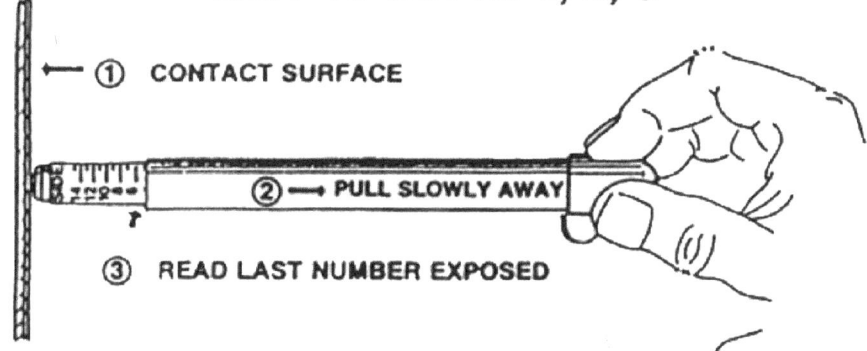

① CONTACT SURFACE
② PULL SLOWLY AWAY
③ READ LAST NUMBER EXPOSED

Read "SIDE" SCALE on side panels such as sides of fenders, doors or any other vertical surfaces.

TIPS ON USE

To insure accurate, predictable readings:

A. Allow gauge to center itself. Hold gauge loosely by cap – as it is pulled out, it will center itself squarely to the panel.

B. Odd numbers are short lines, even numbers are long lines. The reading shown is .005, five thousandths of an inch. (5 mils)

C. Read "TOP" SCALE on top panels, such as roof, hood, trunk, or any other horizontal surface.

TAKE THREE READINGS: After a first reading to learn approximate thickness, take 2 more readings pulling gauge very slowly as it nears the first reading.

INSPECT AND CLEAN PARTICLES FROM MAGNET.

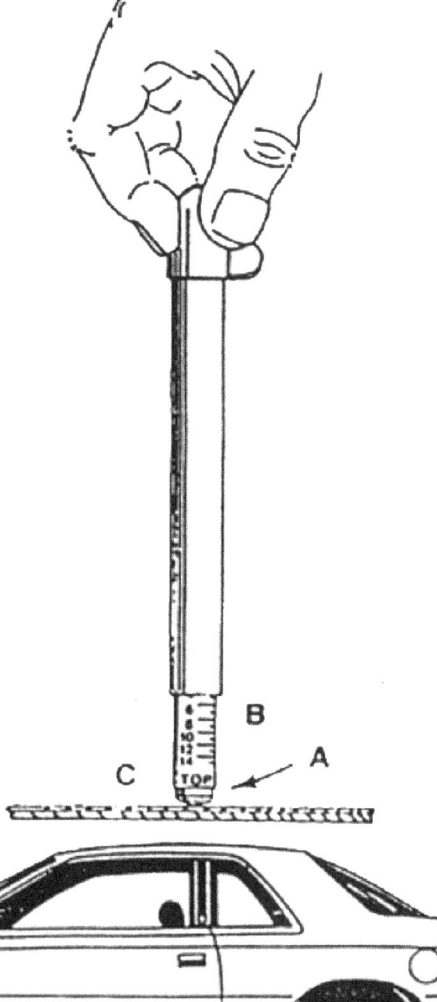

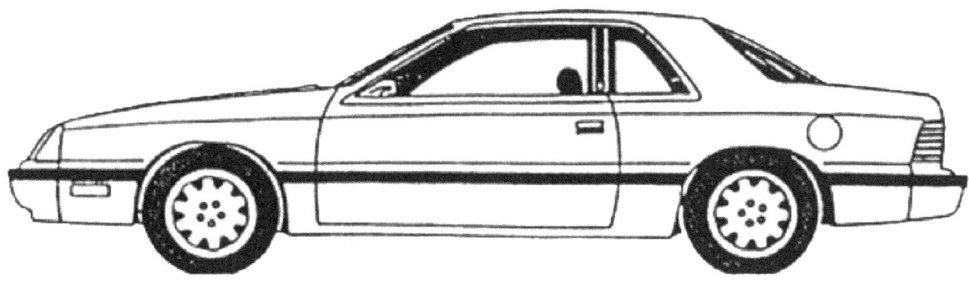

Greg Dumond – Success Training Manual

For a more accurate reading of the thickness of the paint some professional detailers will go to the extreme of measuring the exact thickness of the paint before starting any work on the car especially if color sanding is about to be done on the vehicles painted surface. We will not be covering color sanding extensively in this book, as it requires advanced training and polishing techniques for this type of major paint correction. Here are a couple of examples of the more advanced and more expensive digital type of paint measuring devices, made by Highline Meter.

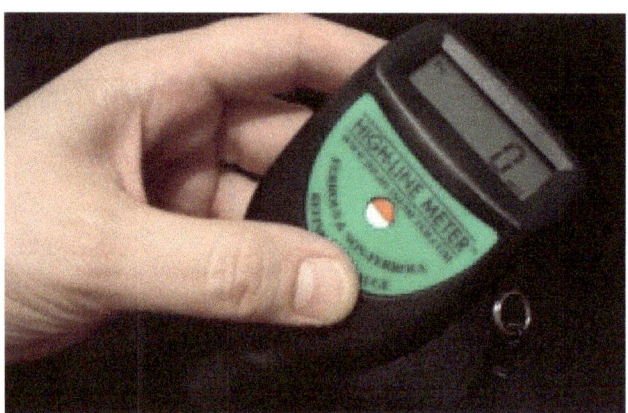

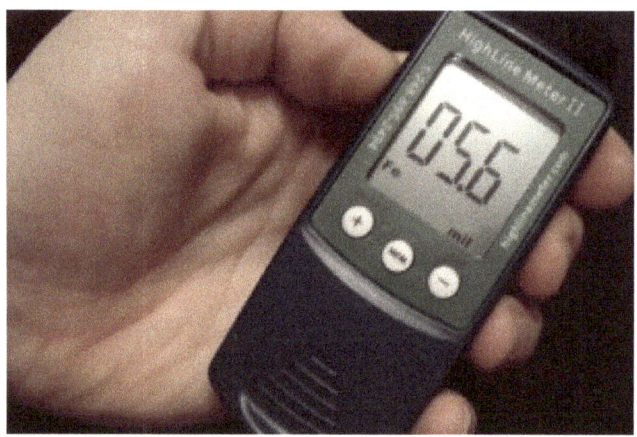

Polish: Non-Abrasive And Abrasive

There are several types of abrasive polish; the most popular are:

1. A Polish which is a mild abrasive chemical cleaner safer for clear coat and all other types of paint finishes. This type of polish will contain either a mild amount of micro abrasives or other products containing Diatomaceous Earth. These types of products are best for clear coat finishes and mild oxidation.

2. Polishes that are more aggressive contain more abrasives designed for single stage or non-clear coat finishes. This method of polishing will remove light to medium oxidation, light scratches, and deeply embedded weathering from the cars surface. This type of product will allow for a smooth, clean surface, for subsequent waxing and sealing.

Directions For Applying A Polish.

Apply the Polish on a cool surface, applying three to four rings of polish to the orbital bonnet and work in a 3' x 3' square area. It is important to **NOT** let this product stay on the cars' surface too long. Certain brands of Polish can dry quickly and can be difficult to remove if left on too long. Test the level of difficulty or ease by using the following method. Continue working in 3 foot sections, applying polish with one bonnet, and removing the dried polish with a separate clean towel or bonnet. Your Polish will be easier to remove if allowed to dry 1 to 2 minutes before buffing off the residue. It is always best to try to work on a cool to the touch surface.

Remember your more aggressive products will smooth the surface of the paint pores by drawing out the dirt left in the valleys and removing the high peaks left on the surface of the paint. In order to achieve perfect paint you will need to level or flatten down the paint so that the light will reflect off at a perfect angle.

Review the different options in your Chemical Section reference guide for other options when it comes to using Polishes, Compounds, Waxes and Sealants. I also recommend researching various manufacturers and suppliers who can offer you sample or smaller trial sizes to try out. You can also refer to my "Product Resource Guide" in the back of this book for more information on these companies.

The same divide and conquer method should be used when applying your combo waxes and sealants. Always follow the directions on the bottle for the best application method as well as curing time. There are differences between manufacturers and knowing these differences can save you time and produce your best results.

> **NOTE:** Most dark colors such as Maroon, Black or Dark Blue, tend to show more streak marks than light colors, due to the depth of color and reflection.

Should you decide to go after the new dealer market, as you can guess, these cars would not need much polishing or compounding. Car dealerships main focus is to deliver a sparkling clean car to their customer. Since the prep time is less involved in detailing new cars, auto dealerships usually expect wholesale volume discount rates. In this case I would recommend using a Production or Speed Wax to detail these cars if you are going to be discounting or wholesaling your services. Longevity is not as important to the dealership the way a retail customer would come to expect. They just want them looking good going out the door.

Compounding And Buffing Procedures

So far we have covered how to recognize many different paint problems and the differences between waxes, sealants, and polishing compounds. Let's take a look at the polishing techniques and how to perform the actual compounding and polishing process by using your professional orbital polisher. Keep in mind that there is no absolute right or wrong method of polishing and compounding paint. Some detailers prefer to polish and compound by hand, however, as we discussed earlier, unless you have had a lot of experience and understand the importance of evenly distributing pressure points you will likely achieve better results by using an orbital polisher.

As mentioned earlier, achieving perfect paint is the result of removing oxidation and dead paint and abrading or leveling the paint until it is optically flat. It is important that you learn and recognize the different levels of products used throughout the detailing process.

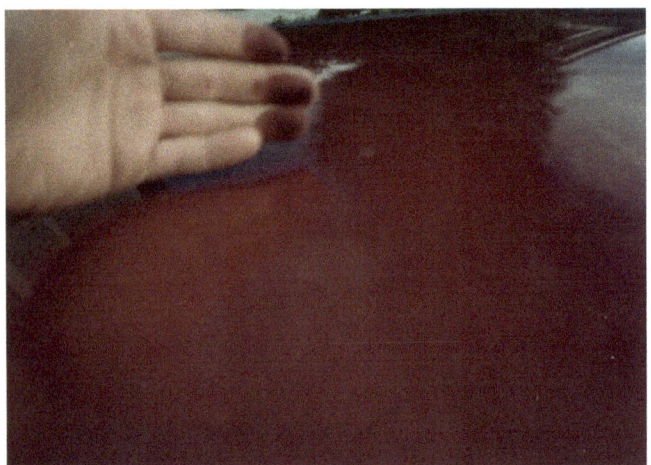

Should you decide to start with compounding, ensure you remove only as much paint as necessary in order to remove the dead paint and heavy scratches on non-clear coat (Single Stage) finishes. You will see that severe oxidation is apparent when you can take your finger, run it across the surface and pick up colored paint chalkiness or another sign to use compound would be if the finish has absolutely no reflection at all. This will help you when deciding what level of compound or polish that you will proceed with.

Divide And Conquer Procedure

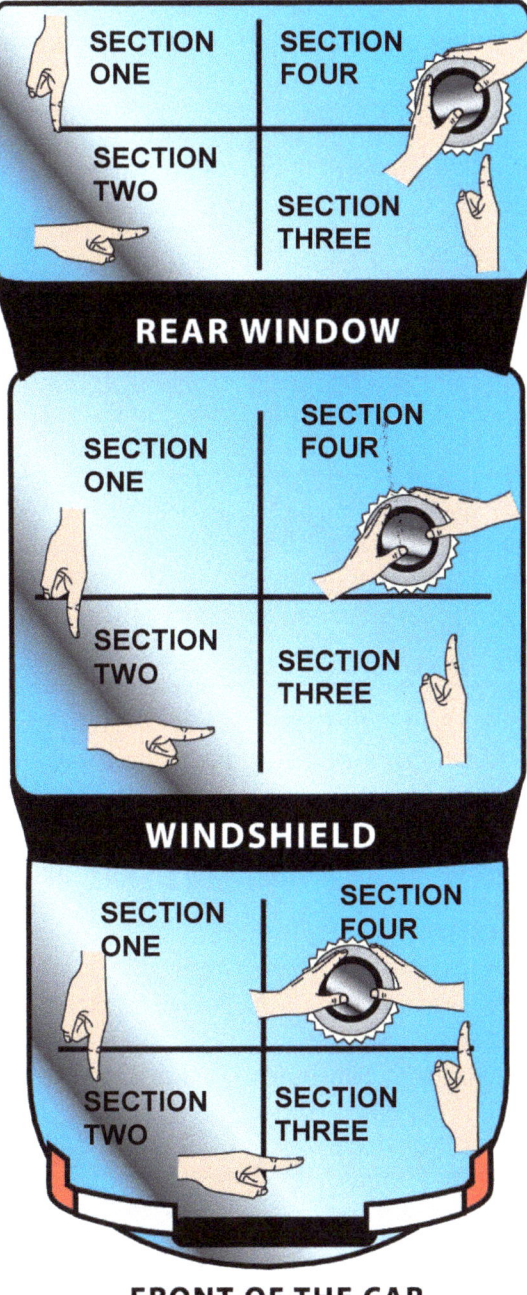

1. Divide the panel into four sections as Illustrated.

2. Proceed to buff and wax the car in the order shown, starting with section one.

3. Always overlap the buffer onto each section to obtain an even application of polish or wax.

Divide and conquer procedure – Divide each panel into four sections for polishing. Start at the top front of the vehicle completing panels 1, 2 and 3. Lastly polish the bottom, sides and bumper areas of the vehicle.

Directions: I highly suggest you remove any rings, watches or belts before starting your work. Be sure to place the electrical cord over your shoulder to keep it from coming in contact with the paint as it can cause scuffing or mar your work. This will also ensure the cord stays out of your way as you work. I recommend you have an extra bonnet and finishing towel close at hand as well. Tip: By wearing a Detailer's Apron, you can keep these items close at hand, including your bottle of polish, wax and other miscellaneous items.

Decide what level of polish or compound will be used based on the previous conditions mentioned in the polishing and compounding sections. During your professional career you will be able to quickly judge the degree of compound to use, just by looking at the vehicle's surface. Remember to test a small area if you are unsure as to the level of abrasiveness necessary to do the job. Be sure to test different compounds and polishes side by side for both abrasive and non-abrasive. Should the finish have no reflection or has a heavy chalky residue then I suggest you start off with a heavier Rubbing Compound. This product is the most aggressive and will quickly get to the problem faster than any other product. Or you may only need to use a milder abrasive compound agent, again depending whether or not you are polishing a clear or non-clear coat finish. Either way, don't be afraid to use your aggressive compound when necessary. Keep in mind that micro scratches from the grit in the compound will be leveled out and removed with the less aggressive Polish later on in the process.

Directions: USING YOUR ORBITAL POLISHER

Use the divide and conquer method until you have covered every section of the vehicle. Now place the orbital polisher on its backside, so that the drive pad is in the up position. Place 3 or 4 rings of compound directly onto the bonnet.

Be very careful to not set the buffer drive pad portion onto the ground as it could pick up grit or small rocks and severely scratch the surface. Keep in mind that the buffer will seem a little awkward at first, so be patient when working with your new equipment. Once you start getting the feel of the machine you will see how it will do the majority of the polishing, saving you a tremendous amount of time as well as body fatigue. Be sure to smear the product on the bottom of the pad back and forth across the surface before you turn the buffer on. This will help prevent the product from spinning off, over spraying yourself, and other areas you may have already cleaned. Start at the front of the hood and work the buffer towards the back. The best and most comfortable position is to hold the buffer directly in front of you and move your arms back and forth across your body. If you start at the left or right front fender, stand to the side of the car and work the buffer towards the front windshield. Ensure you overlap each area by crisscrossing the buffer pad over every square inch of the paint. In other words, if you start at the hood work the buffer towards the center. Should the hood have a chrome strip divider down the center of the hood, use this as your imaginary line down the center. You can use other areas as stopping points, like the crack between the front top fender and the hood. Some detailers will actually take their time by taping off sections of the vehicle before proceeding.

Tip: If you are going to tape off sections of the car, go ahead and apply painter's tape over any rubber trim that could become contaminated with drying compounds or wax. Also run your tape over gaps such as hood and door closures where wax or compound could get into. Also run tape along window frames and the rubber seals around the windows. By taking this extra step you will really impress your customers that you are a true pro. You will also find that this procedure will save you valuable time by not having to spend so much time cleaning out the door and trunk jams or removing excess residue off of the rubber trim and weather stripping.

If you elect not to tape off sections, Use these gaps as a stopping point, you will save time if you do not allow the buffer to embed the compound into the gaps and seams which you will have to remove later with a toothbrush. Be sure to operate the buffer slowly and methodically. Use your wax pad applicator to <u>methodically apply the compound parallel to the gaps and seams.</u>

You may be able to compound an entire half section at a time, if the surface has a lighter amount of oxidation. However, should the oxidation be heavy or severe then only compound a 3' x 3' area at a time. Be sure to check your bonnet after each section and turn the bonnet inside out if it becomes saturated with oxidized material. For foam type of orbital polishers you may need to periodically put on a clean new pad as it becomes saturated with oxidized paint. Continue compounding the next 3' x 3' section. More than one application may be necessary for severe oxidation. Should you find that any heavy scratches or scuff marks are still present, apply a small amount of compound directly onto a wax applicator pad and aggressively rub directly onto the scratch. Caution: Be careful not to apply too much pressure for a long period of time when using the compound. The aggressive micro abrasives in the product could wear through thinning paint.

The following is a demonstration of polishing a 3X3 area while working the buffer back and forth, once vertically and then horizontally. It doesn't matter which direction you start off in just remember to crisscross so each section is buffed in both directions at least one time.

Keeping Bonnets And Towels Clean

Frequently check your bonnet to be sure it is not over-saturated with oxidation. The whole idea behind compounding is to loosen, lift, and absorb the dead oxidized paint onto your bonnet. It's best to use both sides of your bonnet, so once you have saturated your bonnet with a large amount of oxidized paint turn it inside out and continue compounding until this side is saturated as well. Traditional or non-clear coat paint will be absorbing and removing color, which will contaminate your bonnets or towels.

Over time you will be able to recognize when it's time to change your bonnet. Dirt and paint will contaminate the bonnet smearing the paint surface if your bonnet is not changed in between applications. I suggest you use the orbital polisher on the majority of the vehicle when applying the compound. This will save you time and be much more efficient.

Be sure to wipe off any remaining residue with your terry or micro fiber towels using the cleanest side possible. A haze free, uniform look without streaking is a clean surface. During the compounding process you may notice a black residue on your bonnet which is simply from the black rubber window seals and rubber side moldings. This residue can stain the paint and render your bonnets useless. In order to avoid this issue I recommend you compound around these areas first staying away from any of the rubber areas of the vehicle. When you've applied the compound with the buffer to the surrounding area, finish by using a wax pad applicator and guide this along the door, window, sunroof weather stripping, and window seal areas. Use the palm of your hand and fingers as a guide to help prevent globing excess product onto and contaminating the rubber. You can also use the wax pad applicator for the hard to reach areas, such as the windshield wiper arms, window frame edges, door handles, emblems, side moldings etc. Allow the compound to dry to a chalky white haze and then wipe it off with your terry towel. It's best to fold the towel in half and use circular buffing motions to remove the compound turning the towels over, and inside out, if necessary. Continue to buff off any remaining compound powder until the surface is free of residue. Keep in mind that the compound is aggressive by formulation, and will leave fine scratches which can be removed and sealed later.

Once you have completely buffed and toweled off one side move to the opposite side and continue using the same procedure as before. I recommend that you finish with the uppermost areas first, before you proceed to the side areas of the car. For those hard to reach areas, such as the roof, try opening the side doors and step up on the running board to give yourself a better angle and viewpoint.

Tip: Place a towel down on the floor board when stepping up to clean the roof. This will keep dirt and mud from grinding into these areas.

As before, work your way from top to bottom. Be sure to compound the window frames as well (if painted). This would also be a good time to finish compounding any of those hard to reach areas by hand that your orbital buffer cannot reach. These could include; window frames, antenna, around door handles, hood emblems, license plate areas, front and rear bumper, outside body edges, windshield wiper blades, fender wheel areas, and along the side molding. This will help to greatly reduce the likelihood of smearing compound into cracks and seams. You will only need very little compound when doing these areas, which can then be removed by using your terry or micro fiber towel. Now continue to work your orbital polisher along each side of the car and the remaining larger areas of the vehicle.

Ensure you operate the buffer at eye level when doing the sides of the vehicle avoiding any rubber side moldings and older porous rubber areas as these areas will be difficult to remove compounds and waxes once contaminated. A rolling seat is perfect for getting at eye level with your side work.

For many normal blemishes you will need to apply more pressure in order to remove them. These could include scratches caused by trees, paint scuff marks, road paint splatters, door dings, and stains from water drip marks. The term used when applying heavy pressure with either hand or machine polishing, using an abrasive cleaner, is commonly known as cutting or burnishing the paint. I recommend you use the orbital buffer whenever possible in order to apply as much pressure as necessary to remove these marks. You can angle your buffer by tipping it at a sharp angle almost on its side to really get out stubborn marks or blemishes. This technique works very well and can save you valuable time.

Sealing

Before beginning this process you will need to first decide if a conditioning sealant needs to be used. In most cases a conditioning sealer is used in combination with an abrasive compound. As noted in previous sections, you would need to protect any freshly exposed paint from further oxidation, especially after using a compound. There are several products on the market. You will want to look for products like finishing glazes. These glazes have specific conditioning oils in them that will fill and hide small hairline scratches and imperfections on the paint remaining from the compounding process. Once the paint has been conditioned the final step will be to apply the top coat of wax or synthetic sealant.

PAT YOURSELF ON THE BACK, because you have just completed the first stage of achieving perfect paint, and establishing a good foundation for polishing and waxing.

Combination One Step Products

Combo products really make a detailer's job much easier with the combination of mild cleaning solvents, micro abrasives and a blend of waxes or synthetic sealants saving you valuable time. Ideally, the best candidate for combo products would be a vehicle that is brand new or has very little oxidation or haze in the paint. Since most of these finishes are already in good condition they really only require simple maintenance. These type of conditions will require only a once over making combination products perfect for these types of situations while still providing long lasting protection.

You would use the same procedure divide and conquer as was used when applying any other polish or sealant. Remember to start with one section at a time working from the top to the bottom of the vehicle. The benefit of applying a combo product and polishing agent is that you can apply them to the entire surface without having to work in a small section at a time. In fact you will achieve a better bonding effect when left on for a longer period of time. Always check the manufacturer's product label for application methods and curing time. Products may vary.

You can either apply these combo products by hand or by using your orbital polisher. When using your orbital polisher its best to first dispense approximately 3 or 4 rings of product onto the velour bonnet or foam pad. Don't forget to drape the cord over your shoulder giving you plenty of space to work. Also, remember to not turn the polisher on until it has come in complete contact with the surface. Once you turn the polisher on make wide sweeping motions to distribute the product

evenly. Work in one direction and then crisscross the polisher to overlap the same section working in even and systematic motions.

Remember to be careful when distributing the product to ensure you don't overlap on grooves, windshield wiper sprayers, or hood ornaments. When done properly the bonnet will remain moist and glide over the surface without much resistance. Be sure to apply enough product to the bonnet or foam pad or you will be polishing with an insufficiently moistened applicator. You will catch this problem right off the bat when the orbital polisher seems to be skimming erratically across the surface or the product dries too quickly and starts balling up before you've completed the section. Be sure to turn the orbital polisher off before removing it from the surface. This will help to avoid any spin off onto yourself or other sections of the vehicle. Continue this process until the vehicle is completed. Be sure to go over any hard to reach areas by hand using a wax applicator pad.

> **TIP:** I recommend you only apply small amounts of product when buffing hard to reach areas and tip the polisher at a sharp angle allowing you to get a better angle. By avoiding the use of too much polish you will avoid polish spin off. You can also avoid spin off by placing the pad on the surface. Then gently smear and distribute the polish around a 2X2 area before turning on the machine.

Remember to frequently change out your bonnet and towels to avoid over saturation. Even if the paint is relatively new combo products will still pick up small amounts of oxidation in the paint. This is normal, however should you notice swirl marks in the finish as you're polishing, stop the buffer and examine the paint and the bonnet. This could be due to the possibility of picking up a small grain of dirt or sand which could scratch the finish. Be sure to always keep a close eye on your work and continue applying the products with a clean bonnet or towel.

Use the flat palm of your hand when applying your combo products by hand. The idea is to simulate the same action as the orbital polisher, as close as possible. This will help to avoid fingertip pressure points which could create smears or swirl marks. If you decide to apply by hand then fold a micro fiber towel in half sections until it's about palm size or you can use a wax applicator pad. It's important to apply enough product to the pad in order to be able to spread it out over a 3' x 3' section. As with an orbital polisher, apply the wax or sealer in small circular movements ensuring you overlap each circle. It's important to use enough pressure and product in order to avoid streaking.

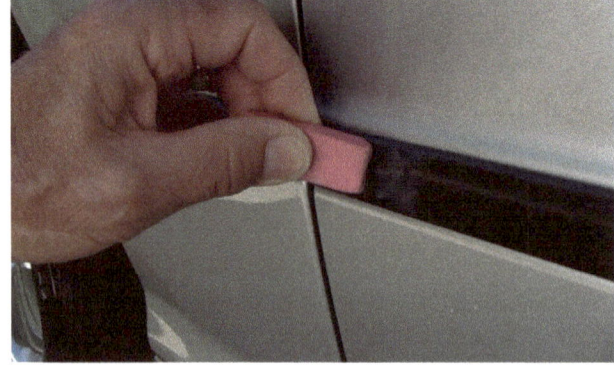

You can use your wax applicator pad whenever applying product along tricky areas, such as door edge closures or rubber side moldings. Use straight back and forth movements guiding the flat outside edge of the pad along the outer edge of the molding. Be sure to avoid getting any wax onto the rubber molding or crack openings. Take your time rather than rushing through any job. This will help you to save time from having to go back in to clean up sloppy work. **Here is a tip**; you can use an ordinary pencil eraser to easily remove old dried up wax embedded in rubber moldings. It works like magic!

Base Coat/Clear Coat Paint

Since 1985 the EPA passed laws for paint manufacturers to come up with new paint formulas that produced less lead and other hazardous solvents found in traditional single stage paint finishes. These hazardous materials were found to escape into the Earth's sensitive ozone layer which was a big concern to the environmentalists. The new 2 stage clear coat finish was born and is primarily used for production of all new cars both in Europe and in America. Today's clear coat finishes are very durable and resist chipping.

The process used for applying base coat/clear coat paint uses a thin layer of pigment or paint color (base coat) which is sprayed on the vehicles surface and then a second layer of clear acrylic urethane (clear coat) similar to a hardened plastic is sprayed over the first layer of color. A vehicle treated with clear coat almost takes on a dimension of seamless glossy paint with no noticeable blemishes. The clear coat is a thin transparent layer taking on the look of a mirrored surface. In this case you will typically not find the orange peel effect as that found in non-clear coated finishes. However, clear coat finishes do have a downside. Similar to the hardened plastic, which is somewhat softer, it can scratch easily. Many of these clear coat finishes are prone to scuffing and scratching eventually clouding the finish.

With this said, clear coat finishes must be treated with respect and understanding. Even though the base coat/clear coat acrylic urethane finishes are much thicker than the color paint base, it is actually only as thick as a piece of wax paper, roughly *1.5* to *2.0* mils thick. Because of this fact, it is important to not over polish the surface as it may cut through the clear coat and reach the base coat underneath. That's why I highly recommend you invest in a paint thickness gauge. Even though the paint gauge is more effective on traditional non-clear coat finishes, it can still give you a more accurate evaluation of how much paint is on the surface. Knowing this can help reduce the risk of damaging the paint.

Paint Type Analysis

PAINT TYPE ANALYSIS EXPLAINED

BASE COAT/CLEAR COAT FINISHES are created using a 2 or 3-stage paint finish. The first layer sprayed is the primer coat. The second layer sprayed is the color or base coat. The top and final protective coat is a hard, plastic-type Urethane finish.

Pearl Essence Paint finishes use a 3 stage process.

Almost all of today's automobile manufacturers are using this type of finish, both domestic and import. This type of finish is somewhat easier to polish due to the fact that there is no oxidized paint lifted off the car during the polishing procedure. However this type of finish is more easily stained and scratched because of its plastic type of coating.

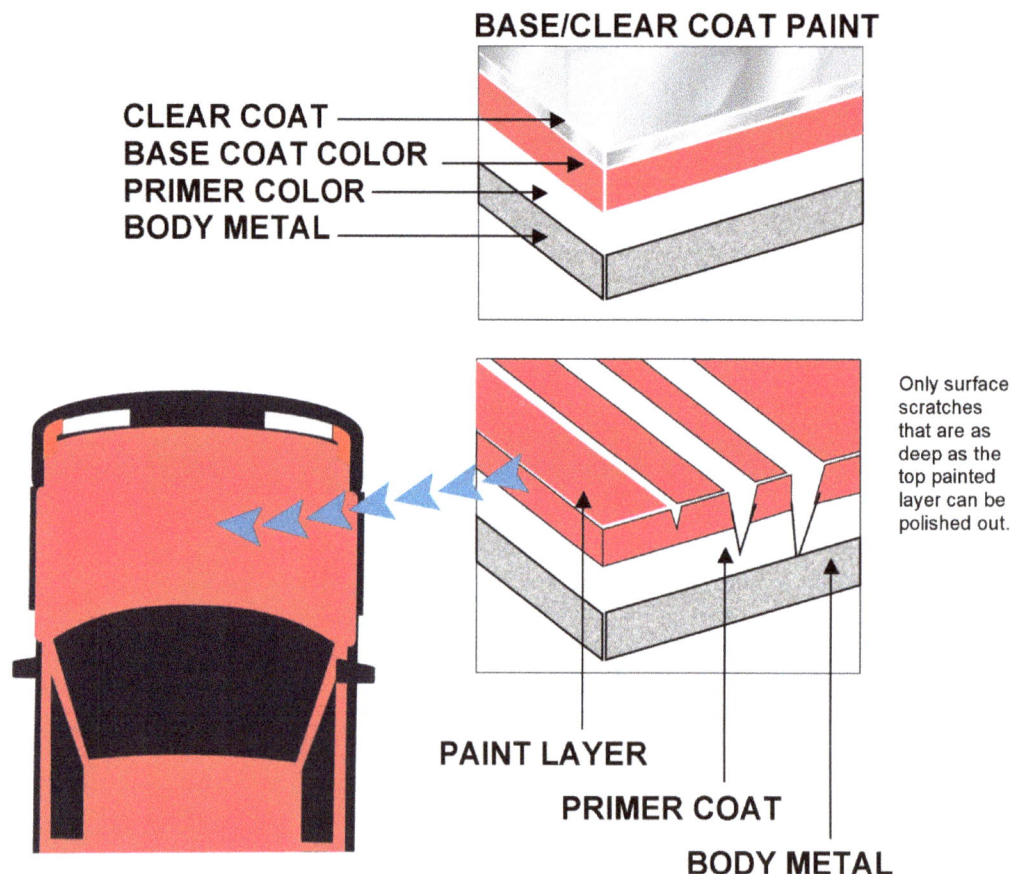

Only surface scratches that are as deep as the top painted layer can be polished out.

TRADITIONAL PAINT FINISHES such as enamel, acrylic, lacquer, metallic, imron, glasurit are all non-clear coat paints. These types of finishes can be polished out using compounds, polishes and combo wax products. NOTE: A good test to check whether or not you are dealing with a non-clear coat finish, apply a dab of Compound to an inconspicuous area on the car. Rub vigorously and inspect the towel. If there is evidence of colored paint on the towel this shows that the car's finish *does not* have a clear coat finish.

A two part paint system consists of 1) color with binders and 2) an active reducer with a hardening catalyst.

Greg Dumond – Success Training Manual

The Clear Coat Test

You can test a vehicle for clear coat by rubbing a small amount of Polish onto the surface of the vehicle. If **NO** visible color bleeds onto the towel, then this is a good indication that the vehicle has a <u>Clear Coat Finish</u>. When you first start out in the business I suggest you get as familiar as possible with each automotive manufacturer to determine what type of finish you are dealing with. Any automotive dealership could help you get an accurate answer as to what type of finish is on the car. Before calling, be sure to have the make, model, and year of the vehicle to get the most accurate information. You may also ask your customer if the car has ever been repainted, especially if it's an older model. This can be very helpful information when bidding out a job over the phone. Over time you be able to easily determine whether or not the vehicle has a clear coat or traditional single stage paint finish.

Compounding Base Coat/Clear Coat

Based on the information noted in the Base Coat/Clear Coat section, clear coats must be treated differently than traditional paints. Without exception, you should never compound or use any type of abrasive cleaner on a clear coat finish. Keep in mind the acrylic urethane coating is very susceptible to swirl marks, scratching, and scuffing. You can cause severe and permanent damage to the finish by using a compound or abrasive cleaner that is too harsh. The best approach to polishing clear coat finishes is by the use of specifically designed polishes and waxes. These are designed to remove scratches and scuffs, while adding a protective layer to the existing clear coat layer. If you are going to use a compound on a clear coat finish be sure the product is marked clear coat SAFE. These products do not contain heavy abrasives and are scientifically formulated using diminishing compounds that do not scratch or swirl the surface of the vehicle. It is also very important to understand the importance of following proper polishing and buffing techniques in order to avoid problems from polishing anything more than the clear acrylic surface above the base coat. Remember; there are limits and too much polishing can wear through the clear coat and permanently damage the base coat below.

However, the upside to working with clear coat finishes is that they are much easier to maintain and there's no need to worry about paint oxidation as found with single stage traditional paint. There is also no need to use reconditioning oil products as that used with traditional paint finishes. Keep in mind that the idea is to lock in a protective barrier over the thin layer of paint. The following problems that you will typically encounter with clear coat finishes as well as correction methods you will need to learn as a professional are:

- * Peeling and flaking on the surface
- * Bird droppings and staining
- * Acid rain and sprinkler water spot removal
- * Scratches, scuffs and swirl marks
- * Buffer swirl marks
- * Holograms

There are three areas to be aware of when working with clear coat finishes:

Number 1: You may not be able to produce the same dramatic results as you can with traditional paints. You will be polishing a clear finish as opposed to paint pigment.

Number 2: Some scratches may be too deep to remove, since the clear coat is made up of a hard plastic material. A vehicle that is severely affected with scuffs and scratches may not respond as well as traditional paint that can be cut and polished out without the protective clear layer.

Number 3: Both waxes and sealers will not cling and lock in protection as well as with traditional paint surfaces that have deeper surface pores. Even though there are many misconceptions that clear coats should never need waxing primarily from uninformed salespeople selling cars at the dealerships, these paint surfaces are still susceptible to the harmful environmental elements.

Without a protective sealer coat or wax the same smog, sulfides, calcium, and detergents will break down a clear coat finish as well. However, it's far more costly to repair a clear coat finish than to repaint a traditional paint surface. Both the clear and color base coats would have to be completely stripped before any repainting is done. That's why it's very important that both you and your customer realize the importance of maintaining a healthy coat of protection.

Water Spots

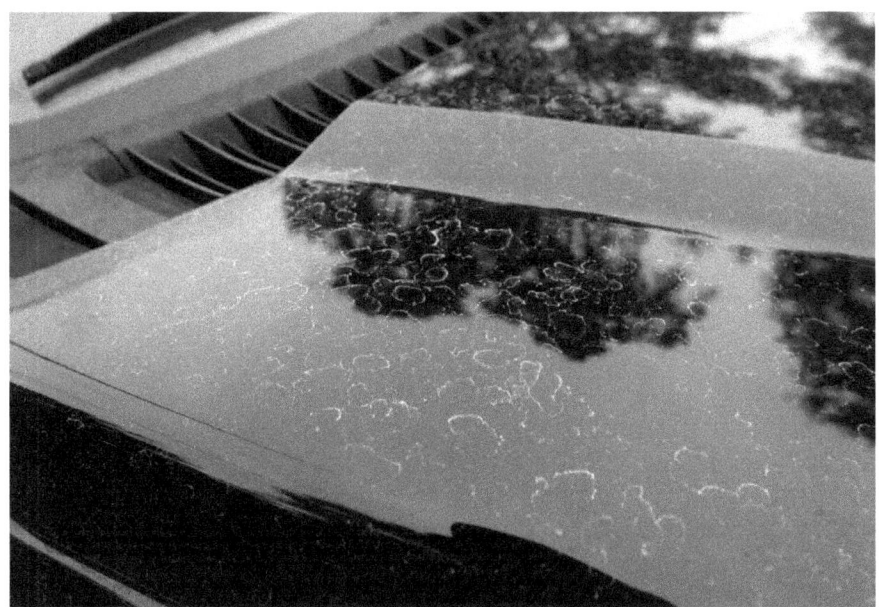

We all dread the issue of water spots; however water spotting is not just caused by rain, but also by a simple car wash or overspray from a sprinkler system. The contaminants found within the water is the real problem with water spotting, such as acid that is found in rainwater. As the water dry's on the surface it creates etching marks. Many of these paint blemishes can be compounded out with little effort, however in more severe cases the acidic water combined with direct sunlight can cause these water droplets to etch themselves all the way down to the primer coat.

To better understand this imagine place several sheets of paper towels on top of each other and drop some water droplets onto the paper towels. You will notice that as you lift each individual paper towel, the water ring becomes less and less noticeable. This is the same concept used when removing water spots with a compound product. By applying enough compound or polish on the mark you should be able to remove the mark. Start off with the least aggressive compound to remove as much of the top layer of the etched area first then move to the next step of a finer compound and polish, and lastly seal the surface. In some cases, you may not be able to completely remove the spots especially on old severely damaged surfaces.

Even with sprinkler systems that contain Alkalis and Calcium deposits, when dried on the surface they can etch the paint in very much the same manner as acid rain. In most cases these types of deposits are usually less severe and can be polished out completely. However, glass windows produce a different problem. Even though glass is much harder than a painted surface, it is not immune to the same etching issue. Chemicals like alkali, calcium and acid rain can actually eat into glass. These water spots can cause permanent glass etching if left on windows for any length of time. However, some of the spotting can be improved by using some steel wool. I recommend using a **Triple 0** rated steel wool you can purchase from any hardware store. Explain to your customer the importance of removing water spots from their windows immediately in order to avoid this issue. You may not be able to get out all the stains, just do your best.

Here's a trick you can try however use CAUTION if you attempt this process. For removal of water spotting both on glass as well as paint, pre-spray the surfaces with water, spray a liberal amount of a ready to use **acid based wheel cleaner** onto the surface. Next take your bug sponge and vigorously rub onto the surface. You can use a piece of Triple 0 steel wool instead of the bug sponge on **windows only**! Only the bug sponge should be used on the painted surface. Allow the product to dwell for approximately one minute then thoroughly rinse and soap wash these areas. The acid in the cleaner will help dissolve the crusty calcium buildup making it much easier for removal and less work for subsequent polishing and waxing.

Treating Chemical Fallout, Acid Rain And Water Spots

ACID RAIN

Acid rain damage accelerates the deterioration and oxidation process and is a real problem that needs to be addressed. In many cases acid rain damage is difficult to remove without compounding and polishing the surface first. This is especially difficult to minimize with sensitive thinner base/clear coat finishes. Product knowledge and procedures will be extremely important for addressing this situation.

You may want to consider investing in additional training and a high speed polisher in order to attack special situations such as acid rain spots, water spot removal and fall out damage. However the good news is that you can minimize and in many cases eliminate these problems with the right compound and your orbital polisher. It will just take more time and patience to correct these problems.

Generally there two methods to treat acid rain spotting.

One: Give the vehicle an alkaline based wash designed especially for acid rain spot removal and then follow it up with a neutral Ph balanced wash. You will then need to buff out the paint using a cleaner polish and then a final coat of sealant to form a lasting protective finish.

Second: This is the most aggressive method involving color sanding. As mentioned in previous sections of this manual, color sanding involves the use of hand or machine sanding with 1500 to 3000 grit grain paper and water. Until you have become proficient in the art of auto detailing, this process should only be done by professionals who have been trained in color sanding and high speed polishing methods. Follow the same procedure as above. The vehicle goes through an alkaline wash, the surface is hand rubbed out using 1500 to 3000 grain sanding paper, followed up with a neutral Ph balanced wash, and then buffed and waxed with a sealing glaze or wax.

Industrial Fallout

Industrial fallout affects almost every vehicle on the road today. However, it's more apparent on light colored vehicles. Fallout is more noticeable on the upper most portion of the car, such as the hook, trunk, and topside areas whereby you will notice hundreds of tiny red specks scattered over the surface of the vehicle. This condition is caused by a combination of industrial pollution from smoke stacks and acid fog or moisture, and is commonly mistaken for paint overspray. The surface is rough to the touch similar to grit, but its characteristic color is rust or tiny reddish looking dots. As with paint overspray this issue can be very difficult to remove. Even though there are specific products made especially for removing industrial fallout, they are made up of an acid base and unless you are very experienced in removing this type of contaminant, we recommend following a safer regiment of removal processes. You can achieve excellent results in removing industrial fallout by using a Detailer's bar of clay made for removing surface contamination. There are different levels of aggressive clay much like comparing the difference between 1500 grit to 3000 grit sandpaper only much safer, but be prepared to use a lot of elbow grease as sometimes you will need to go over every inch of the car. I recommend you adjust your pricing accordingly to account for the extra time you will spend on this type of situation as it can involve taking up to an extra hour(s) worth of work. I treat this extra time as over and above normal detailing and you should charge your customers accordingly. How much you charge should be based on your hourly labor fee.

Paint Overspray Removal

One of your first indications of evaluating any paint finish is by the feel of the car's paint surface. Even though a paint job may look great and shine, you may find it feels rough to the touch. This is commonly known as paint overspray. Paint overspray can be caused by many different situations; 1) paint drift from paint and body shops; 2) a commercial/residential painter air spraying homes or buildings nearby. If you come across a vehicle that has paint overspray on the surface – STOP!! Most likely your customer has not even noticed this and you want to bring this to their attention before you begin any detailing. It's possible they can get the building manager or company to pay for this issue so it's not out of your customer's pocket to pay you to correct this problem. Again, this is above and beyond what is included with an average car detail and should be treated as an add-on service and service fee.

You want to give your customer the option to discuss your fees and whether or not they want the over-spray removed or left on the vehicle. Give them the chance to either accept or decline. This will help save you a lot of time and grief upfront. Be sure to discuss the reason for the higher rate and the time involved to remove it.

Remember you are like a doctor. You have specialized knowledge. Your customers are paying you for your skills and expertise. You can price out the extra work based on your hourly rate or you can price it out as a specialty skill charging a much higher rate.

Paint Transfer

You've seen it. You come back from the store and all of a sudden a smear of paint from another colored vehicle has somehow managed to get onto your vehicle. Or you were backing out of your garage and you managed to bump up against the side wall.

This type of scuff can be removed either by a more aggressive compound or try this technique, gently wipe the surface with a paint solvent such as DuPont Enamel Remover or Acetone. First determine what type of paint you are cleaning. Most painted surfaces such as enamels, latex, or the toughest epoxy based paint will react well. **USE CAUTION** when applying these solvents to plastic or fiberglass bumpers or aftermarket parts and soft materials like rubber, black window trim and vinyl coated side mirrors as this process can strip out color as in the mirror shown here.

When you apply the solvent pour a small amount onto a towel, **NOT DIRECTLY TO THE PAINT** and rub gently by hand. Always rewash the area with soapy water and follow up by polishing and sealing the paint. It's essential to learn the use and application of these powerful chemicals. With practice, you can make huge profits in the "Paint Removal Market"!

Wood Grain And Aerodynamic Body Parts

Most vehicles have some sort of accents including stripping, vinyl mirrors, flare kits, running boards, chrome trim, and simulated wood grain applications. Although attractive, these accents can really set the vehicle off if blended well with the right application. Most of these accents can be polished and waxed.

On older model cars or wagons wood grain accents are usually made of a sophisticated vinyl contact sheet applied by hand to the surface. Even though the appearance of wood grain is an attractive feature it can fade and peel over time. You would treat the wood grain paper the same as painted metal with the exception of not using an abrasive polish, which can dull and permanently ruin the protective coating. I recommend the use of a nonabrasive one step cleaner wax or sealant in order to clean and polish the surface safely. For situations where the vinyl paper wood grain begins to break apart and develop small cracks you can usually improve the appearance by applying a vinyl protectant dressing with a small wax pad to the simulated wood grain instead of waxing. This will temporarily condition the simulated wood finish, dramatically improving the appearance by adding a nice shiny gloss. Be sure to apply the dressing or sealer by hand working the product back and forth in even strokes. Ensure you allow the product to penetrate for several minutes before buffing off the excess residue with a soft towel.

* * * * * * * * * **CAUTION** * * * * * * * *

Avoid direct spraying with your Pressure Washer when cleaning this area for Wood grain that is chipping, peeling or cracking. This could cause further damage removing sections of the paper vinyl. Keep in mind that damage to simulated wood grain is irreparable so ensure you use caution when washing and polishing these problem areas.

Another trick for bringing back extremely dry, dull and chalking blackened surfaces is to use a silicone based aerosol product to treat these surfaces.

For aerodynamic body parts that are made of fiberglass or plastic, you also need to polish and clean these areas. These are the wheel flare kits, front and rear spoilers, and side plastic moldings, etc. Similar to the simulated wood grain, these materials are more sensitive to breaking down over a shorter time frame than painted metal parts. The painting process used to treat many aftermarket body parts combine a flex agent to a vinyl paint base. Over time, the continuous washing and treatment using solvent or alcohol based products will cause the paint to lose its pliability and become dry and brittle. This issue can be detected when you see a whitish finish and the developing of a crazing (small cracks in the paint) effect. I recommend you treat these areas with the appropriate one step combo wax or nonabrasive sealer. It's best to <u>avoid</u> using any abrasive compounds on these areas. As noted before, plastic and fiberglass is a soft material that can be scratched and dulled permanently by the use of abrasive polishing agents. There are a number of plastic polishes such as Plexus and Meguiar's PlastX that do a great job on cleaning and polishing small accent and other plastic areas.

Special Notes Page

Section 10

Exterior Polishing

Finishing Touches	201
Wheel Polishing	203
Chrome Work	204
Antennas	205
License Plates	205
Toothbrushing	206

Finishing Touches

It's important to have a keen eye to detail and scrutinize every inch of the car. Keep in mind that your customer will notice any flaw particularly if the client has a high end car and is expecting perfect results.

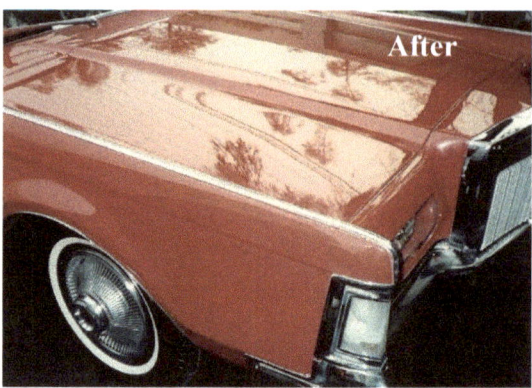

However, there may be situations where no matter what you do to make a real disaster look good it's just not possible. But keep in mind that most of these customers don't expect miracles, so anything you do to make it look better will most likely receive accolades. In fact, in most cases you will find your customer will believe that you have performed nothing short of a miracle by making their car look much better than when they originally dropped it off.

Just be sure to spend extra time on those areas that look worse for the wear, such as the engine or chrome bumpers. Remember that even though you may not be able to bring the car back to its new luster, it will still look better then when the customer first dropped it off. Work hard, do your best, and be sure to point out the areas you were successful with.

The customer will zero in on both the paint and wheels, as these are the first things they will notice up front. Once you have wowed them here, you've won half the battle. It's attention to all of the other details that will set you apart from the amateurs. I suggest you have a check list available noting both the interior and exterior finishing touches to ensure you have not missed anything as well as a way to give you an opportunity to review what has been done with the customer.

Keep in mind that finishing work is just that. By adding those finishing touches it can really make a car stand out.

Now that you have cleaned the paint, rubber and chrome it's time to put on the finishing touches.

Directions: Apply an ample amount of **Vinyl Dressing** with a soft clean micro fiber towel to the tip of the cloth and dress all the rubber, side moldings, trim, rubber bumpers, window seals, door edge, and trunk seals. Be sure to also take time to dress the spare tire.

Be careful to avoid spreading the dressing onto the paint

or windows by using the tip of the micro fiber towel. A small wax applicator pad works well for these areas. Remove any dressing residue from the non-rubber parts after treating these areas with a separate dry towel. Do the same around the base of the antenna rubber boot and vinyl or plastic side view mirrors. Should the side view mirrors be made of chrome then it would be best to use a **Chrome Polish** to clean this area.

A good tip is to polish, not dress plastic mirrors since the plastic side mirrors are made of a hard vinyl material, and are not absorbent like rubber. They are usually black in color and are dull from fading. By dressing these you will improve their look, however, to get the best results and to bring them back to life you should polish them with a mild compound and follow up with a sealant to get them to shine.

Before

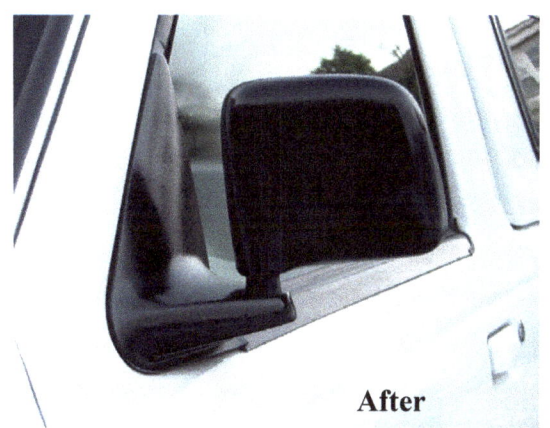

After

Directions: You can bring the shine back to dull hard plastic by using a small amount of **mild compound** on a terry cloth towel and rub vigorously. Rub until the dull mirror takes on a glossy shine. Once the mirror has been polished, apply a wax or sealant and buff to a brilliant shine. You will find that many side view mirrors collapse inward, so be sure to push them forward in order to the best possible angle.

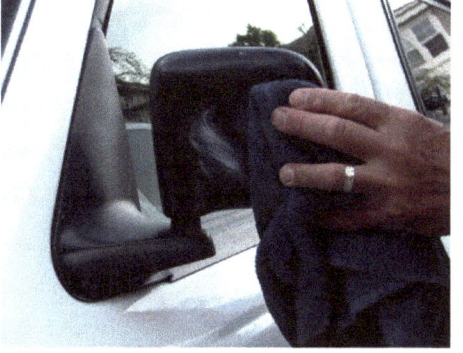

Be sure to use a separate clean terry cloth towel when cleaning the tire and rubber bumper areas. At this point you will be removing the excess vinyl dressing by folding the towel in half and lightly wiping over the rubber tire.

This process will help to prevent spin off onto the paint from the oils in the dressing. As you recall, you soaked the tires by spraying a Vinyl Dressing directly on after the washing sequence. At this point the tires have had enough time to absorb the silicone oils. Also, be sure to remove any puddles or excess dressing by wiping the rubber bumpers.

Wheel Polishing

Now it's time to remove the excess silicone oils from the wheels. Wipe off as much residue as possible with a clean terry cloth towel. Be sure to use a good Chrome Polish for chrome wheels.

Apply the polish directly onto the chrome wheel by using a clean towel or wax pad and allow the polish to dry. I would suggest you apply the polish to all the wheels in order to save time. This will allow all the wheels enough drying time before you start buffing off the excess polish with a separate clean dry towel. For faster clean up you can pre-clean the chrome with a window cleaner first containing some ammonia which will help cut through the over sprayed oil on the rims.

I suggest you use an **Aluminum Polish** like Mother's Mag Polish for aluminum wheels. Let's start by applying the polish using the same technique used in applying the chrome polish. However, you will need to work the product into small sections at a time using a clean towel. Ensure you aggressively rub the Aluminum Polish into the wheel. Continue to turn the towel over to a clean side, as it becomes saturated with oxidized aluminum, and proceed with the rest of the wheel until completed.

You will notice that on raw aluminum (No Clear Coat) your towel will turn black as you polish so it is important to continue turning the towel to a clean side as your working in the polish. With a separate clean towel buff the excess blackened cleaner off, until the aluminum is bright and clear.

NOTE: If the factory wheels have been protected with a clear coat sealant you will not see any black oxidized material on your towel when polishing and therefore will be far easier to clean.

Chrome Work

Like a diamond, chrome sparkles and really sets off the car's appearance. Unfortunately, many of the newer production vehicles are accented with much less chrome than the earlier made vehicles. Have you noticed how chrome is being replaced with cheaper, lighter plastic, and rubber accents? Regardless of this fact, most cars do have some type of chrome appliqués usually found as emblems, side pocket mirrors, window trim, wheel well rims, license plates, grill, light areas, front and rear bumpers.

Chrome becomes susceptible to weathering and staining over time with rust deposits, exhausts, film, and the worst culprit of all, small insects. These little pests excrete a mild acid that can blemish the chrome if not removed immediately.

Note: You can bring the life of chrome back by using a Chrome Polish, which is specially formulated to remove haze, rust, and other natural elements in one easy step.

Directions: I recommend you use the Chrome Polish while rubbing with a piece of #000 steel wool for chrome that is pitted or crusted with rust stains. Simply apply a small amount of the Chrome Polish to the steel wool and rub vigorously using brisk movements to work off the rust loose. Now buff the chrome clean by using a separate clean towel. You can also use the steel wool to remove bugs stuck to the chrome front bumpers or chrome grill. Most of your higher end vehicles, such as the Cadillac, Jaguar, and Rolls Royce, you will find a chrome grill made up of long narrow slots or fins.

You can clean these fins by using a Chrome Polish and applying a small amount to the tip of a micro fiber towel. Use your finger to work the product in between the fins running your finger up and down until all the fins have been treated. Now buff the area clean with a separate dry towel. Remember, a perfectly polished front end will really improve the overall look of the vehicle.

By using the divide and conquer method, continue working around the vehicle until all of the chrome is perfectly polished.

Other areas to pay special attention to are:

Antennas

Often times this area is overlooked, so be sure to remove any grease or oil by using a solvent made for removing gum and tar. Sometimes an Engine degreaser works well for removing grease on antennas. Follow up by polishing the antenna with your Chrome Polish or Window Cleaner.

License Plates

The license plate area is a difficult area to clean, so I recommend you remove the license plate first before you begin. Ensure you have the appropriate tools to do so first. Clean this area and then apply one of your combo products to polish the area clean. Now reattach the license plate, however be sure to polish the license plate frame before doing so. Use your Chrome Polish for chrome frames or your Aluminum Polish for brass frames.

Take that extra step by cleaning and degreasing the inside of the gas filler cap area. As you can guess this area is usually contaminated with a thick film of fuel and oil. Be sure to clean and polish the inside door cover as well or dress the rubber gas cap flap, should there be one in place. Your customers will really be impressed when you point this attention to detail out to them!

Toothbrushing

By being meticulous in your work you separate yourself from the amateurs putting yourself in a category of true professionals! Attention to detail is key by ensuring you leave no traceable wax in the crevices of the car. With this said, I recommend you use a toothbrush to get in between all those hard to reach areas. I like to use 2 types of tooth brushes. The first is a standard looking toothbrush with stiffer bristles to loosen stubborn wax in cracks and emblems. The second is a paint style brush with the bristles cut short.

This type of brush is softer and will reduce brush scratches when removing wax from the trunk, hood, and other areas that are susceptible to showing marks like that found on darker colored vehicles.

Let's start by tooth brushing from the top of the hood down remembering that there are two sides to everything. Be sure to also open the trunk and hood, and wipe the edges including the inside track on the body of the car. Also, don't forget to remove any visible wax in between and around the door jambs, vents, body edges, window frames, car handles, emblems, etc.

Special Notes Page

Section 11

Selling Paint Sealant For More Profit

Long Term Paint Sealant Application ... 209

Some Tips On Cleaning Wool Bonnets And Foam Pads 210

Long Term Paint Sealant Application

The bulk of your work will be in offering standard detailing packages which include interior and exterior cleaning and rejuvenation of the paint and fabrics of the car. However you should also consider offering additional protection packages such as a **Premium Long Term Paint Sealant**. Paint sealants are sold in a variety of ways and some are over hyped particularly at the car dealerships where you purchase a new car. The biggest hyped product sold is a **Teflon Paint Sealant.** The company DuPont is the manufacturer of Teflon. Their scientist's note that Teflon must be heated up to 700 degrees Fahrenheit before it will stick to a pan let alone a car paint finish. So unless you are dropping pellets of Teflon on the car with a Bunsen burner, well you get the picture!

The car salesperson knowingly or perhaps unknowingly will offer their customers a 5 year paint sealant and interior protection package usually for an astronomical price. This so called protection package comes with an unrealistic 5 year guarantee that the customer will never have to wax their vehicle again or a least for 5 years. They also verbally claim the paint protection package and interior stain prevention package is guaranteed to last for the period claimed by the salesperson. The real story here is if you read the contract you are many times required to bring the car back to the dealership at least once a year for re-application of the products used for the protection package to maintain the factory warrantee.

However, as you read the fine print you will notice for example: the warrantee does not cover damage from bird droppings, paint peeling, paint fading, interior staining, etc. Basically they are taking your hard earned money and gambling that more people than not will come back for the re application of product. **MARKETING AND PROFIT**

As a professional, you want to offer products that set realistic expectations. Offering a long term paint sealant and interior protection package is a great up sell to add more profit to your bottom line. I recommend offering a product containing a polymer based formula. Polymers have been proven to outlast ordinary wax such as Carnauba, Monton, and Bees Wax based products. They typically withstand much higher temperatures so the melting point of this product is much higher. The bottom line is polymers hold up and wear much longer than typical over the counter products or paste waxes. Polymers also form a harder and more slippery finish and feel. A realistic life expectancy of a polymer paint sealant application is 6 months with stretching it to one year if the car is usually garaged. So again this product should be offered as a separate service over and above a standard exterior detail. The additional price will vary from detailer to detailer. It will be up to you to charge whatever you feel will be a fair price. The application of this product takes about the same amount of time as applying any other wax product, so your labor will be about the same. Expect to pay a little more for this product as you are purchasing higher quality ingredients from the manufacturer of polymer products.

Other businesses you can sell your long term protection packages are rental car agencies, fleet owners, government vehicles, Police cars and other public service vehicles and school buses. They are willing to pay a premium price for a long term protective coating. This is a cost savings investment as it saves them maintenance time on their vehicles. Many company cars, trucks or vans are also great candidates as their vehicles are used as company billboards to advertise their business. You might even want to advertise in your local newspapers and compete against your local car dealerships who are selling very expensive protection packages. Many car dealerships sell their protection packages from $400.00 to $1,000. Do you think you could make a profit at a substantially reduced cost to that same customer? Plus think of the repeat business you will have by running an honest business selling realistic services.

Some Tips On Cleaning Wool Bonnets And Foam Pads

Plan on washing your bonnets and pads daily when using a polymer based product. Polymer is a viscous and very sticky product. If you are using a bonnet, slip it off the foam drive pad and use the reverse side to reapply more product.

If you do not plan on washing the bonnets or pads right away, toss them into a bucket of water after you finish using them. This will keep the bonnets or pads from becoming dry and stiff.

Never wash wool bonnets with granular soap!! Invariably small particles of soap may not dissolve and lodge itself in the fabric causing you to leave swirl marks on the next job you do.

Always use LIQUID soap concentrate. In addition, add 1/2 cup of liquid ammonia to the wash water to help dissolve the waxes, polishes, and sealants while washing the bonnets.

For Foam Pads there are granular products specifically made and sold by professional suppliers. I personally presoak them in liquid dishwasher soap in a bucket of water for at least an hour and then wash them clean by using the garden hose spray nozzle. For really heavily stained foam pads you can wash them on delicate in your washing machine. This should be a last resort as this method can weaken the velcro material that holds the foam in place.

Never use a high pressure sprayer machine to clean them otherwise you will rip apart the foam pad.

Special Notes Page

Section 12

Window Cleaning

Glass Cleaning 214

Plastic Rear Windows 218

Cleaning And Polishing Diagram
For Windshields And Windows 219

Vehicle Detailing Summary Steps 221

Glass Cleaning

One of the most difficult tasks in auto detailing is to attain perfect glass. A driver should be able to look through the glass as if there was nothing there. A good detail job can instantly be ruined by streaks and smears. Remember the last time you went through a drive thru car wash and everything looked fabulous until you noticed those stubborn streaks and smears in the window. A clean window takes both patience and perseverance to achieve perfect glass with a combination of skill and using the right product. There are many different formulas to choose from including a few garage made products. The old ways of cleaning windows consisted of using a combination of water and ammonia, followed up with a good wipe down using newspaper. The ink in the newspaper acted as a fine chemical compound when cleaning the glass. However, many times the ink from the paper would bleed and stain the interior fabric of the car. Instead I recommend using a couple of different professional and less messy products.

Your standard **Blue Glass Cleaner** will clean most ordinary jobs. I recommend that you purchase a concentrated formula from a professional chemical company. **Here's the trick to mixing a perfect formula**…never add regular tap water to the concentrate. Regular tap water contains minerals which can lead to clouding and streaking of the glass. Instead pick up some Distilled water at your local grocery store and add this to your concentrate. All the minerals have been removed from this type of water and you will have much more success achieving perfect glass!

The other product I would keep in your arsenal is a bottle of **Glass and Chrome Polish.** It is a stronger glass cleaner very similar to the old type of glass wax used containing ammonia and special polishing compounds that strip away heavy film and oil normally too stubborn to remove with the blue glass cleaner. It is especially effective for removing oils, grease and nicotine stained glass from heavy smokers. Nicotine tar vaporizes and attaches itself to the inside windows. The best method for applying the Glass Polish is to use a super clean wax pad. Keep in mind that this polish wipes on like thick wax and dries to a light pink powder so you may have to lightly wipe off any powder that comes in contact with the interior surface after removing it.

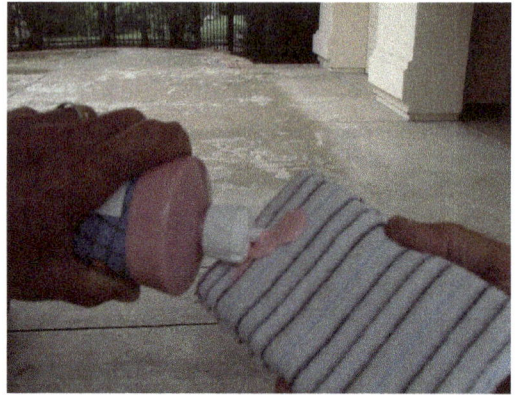

Directions: Begin cleaning by opening all the doors of the vehicle. Start at the top edge of the windows first, cleaning one window at a time. Be sure to use a systematic system as mentioned in previous sections. Ensure you roll down the top edge of all the side windows about 2 inches. Now place a small amount of Glass and Chrome Polish onto the corner of your towel or wax pad and run the edge of your finger along the top edge inside the lip area. Then clean the outside lip area of the same window. Follow the same procedure with all the other side windows. When you are done applying the Glass and Chrome Polish to all the windows; buff off all the excess powder with a separate clean towel. Now that you've completed this process roll all the windows back up into their fully closed position.

For normal cleaning, apply the Blue glass cleaner by either heavily misting a clean towel with your spray bottle or by directly spraying the Blue glass Cleaner onto the window. Should you decide to directly spray the cleaner onto the glass, be sure to hold a separate towel underneath the area to catch the excess liquid since the excess liquid containing ammonia could possibly leave spots on the dashboard or upholstery. This will help to save you time in having to re-clean or re-dress these areas again.

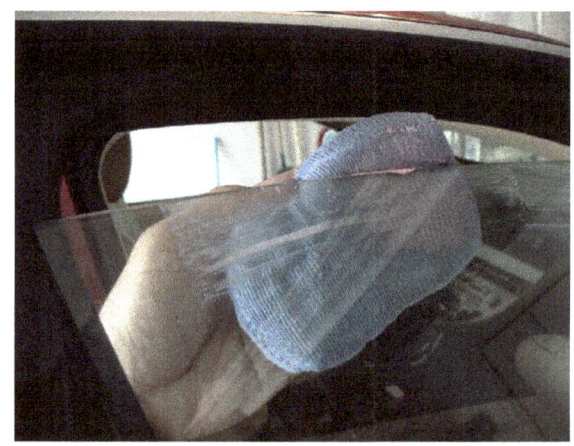

Now clean the inside driver window ensuring you saturate every inch of the glass with the Blue glass cleaner to prevent streaks in the glass. Be sure to fold your micro fiber towel in ½ and then in ½ again for a neat application method and to avoid missing any spots. Using even pressure, work the glass cleaner all the way around the outside edges of the glass ensuring you push the towel up into the corners of the glass. Work the towel in even up and down motions and then by using a crisscross motion go back over the glass in the opposite direction. Immediately follow up by using a clean dry separate micro fiber towel using the same motion to wipe off the glass cleaner just applied. **Tip:** Wipe the window dry with the second towel <u>before the window cleaner has dried.</u>

NOTE: Be sure to clean one window at a time when using the Blue glass cleaner. If you use the Glass & Chrome Polish, be sure to apply the product to the entire glass area on all the windows and then allow the product to dry to a hazy substance, roughly 2 to 3 minutes, and buff residue off with a separate clean microfiber towel.

It is good practice to keep a separate supply of colored towels specifically for cleaning the windows. Remember that silicone oils from dressings or waxes can be very difficult to remove, even after a through washing.

A good rule of thumb is to keep your feet out of the car as this process comes after you have already detailed and cleaned the interior. You don't want to have to go back in and re-do your work when it can be avoided up front. I suggest you either place a large towel on the floor of the car or sit on the seat while keeping your feet outside of the car. Be sure to only clean the glass in front of you. I like to use a bench or my knee placed right in front of my work so I am looking straight at the glass when cleaning it. Once you have finished one side go to the opposite side of the car ensuring you clean in the same manner.

Clean the glass in the same manner for hatchback type of vehicles. In most cases the hatchback window is smaller than the front or rear windshield, so apply glass cleaner over the entire window and buff clean. For large windows such front or rear try dividing the window in half when cleaning.

In many older model cars they come with defogger strips that are not always embedded into the glass. These are fine thin wires glued to the glass. Be sure to test this theory by running your fingers across the glass. Should you find the wires to be on the outside remember these three very important notes:

1. Ensure you never run a razor blade across the window to clean or remove stickers as the razor blade could cut a wire rendering the defogger useless.

2. Be sure to clean the glass in the same direction as the wires run, never against them.

3. Should a customer request you remove a decal or sticker from **non tinted or windows without defogger wires**, you can use a single sided razor blade to remove it. For removing interior stickers try peeling away the sticker in one whole piece if possible leaving only the sticky adhesive to be removed. Stickers remove more readily if they are warm from the sunshine or try pre-warming them up with a hair dryer. The sticky adhesive can now be removed with either a glue and tar remover solution. I have even used a little bit of Lighter Fluid to remove adhesive with great success. Follow up with cleaning this area again with your glass cleaner.

As you are cleaning the inside and outside windows, polish the side view mirrors as well. Don't forget to clean the vanity, sunroof glass and rear view mirrors. Use caution when cleaning around the rear view mirror as some of these mirrors are held on by a flimsy plastic mount glued to the window. If bumped, these mirrors can break away.

TIP: Should the vehicle you are working on have hidden retractable headlights ensure you flip these up to clean the lenses and any surrounding areas. These can be activated to open by turning on the ignition key and turning on the headlight switch.

Most front windshields will have a combination of bugs, water spots, paint overspray and even window stickers. Should your attempts to clean these problem areas, using regular glass cleaner not be effective, try cleaning the glass with some #000 steel wool saturated with some glass cleaner. Vigorously rub the steel wool over the stubborn areas until you have corrected the problem. **Use caution not to come in contact with any painted or plastic areas as the steel wool will certainly scratch these surfaces!**

#000 steel wool works well for also removing stubborn water spots on glass windows!

Once you have completed the front windshield, continue to the outside driver's window, side, and rear windows following the same procedures.

******************* **CAUTION** **********************

NEVER USE STEEL WOOL ON AFTER FACTORY TINTED WINDOWS OR SIDE VIEW MIRRORS MADE OF HIGHLY POLISHED PLASTIC WHICH SOMETIMES LOOKS LIKE GLASS. THE USE OF STEEL WOOL ON THESE AREAS CAN SCRATCH THE PLASTIC.

AVOID USING GLASS & CHROME POLISH ON TINTED WINDOWS. TINTED WINDOWS ARE TREATED WITH A THIN SHEET OF PLASTIC COLORED MYLAR WHICH HELPS TO REDUCE SUNLIGHT FROM ENTERING THE VEHICLE. ONLY

CLEAN TINTED WINDOWS WITH A DAMPENED CHAMOIS OR CLOTH OR NON AMONIA CLEANER AND DRY WITH MICRO FIBER TOWEL.

You may find when cleaning Mercedes coupes or similar type cars that the area behind the speedometer is difficult to reach and get clean. This space is often too narrow to get between the hump and the glass. However, you can take a flexible strip of metal (a Slim Jim works perfect) and tightly wrap it with a few layers of paper towel soaked in the Blue glass cleaner. By using gentle pressure work the cleaner around this area and towel wipe it dry. Be sure to use caution when cleaning this area as too much pressure from forcing or jamming the towel in this area could feasibly crack the windshield. This is the first area of visibility the customer sees so take your time and do a thorough job.

Plastic Rear Windows

In most convertibles or rag tops, plastic material windows are installed rather than hard glass and can be scratched very easily. With this said, **NEVER** use any abrasive materials such as steel wool or scrub brushes to clean this area. You will find that some of the older plastic windows are heavily discolored and scratched making it difficult to bring them back to their original condition. However, there are many plastic cleaners and polishes available that can bring life back to old dull plastic.

Even though there are several good plastic polishes out there we recommend you use **Meguires Plastic Cleaner or Megs Scratch X** for extreme scratch removal. These products contain mild abrasive compounding agents and will remove fine scratches and dull oxidized materials. To start, apply a small amount of the product onto a soft clean towel and gently rub on to the plastic surface. Once done, wipe off the cleaner completely with a clean towel. Follow the same procedure for both sides of the plastic, followed up by polishing the plastic with a separate clean micro fiber towel. Lastly, seal the window with **Meguires Plastic Polish** for optimum clarity.

Cleaning And Polishing Diagram For Windshields And Windows

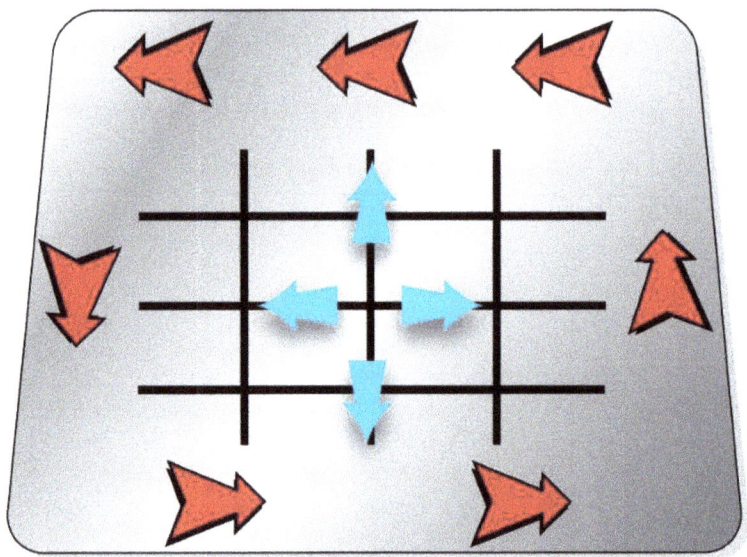

THE CORRECT CLEANING AND POLISHING
PROCEDURE FOR WINDSHIELD AND WINDOWS

STEP 1 - FIRST CLEAN THE PERIMETER OF THE WINDSHIELD OR WINDOW, PAYING PARTICULAR ATTENTION TO THE CORNERS. ALWAYS FACE YOUR WORK STRAIGHT ON TO ENSURE YOU DON'T MISS ANY AREAS. FOLLOW THE DIRECTION OF THE HANDS ON THE ILLUSTRATION.

STEP 2 - THE CENTER SECTION OF THE WINDSHIELD OR WINDOW SHOULD BE CLEANED WITH AN OVERLAPPING CRISS-CROSS MOTION, CLEANING IN THE DIRECTION OF THE ARROWS. USE THE SAME METHOD FOR APPLYING THE WINDOW CLEANER AND/OR DRYING THE WINDOWS.

Special Notes Page

Section 13

Vehicle Detailing Summary Steps

Setup Area And Equipment 221

Engine Cleaning 222

Initial Pressure Washing 222

Detailing The Interior 224

Exterior Polishing 225

Window Cleaning 225

Setup Area And Equipment

- [ ] Canopy
- [ ] Equipment, chemicals, and accessories - close to vehicle
- [ ] Vehicle setup
    - [ ] Customer belongings to container
    - [ ] Check antenna
    - [ ] Remove floor mats
    - [ ] All debris to trash bag – empty ashtrays

Engine Cleaning

- [ ] Make sure engine is warm
- [ ] Cover distributor and sensitive components with plastic bags, if necessary
- [ ] Pre-Rinse engine compartment, sides, and hood of car (**turn pressure down (150 psi) and flutter-wash**)
- [ ] Apply degreaser – use *Engine Degreaser*
- [ ] Hand scrub-brush next – Use *Car Wash Shampoo Mixture*
- [ ] Power wash and rinse
- [ ] Condition engine compartment hoses and plastics - use *Vinyl Protectant*
- [ ] Final touches and engine check

Initial Pressure Washing

- [ ] Wheel, tires, and undercarriage (**do not wash or rinse wheels if car has just been driven, let them cool**)
    - [ ] Carefully examine wheels prior to cleaning - coated alloy, aluminum, steel, plastic or painted types
    - [ ] Use wash pad and soapy water - *Car Wash Shampoo* or *All Purpose Cleaner*
    - [ ] Chrome wheels use – *Wheel* and *Mag Cleaner*
- [ ] Rubber tires and white walls
    - [ ] Spray liberal amount of *All Purpose Cleaner*, scrub with wheel brush
    - [ ] Scrub with white wall wire brush
    - [ ] For hard to clean black curb scuffs use *Tar and Gum Remover*
    - [ ] Clean wheel well area with *All Purpose Cleaner* - if heavy grease in areas use *Engine Degreaser*

- Scrub with fender well brush
- Grill body and undercarriage
    - Spray with pressure washer
    - Pre-spray with *All Purpose Cleaner*
    - Use bug sponge to scrub area
    - Use fender brush and *Car Wash Shampoo* for valance area
    - Rinse thoroughly
- Rear tail light area
    - Spray with pressure washer
    - Pre-spray with *All Purpose Cleaner*
    - Use bug sponge to scrub area
    - Use fender brush and *Car Wash Shampoo* for lower area
    - Rinse thoroughly
- Road tar and sap removal
    - *Tar and Gum Remover* will treat both sap and tar
- Pressure washing
    - Work from top to bottom
    - Clean door jambs
        - Open all doors
        - Spray with *All Purpose Cleaner*
        - Use brushes and bug sponge to clean jambs
        - Blast areas with pressure washer
    - Vinyl tops
        - Flood with water
        - Spray with *All Purpose Cleaner*
        - Scrub with iron carpet brush
    - Power up the suds
    - Hand body wash
        - Work from top to bottom
    - Power rinsing
    - Dry the vehicle
    - After drying spray with *Vinyl Protectant* on tires - be sure to wipe off excess

- While spraying tires simultaneously spray fender wells with *Vinyl Protectant*

Detailing The Interior

- Open up all doors
    - Turn off overhead dome light
- Vacuuming
    - Start at the top and work down
    - Use floor tool and crevice tool and vacuum everything
    - Use *All Purpose Cleaner* for stubborn dirt or grease
- Shampoo the interior with *Carpet and Upholstery Shampoo*
    - Use *Traffic Lane Cleaner* or *All Purpose Cleaner* on soiled area in seats
    - Use extreme caution on headliners as they are very delicate
        - American cars have velour type headliners which are more durable
    - Removing carpet stains
        - *All Purpose Cleaner* aids in dissolving greasy foods, breaks down ink, and cosmetics
        - *Traffic Lane Cleaner* is an excellent general cleaner for all types of spills and stains
- Extracting – Follow up with machine after hand scrubbing
- Cleaning dashboard and gauges
    - Use *All Purpose Cleaner*, towels, brushes, toothbrushes, and cotton swabs
    - Use *Air Fragrance* in vent areas after cleaning
- Steering wheel
    - Clean
    - Apply light coat of *Vinyl Protectant* and buff
- Ashtrays – use *All Purpose Cleaner*
- Seat Belts – use *All Purpose Cleaner*
- Rubber boots and pedals – Use *All Purpose Cleaner*
- Use *Vinyl Protector* on all areas except pedals (**NEVER APPLY DRESSINGS TO FOOT PEDALS**)
- Apply *Fabric Guard* if required

- Interior vinyl – use *All Purpose Cleaner*
- Door jambs – use *All Purpose Cleaner* or *Engine Degreaser*
- Apply *Vinyl Protectant* to all vinyl upholstery areas
- Use *Leather Conditioner* on leather upholstery and trim, you can use *Traffic Lane Cleaner* if needed to pre-clean

Exterior Polishing

- Polishing is a process of pre-cleaning the paint
- Determine products needed and follow procedures – be sure to test for clear coat with *Mild Polish*
- Make sure bonnets and towels are kept clean
- Compound and buff
    - *Heavy Duty Rubbing Compound* is the most aggressive – use on **NON CLEAR COAT ONLY**
    - *Medium Rubbing Compound* or *Light Rubbing Compound* is to be used for clear coat finishes
- Exterior finishing touches
    - Attention to detail is what it is all about
    - Dress all the rubber molding etc., with *Vinyl Protectant* or *Silicone Spray*
    - Dress spare tire if there is one
    - Wipe off excess tire dressing which should have been dressed earlier
    - Wheel polishing – use *Glass and Chrome Polish* or *Aluminum Polish*
    - Chrome work – use *Glass and Chrome Polish*
    - Antennas
    - License plates
    - Tooth brushing
- Paint sealant application
    - Follow product instructions
    - Divide vehicle into six sections
    - Don't rush, take your time
    - Repeat application to the hood, roof, and trunk lid after vehicle is completed

Window Cleaning

- Use *Glass and Chrome Polish* or *Blue Glass Cleaner* as needed

Never use *Glass and Chrome Polish* on tinted windows

Go through checklist and review the vehicle to insure all items were detailed and that the car is completed properly.

Special Notes Page

Section 14

Special Tips And Techniques

Special Tips Section............................ 229

Special Tips Section

This section was created for you as a summary and quick review of just a few Car Tips and Safety Alerts to be aware of. Not all Special Tips or Alerts are listed here but you should find many of these worth noting.

Section 2   **Setting up Your Work Area -** We recommend you use a GFI (Ground Fault Interrupter) for your safety and protection. The GFI is a device designed to protect people from electrical shock.

Section 2   **Setting up Your Work Area -** To keep organized and have everything in reach, consider investing in a Detailer's pouch or what is commonly called a Carpenter's tool bag. The handy compartments in the bag can conveniently store things like tooth brushes, Q-Tips, razor blades, bottles, even business cards.

Section 4   **Chemical Information -** In today's high overhead, smart operators research every way to save money. One easy way to significantly save is to order your liquid products in 4 gallon lots. By doing so you can save from $4.00 to $4.50 per gallon. That is a 22% savings per gallon as opposed to paying in 1 gallon lots.

Section 5   **Equipment Safety -** Be sure to eyeball the polisher for any Bonnet threads or material that may become entwined around the motor shaft. Any build-up that goes unchecked will overload the motor causing damage to the armature, VOIDING THE MAUNUFACTURER'S WARRANTY.

Section 5   **Extractors -** Do not use any detergent or cleaning agent that has not been tested and approved by the manufacturer. You can purchase compatible detergents at your local Janitorial Supply Store.

Section 5   **The Immersion Heater -** You can be simultaneously heating the water in the bucket while washing the car. This can help you save time when setting up. Once the car is washed and dried, your extractor will be ready to use in the next phase of detailing the Interior.

Section 5   **Warning -** High Pressure Sprayers can Cause Serious Injury so ensure you observe all warnings! For Professional Use Only!

Section 5   RUNNING THE PRESSURE WASHER DRY CAN CAUSE SEVERE DAMAGE TO MOVING PARTS. ALWAYS TURN ON THE WATER SUPPLY BEFORE STARTING THE MOTOR.

Section 5   **Equipment maintenance -** We recommend you maintain a LOG BOOK to record your operating hours.

Section 6 **Engine cleaning -** For a great looking engine compartment, while the engine is still wet, apply a nonflammable silicone Vinyl Dressing over the entire engine compartment with your spray bottle. Spray the hoses, motor, battery, radiator, and all metal and rubber parts. This will really enhance the engine's appearance!

Section 6 **Engine Cleaning -** Before stepping into the automobile place a towel on the floor to prevent contaminating the carpet with grease.

Section 7 **Basics of car washing -** It is importance of using the right type of car wash solution in order to prevent water and chemical compounds from sticking to the surface.

Section 7 **Basics of car washing -** When cleaning door jambs pre-spray All Purpose degreaser with spray bottle into all hinge and door openings. Let product dwell for 30 seconds to break down the grease and dirt then rinse off with high pressure washer or hose. This will save a lot of hand cleaning later on. For stubborn grease agitate with your bug sponge.

Section 7 **Basics of car washing -** After degreasing and rinsing the wheel well area spray a liberal amount of Vinyl dressing. These areas pick up a heavy amount of dirt and road tar. Once dressed the Black undercoating behind the tires will stand out beautifully!

Section 7 **Basics of car washing -** Carefully examine the wheels prior to cleaning them as there are many different types and some can only be cleaned with certain types of cleaners. So it is important that you distinguish what type of wheels you are cleaning beforehand.

Section 7 **Basics of car washing -** Since many of your cleaning products contain mild acids or solvents, we suggest you consider the area in which you are cleaning the wheels and tires. These products can permanently stain expensive concrete or custom tile work, so we suggest you bring the car to the asphalt pavement in the street rather than using the driveway.

Section 7 **Basics of car washing - TEST TIP:** If you are unsure if you are cleaning a wheel that is compatible with an acid based Wheel/Mag Cleaner, have running water in one hand and a spray bottle of acid based Wheel/Mag Cleaner in the other hand. Spray a small amount on a tiny section of the wheel. **If the wheel begins to foam, RINSE IMMEDIATELY!** This is a sign that the wheel is NOT compatible with this type of cleaner and permanent damage could occur if not rinsed off quickly!

Section 7 **Basics of car washing -** ALWAYS WEAR PROTECTIVE GOGGLES, RUBBER GLOVES, AND CAREFULLY FOLLOW THE MANUFACTURERS INSTRUCTIONS WHEN APPLYING THESE PRODUCTS.

Section 7 **Basics of car washing** - You may sometimes notice the appearance of rust on the brake drum after treating the wheel with an acid based wheel cleaner. This is a perfectly **normal reaction**. Once you or the customer applies the brakes and the brake shoes come on contact with the drum the friction of the shoes will remove it.

Section 7 **Basics of car washing** - To ensure you have not missed any areas, back up the car to ensure the wheel rotates approximately ½ turn from top to bottom (180) degrees. Rotating the wheel with the top portion of the wheel now on the bottom, will allow you to see if any brake dust or grease was missed.

Section 7 **Basics of car washing** - Remember to work from the top to bottom of the vehicle in order to save you time from having to rinse an area more than once.

Section 7 **Basics of car washing** - Should your tap water have harsh chemicals or you find calcium deposits and water spots after washing, we recommend you invest in purchasing a soft water system tied into your tap water line.

Section 7 **Basics of car washing** - Be sure to use a detailer's towel instead of a chamois cloth, should there be any grease or oil present in the door jamb areas.

Section 7 **Basics of car washing** - Caution: Many Solvent based dressings are flammable and should not be used for treating engine compartments or vehicle interiors.

Section 8 **Interior cleaning** - For Animal hair try using an Animal Hair Removal Stone. Another trick is to use a piece of duct tape or masking tape and by using the sticky side up you can lift the hair out. You can also use a lint brush or clothing sticky roller, usually available at most dry cleaners.

Section 8 **Interior cleaning** - For quick cleaning of dirty air vents, try using a presoaked Q-Tip with All Purpose cleaner. For dusty vents you can use Stoner silicone shine spray along with a soft interior dusting brush. To freshen up the air vents spray a little deodorizer straight into the slots.

Section 8 **Interior cleaning** - For black heel marks on running boards try using a piece of OOO steel wool and some tar remover. You can also use a Mr. Clean Magic Eraser pad for this area as well as other hard plastic areas. Steel wool should <u>not be used</u> on any interior area than the floor boards.

Section 8   **Interior cleaning** - Should you come across either a melted crayon, piece of lipstick or any other cosmetics follow the special procedure for cleaning this problem. Many of these materials are made of a wax like base and can smear and spread incredibly fast. In order to contain the material from spreading lift the bulk of the material with either a putty knife or screw driver and then spray a heavy solution of Spot & Fabric Cleaner directly onto the spot. **IMPORTANT NOTE: DO NOT RUB BACK AND FORTH!** Instead use a blotting approach by taking a thick terry cloth towel and pressing down lightly with your fingertips.

Section 8   **Interior cleaning** - Pour a few ounces of water based Interior Car Fragrance along with the detergent into the Carpet Extractor for an **extra fresh smell. This will last for hours and leave a clean fresh scent.**

Section 8   **Interior cleaning** - Some detailers will use the technique of restoring old, pitted, and rusty ashtrays by repainting or lacquering them. Should you decide to do this as well, we suggest you ensure the ashtray is completely clean and dry beforehand. Tape the outside edges and external area with masking tape. Use a bright aluminum spray paint for metal type ashtrays, which can be found in most hardware stores.

Section 8   **Interior cleaning** - You must never apply any dressing directly onto the foot pedals as this could cause your customers foot to slip off and cause an accident. Always use good common sense and judgment whenever applying the dressing.

Section 8   **Interior cleaning** - Should you experience overspray when spraying Fabric Guard, take a damp towel and wipe off all excess overspray from any of the vinyl, leather or wood grain areas. Avoid spraying any Fabric Guard onto any window areas, as this product tends to resist water and other liquid cleaners.

Section 8   **Interior cleaning** - For general scuff marks try using a Mr. Clean Eraser pad.

Section 8   **Interior cleaning** - For stuck gum in carpet try using a product called Gum Freeze found in your local auto parts store. Use the gum freezes use a flat sided razor blade to scrape off excess. You can also use a gum and tar remover with a plastic razor scraper as well. Just spray, let soak and scrape off.

Section 9   **Exterior Polishing** - A good tool to use is a high powered 10X paint magnifier to closely examine the surface of the vehicle.

Section 9   **Exterior Polishing -** Compounding should be your last resort to cutting an old faded finish. Be sure to first test an area with a mild polish or chemical cleaner before you continue.

Section 9   **Exterior Polishing -** You will greatly reduce the risk of paint damage by knowing how much paint is on the surface of the vehicle prior to compounding. By using a paint thickness gauge you can instantly get an approximate reading of how thick the paint really is.

Section 9   **Exterior Polishing -** Most dark colors such as Maroon, Black or Dark Blue, tend to show more streak marks than light colors, due to the depth of color and reflection.

Section 9   **Exterior Polishing -** I highly suggest you remove any rings, watches or belts before starting your work. Be sure to place the electrical cord over your shoulder to keep it from coming in contact with the paint as it can cause scuffing or mar your work.

Section 9   **Exterior Polishing -** By wearing a Detailer's Apron, you can keep these items close at hand, including your bottle of polish, wax, brushes and other miscellaneous items.

Section 9   **Exterior Polishing -** If you are going to tape off sections of the car, go ahead and apply painter's tape over any rubber trim that could become contaminated with drying compounds or wax. Also run your tape over gaps such as hood and door closures where wax or compound could get into. Also run tape along window frames and the rubber seals around the windows.

Section 9   **Exterior Polishing -** Place a towel down on the floor board when stepping up to clean the roof. This will keep dirt and mud from grinding into affected areas.

Section 9   **Exterior Polishing -** I recommend you only apply small amounts of product when buffing hard to reach areas and tip the polisher at a sharp angle allowing you to get a better angle. By avoiding the use of too much polish you will avoid polish spin off.

Section 9   **Exterior Polishing -** You can test a vehicle for clear coat by rubbing a small amount of Polish onto the surface of the vehicle. If **NO** visible color bleeds onto the towel, then this is a good indication that the vehicle has a Clear Coat Finish.

Section 9   **Exterior Polishing -** To quickly remove paint overspray and other surface contaminants try using a bar of Professional Detailer's Clay. Typically Blue clay is for mild overspray and Red clay is for heavy overspray. Clay is a safe and effective method.

Section 9   **Exterior Polishing - Here's a trick you can try however use CAUTION if you attempt this process.** For removal of water spotting both on glass as well as paint, pre-spray the surfaces with water, spray a liberal amount of a ready to use (Diluted) **acid based wheel cleaner** onto the surface. Next take your bug sponge and vigorously rub onto the surface. You can use a piece of Triple 000 steel wool instead of the bug sponge on **windows only**! Only the bug sponge should be used on the painted surface. Allow the product to dwell for approximately one minute then thoroughly rinse, then re-soap wash these areas again. The acid in the cleaner will help dissolve the crusty calcium buildup making it much easier for removal and less work for subsequent polishing and waxing.

Section 9   Exterior Polishing - Another trick for bringing back extremely dry, dull and chalking blackened surfaces is to use a silicone based aerosol product to treat these surfaces.

Section 10   Exterior Finishing Touches - You can bring the shine back to dull hard plastic by using a small amount of **mild compound** on a terry cloth towel and rub vigorously. Rub until the dull mirror takes on a glossy shine.

Section 10   Exterior Finishing Touches - You will notice that on raw aluminum (No Clear Coat) your towel will turn black as you polish so it is important to continue turning the towel to a clean side as you are working in the polish. With a separate clean towel buff the excess blackened cleaner off, until the aluminum is bright and clear.

Section 10   Exterior Finishing Touches - I recommend you use the Chrome Polish while rubbing with a piece of #000 steel wool for chrome that is pitted or crusted with rust stains.

Section 10   Exterior Finishing Touches - Before delivering the vehicle to the customer once done, remove any light dust or lint by going over the paint with either a Tack cloth or a rope type dusting brush that has been treated with paraffin wax like the California Car Duster. Don't forget to use your tooth brush to remove any remaining wax in the cracks and emblems.

Section 10   Exterior Finishing Touches - It's the small details like polishing a license plate frame the really sets you apart as a perfectionist and a Pro. For Chrome frames use a Glass and Chrome Polish. If the vehicle has a brass or aluminum plate holder use an Aluminum polish.

Section 10   Exterior Finishing Touches - An easy and safe solution for removing old stubborn and dried wax from rubber molding is an old fashion school rubber eraser. An eraser block also can remove light paint scuff marks.

Section 11   Selling Paint Sealant - Never wash wool bonnets with granular soap!! Invariably small particles of soap may not dissolve and lodge itself in the fabric causing you to leave swirl marks on the next job you do.

Always use LIQUID soap concentrate. In addition, add 1/2 cup of liquid ammonia to the wash water to help dissolve the waxes, polishes, and sealants while washing the bonnets.

Section 11   Selling Paint Sealant - Other businesses you can sell your long term protection packages are rental car agencies, fleet owners, government vehicles, Police cars and other public service vehicles and school buses. They are willing to pay a premium price for a long term protective coating.

Section 12 **Window Cleaning** - Your standard **Blue Glass Cleaner** will clean most ordinary jobs. I recommend that you purchase a concentrated formula from a professional chemical company. **Here's the trick to mixing a perfect formula**...never add regular tap water to the concentrate. Regular tap water contains minerals which can lead to clouding and streaking of the glass. Instead pick up some Distilled water at your local grocery store and add this to your concentrate. All the minerals have been removed from this type of water and you will have much more success achieving perfect glass!

Section 12 **Window Cleaning** - Never run a razor blade across the rear window to clean or remove stickers as the razor blade could cut a wire rendering the defogger useless.

Section 12 **Window Cleaning** - Should the vehicle you are working on have hidden retractable headlights ensure you flip these up to clean the lenses and any surrounding areas. These can be activated to open by turning on the ignition key and turning on the headlight switch.

Section 12 **Window Cleaning** - #000 steel wool works well for removing stubborn water spots on glass windows only!

Section 12 **Window Cleaning** - NEVER USE STEEL WOOL ON AFTER FACTORY TINTED WINDOWS OR SIDE VIEW MIRRORS MADE OF HIGHLY POLISHED PLASTIC WHICH SOMETIMES LOOKS LIKE GLASS. THE USE OF STEEL WOOL ON THESE AREAS CAN SCRATCH THE PLASTIC.

Section 12 **Window Cleaning** - You may find when cleaning Mercedes coupes or similar type cars that the area behind the speedometer is difficult to reach and get clean. This space is often too narrow to get between the hump and the glass. However, you can take a flexible strip of metal (a Slim Jim works perfect) and tightly wrap it with a few layers of paper towel soaked in the Blue glass cleaner.

Section 12 **Window Cleaning** - In most convertibles or rag tops, plastic material windows are installed rather than hard glass and can be scratched very easily. With this said, **NEVER** use any abrasive materials such as steel wool or scrub brushes to clean this area.

Section 18 **Walk Around** - Leave a lasting impression with your customer. They are thrilled to have just spent their hard earned money and have been rewarded with your professional skills at transforming their vehicle to like new. Now WOW them by giving them something they never expected. For example: A nice touch would be to leave a Carnation or Rose on the dash. Or a desk top calendar with your name and company logo or how about leaving a business card or mailing them a picture of their beautiful detailed car in the mail with a thank you note. Be creative!

Special Notes Page

Section 15

Recreational Vehicles

Rv's 238

Interior Cleaning Will Consist Of: 238

Potential Customers Are: 240

Rv's

Since many individuals who own motorhomes usually have disposable income, the RV market is potentially a very profitable market. These projects can be a huge undertaking for most individuals. This is where both your expertise and professional advantage can really help you to tackle these big jobs thanks to your knowledge and equipment.

Your average RV job will usually range between 3 – 6 hours for one person to complete, however the good news is that the cleaning process is very similar to cleaning an automobile. I have some great advice and that's to invest in a good pair of white rubber soled tennis shoes, due to amount of water you will be using. It could get slippery especially when you're working on the top of the RV.

Interior Cleaning Will Consist Of:

Shampooing and extracting of carpet and upholstery.

Vinyl dressing on all vinyl surfaces, which can also be used on wood grained cabinets.

Cleaning windows and dash board.

Cleaning kitchen sinks, counter tops, stoves, and table tops.

Usually refrigerator, bathroom and showers are not included except for shampooing carpeted areas.

Fabric Guard protection is an extra add-on service.

TIPS:

1. Carry a full load of water at all times, since you will be washing a very large vehicle. I recommend at least 100 gallons.

2. Most RV's are made of either aluminum or fiberglass sidings, which are normally simple to polish. However, many RV's unfortunately sit idle throughout the year and many unprotected from the sun and elements. You will come across many RV's with moderate to severe oxidation because of this. Fiberglass is very porous and can become dry and chalky as it ages. When the RV is in this kind of condition, be sure to work in 3X3 foot sections at a time. Apply wax or polish and <u>towel dry immediately</u>.

3. With some of the older RV models, such as the Pace Arrow, have what are called

CAPS which are located at the front and rear sections of the RV. These are made of color added pre-formed molded fiberglass end caps. You are able to polish these as well, but you won't be able to achieve the same high polished look as you would with other RV models. On the other hand, aluminum siding is painted with a similar painting process as found on automobiles.

The best polishing methods for these CAPS are as follows:

- Have one polishing wax pad in one hand and a separate towel for drying in the other. Apply wax to a 2 by 2 foot section, wiping the areas off immediately as you go. Or instead of the wax pad apply wax with an orbital polisher. It's imperative that you DO NOT allow the wax to dry on the surface, as this will bond with the surface making it very difficult to remove especially on older porous finishes.

Potential Customers Are:

Advertise to Private Individuals

RV Sales and Service Facilities

Pass out flyers in RV Parks

Join RV Clubs (like the Good Sam Club)

Special Notes Page

Section 16

Boats And Airplanes

Marine 243

Potential Customers Are: 247

Price List For Detailing Boats 248

Overview Of The Steps For Detailing Aircraft: 249

Suggested Price Schedule For Aircraft Detailing 252

Marine

Should your Marine Market be large enough, you could feasibly set up a full time operation devoted specifically to boats. However, a residential mobile service can be highly profitable as well as many homeowners store their vehicle at their homes.

The size of boats are much larger in comparison to automobiles allowing you to have a higher per unit profit producer. The cleaning process is simply made up of polishing the fiberglass, cleaning the trailer, shampooing the carpets, cleaning upholstery, window glass, trim and detailing the console. For larger boats or yachts, you will need to also clean the inside mirrors, table tops, kitchen, and sink counters and if applicable, the galley.

You can dress up Teak wood with a Vinyl dressing or Teak wood oil, found in most marine shops. However old worn out teakwood may not respond well to detailing. To properly bring back Teak wood it needs to be bleached, sanded and re-varnished.

Railing can be polished with an Aluminum Polish. I suggest you use your orbital polisher for waxing large surfaces to make it a much easier process. Since most boats are made of fiberglass or gel coated materials you can use a good one step cleaner wax for most of the surfaces. In those cases where the surfaces have high oxidization I suggest you spend the time compounding these areas prior to applying your wax or sealant.

Ensure you check with your customer beforehand to see if they would like the trailer polished as well so that you adjust you're pricing to include this. The whole process will take roughly 2 – 4 hours to complete with a 1 – 2 man crew.

TIPS:

1. I suggest you contact the marine operators or service managers to provide you with leads for those who charter boats for private or public excursions.

2. Should the boat be on a trailer, ensure you clean the underside of the hull as well. This area usually contains algae, road tar, crusty hulls and other heavy weathering dependent upon how they are maintained by the owner. Most of these areas can be cleaned by using your bug sponge and a strong compound made for fiberglass cleaning. A mechanics creeper works well to lay on while working on this hard to reach area.

3. Mix a solution of Car Wash and 25% of a strong All-Purpose Cleaner to pre-wash the boat. I suggest you use a boat hull cleaner, (you can pick this up at one of your local marine stores). For severe algae, rust or crusty hulls, some hulls cleaners use an acid based solution. Use caution with this product as it is extremely toxic and may require rubber gloves and a respirator.

4. Below are a few things to remember when bidding your job. Consider the amount of time, products, and labor when offering your bid.

    - How long has the boat been in storage?

    - Is there evidence of heavy oxidation, rust, or severe contamination?

    - Is there a heavy amount of salt residue present?

    - Is there a Galley or Cabin area that will need cleaning?

    - Is there a lot of teak wood that will need cleaning and treating?

    - Is the surface in need of an acid based hull cleaning?

5. You will need the following supplies when detailing a boat:

   - A fiberglass compound and one step cleaner wax made for Marine use.

   - #000 Steel Wool and Aluminum polish for the railing, tie downs, props, ladder rails, horns, running light fixtures, etc.

   - Teak wood oil or Vinyl dressing for the wood.

   - Carpet Shampoo and All Purpose Cleaner for the interior.

   - Meguires Plastic Polish for the plexiglass windows.

   - Vinyl protectant for dressing any vinyl upholstery.

   - Blue glass cleaner for glass windows, chrome wheels, etc.

   - Silicone spay for dressing console area and outboard motors

   - 6 ft ladder for tall boat cleaning

6. Ensure you **DO NOT** remove gear grease when cleaning outboard engines as this is used for lubricating all of the moving parts. Most of your newer outboard motors, (Evinrude, Force, and Mercury) are covered with a Basecoat/Clearcoat finish. Polish this area with a good marine wax or sealant

7. You can use your Engine Degreaser to degrease inboard motors, however use caution to

clean around the distributor caps, air cleaners, etc. Valve covers and air cleaner covers are usually made of aluminum so polish these as well with any Aluminum polish. This procedure is similar to cleaning a car's engine, as noted in **Section 6**.

8. Most boats have indoor/outdoor carpeting on the floors. I suggest you use your Pressure Washer to quickly remove dirt, lint, fish scales, etc. Shampoo as needed. You can use the Bilge Pump on the boat to drain the excess water, however if there is no Bilge Pump then use your Wet/Dry Vacuum.

9. You can also use your Pressure Washer to clean upholstery, just be sure to remove seats and cushions whenever possible. Use your All Purpose cleaner and carpet/upholstery brush to clean the upholstery followed up with a power rinse. Once this has been completed be sure to seal the upholstery with a vinyl dressing.  For larger boats with a galley or cabin sleep area pay close attention to these interior areas that have sinks, mirrors, interior carpets, fabric seats or couches and other locker and storage areas that need cleaning.

Whether you're detailing a yacht, sailboat, speedboat or a personal watercraft, boat detailing can be a lot of fun and profitable.

Potential Customers Are:

- Private Owners
- Charter or Rental Boats
- Yacht Clubs
- Yacht Brokers
- Boat Storage Yards
- Boat Repair Shops
- Chandleries
- Boat Race Events
- Personal Watercraft

Price List For Detailing Boats

Boats (under 21 ft) — Exterior Only $7.50/ft to $10.00/ft

— Ext. & Interior $10.00/ft to $12.00/ft

Boats (over 21 ft) — Exterior only $10.00/ft to $12.00/ft

— Ext. & Interior $12.00/ft to $14.00/ft

Trailors $25.00-$50.00

Planes

Planes are a bit trickier as there are certain areas that you must be aware of when cleaning and polishing.

Overview Of The Steps For Detailing Aircraft:

- Preparation .... washing the Aircraft.

- De-bugging .... removing bugs and bird droppings from leading edge of wings.

- Pre-cleaning........... horizontal and vertical stabilizers, Cowling, Engine Nacelles, Flaps and surrounding Landing Gear area.

- Degreasing .... remove excess grease and road tar from Belly and Landing Gear.

- Deoxidizing .... removing oil film, pipe exhaust, and oxidized paint.

- Sealing or waxing .. applying a long term weather resistant finish.

- Window cleaning.... applying the appropriate plastic window cleaner and polish.

- Metal polishing .... polishing propellers, spinners, aluminum siding, and chrome.

- Treating rubber ...... apply dressing to tires, rubber seals, and deice boots.

- Interior detailing ..... cleaning carpets, upholstery, seats, windows and light dash area cleaning or dusting.

Note: When working around the antenna and wire areas use caution especially around the static ports. Avoid getting water or wax in these holes, located on the side of the plane. Be sure to leave the grease on the landing gear, grease fittings, etc.

Since the paint is sometimes thin on these areas, use Caution when buffing around the aircraft rivets.

Most of the windows and windscreens used on planes are made of Plexiglas and can scratch easily so I suggest you only use water and a soft towel. Another safe product that is popular for use on Plexiglas, Lucite, Lexan and Acrylite type windows is **Plexus** an anti-static cleaner, protectant and polish all in one. **NEVER USE ANY TYPE OF GLASS POLISH** as the abrasive compound in this product can scratch these softer plastic type of windows.

When polishing, be sure to work in smaller sections, using a one step cleaner wax or sealant. Use an Aluminum polish for any aluminum panels, usually located on the sides of the plane. Most planes have interiors similar to cars, and can be cleaned in the same manner. **However, it is highly recommended that if you are not a pilot to stay away from the cockpit or instrument panel.**

Ensure you use **only cold water** to clean any of the carpeting and upholstery as these areas are usually pretreated with a flame retardant that can be removed if hot water is used such as with a hot water extractor.

The wings of the plane, better known as the "Leading Edge", should be treated with a double coat of wax, using either a one step wax or better yet a polymer type of sealant. A polymer is best as it contains thermal plastic resins which withstands higher temperature changes and has better wearing properties. By using this simple procedure will help to make future maintenance and cleaning of bugs, road tar and dirt a much easier process. In many cases, this can be one of the hardest areas to clean if this area has never been routinely cleaned. Upfront you may have to pre-polish or compound this area to get a smooth waxable surface.

You can use your Engine Degreaser or All Purpose Cleaner to remove smeared landing gear grease. Be sure to clean and dress the tires as well.

When cleaning the cockpit windshield use a soft micro fiber towel with a product like MEGUIRES PLASTIC POLISH, PLEXUS or WATER. This is the best method for cleaning this area.

Most propellers can be cleaned and shined with a mild polish followed by a wax or sealant. You can use an Aluminum polish for stainless steel props.

Most companies that specialize in painting planes use a more durable and weather resistant Imron paint. A small single engine plane could cost around $3,500.

With this said, you can see why it pays to have your detailing service maintain and protect your customer's investment.

Many small private airports are a great source of business, which also requires persistency when marketing your detailing services. However, you can initiate a monthly maintenance program of washing and/or detailing by inquiring at the front desk about obtaining a Pilots Association list. I suggest you check into attending one of their meetings in order to introduce yourself and services. Don't forget to distribute your business cards or flyers to interested parties. Should you decide to mail out flyers or brochures I suggest you stress the fact that you conveniently carry your own water and power on board your detailing vehicle. Since most airports don't have washing facilities nearby, you can take advantage of this based on your portable service. Many will appreciate the convenience of your detailing business.

Suggested Price Schedule For Aircraft Detailing

- Planes - Single Engine .... $200.00 to $275.00

- Planes - Small Twin Engine .... $300.00 to $375.00

- Planes - Large Twin Engine .... $300.00 to $550.00

- Planes – Turbo Prop Type .... $325.00 to $600.00

- Lear Jet/Citation .... $375.00 to $425.00

*Note…For unusual and large aircraft price per ft. or $60-$80 per hour

Special Notes Page

Section 17

Checklist And Retail Service Price List

Vehicle Checklist.................................. 255

Vehicle Checklist

Ashtrays Cleaned	
Carpets Shampooed	
Chrome Polished	
Console Cleaned	
Dash Glass	
Dashboard Cleaned	
Door & Trunk Jambs Cleaned	
Door Panels	
Engine Cleaned	
Fabric Protection	
Gas Lids	
Glove Box	
Grill & Front Section	
Interior Chrome	
Interior Dressed	
Interior Fragrance	
Interior Vacuumed	
Kick Panels	
Name Plate & Emblems	
Rocker Panels	
Rubber Moldings	
Spots Removed	
Steering Wheel	
Tires, Bumpers Dressed	
Tooth Bruch Cracks	
Trunk Cleaned	
Under Bumpers (Spoilers)	

Upholstery Cleaned	
Vinyl Top Dressed	
Visors	
Wheel Wells Cleaned	
Wheels Cleaned	
White Walls Cleaned	
Window Edges	

DETAIL MASTERS of America
Professional Mobile Car Cleaning Services

CARS, TRUCKS and VANS	Exterior	Interior	Full Detail
2dr. Import Car........(Porsche/Miata)	$90	$85	$160
4dr. Mid-Size Car....(Accord/Camry)	$95	$95	$165
Full Size Car..........(Jag/Lexus/Merc./BMW)	$95	$95	$175
Mini-Pick Up w/o Shell	$90	$75	$160
Full Size Truck Standard	$110	$85	$170
Full Size Truck Extra Cab	$125	$90	$185
Mini Van................(Caravan/Astro)	$135	$125	$225
Full Size Van	$150	$145	$250
Full Size ....(Blazer/Bronco/Durango)	$125	$125	$190
Explorers/Jeeps/Landcruisers/4Runner	$125	$125	$185
Yukons/Expeditions/Landrovers	$135	$135	$210
Suburbans/Excursions	$135/$150	$150	$225/$250

ALL BLACK VEHICLES ADD $10.00

10% DISCOUNT ON 2 CARS OR MORE

DETAIL MASTERS of America
Professional Mobile Car Cleaning Services

DETAIL MASTERS PRICE LIST

BOATS	Exterior	Full Detail
19 Ft. and under	$7.50/Ft.	$10.00/Ft.

Includes hand washing of trailer, wheels polished & tires dressed
*To wax trailer is an additional................$25.00
19 Ft. and up................$10.00/Ft......$12.00/Ft.

RVs
Exterior Only (Flat Surface)................$10.00/Ft.
Interior Only................$4.00/Ft.
Full Detail................$12.00/Ft.
*Over 5 years old add $2.00 per Ft.-Ribbed siding add $4.00 per Ft.
R.V. Wash................$125.00

CAMPER SHELLS
Truck Camper Shell Small................$25.00
Truck Camper Shell Large................$30.00

*EXTRA SERVICE CHARGES
(Based on $30-$40 Labor per hr.)
*Heavy Oxidation................$30-100
*Paint Overspray or Heavy Tree Sap................$30-75
*Interior heavy stain removal with steam extraction................$25-30

*Gift certificates available. *Weekly wash & detail services starting at $165.00 Per Month.

Special Notes Page

Section 18

Equipment And Supply Check

Supply And Equipment 260

Final Walk-Around 261

Inspection And Payment 261

Sample Invoice 263

Supply And Equipment 258

Supply And Equipment

Keep the following points in mind when running your detailing service:

- Be considerate of others.

- Respect the environment and surroundings you leave behind after your detail job.

- Be sure to always pick up all of your belongings and equipment.

- When operating a mobile service ensure there is no evidence left behind.

- All trash and debris should be picked up and stored in a separate container within your work vehicle.

- Remember to pick up even the smallest bits and pieces of paper etc. from the ground. You don't want to leave a bad impression especially when working at an office complex.

- Being a clean thoughtful detailer will make you stand out amongst the competition by respecting the work area you work in regardless of where that may be.

- Don't forget to disconnect your machinery and store them in a safe clean place.

- Pick up all bonnets and towels and place them in a separate container to wash later.

- Refill all your chemical products so that you will be ready for the next detailing job.

- Clean and check all of your detailing tools, brushes, Q-Tips etc. Refill as necessary.

- Like prepping a car, prepping and stocking your area with supplies is just as important.

- Always make a good impression by keeping your work area spotless and take pride in your business/service.

Final Walk-Around

Once you have completed the finishing touches, thoroughly inspect the car for any flaws. Should you have the vehicle under the Detailer's Canopy, be sure to pull it out now to get a better look in the natural sunlight. Always remember to wipe your feet off before getting into the car and place a towel on the floor before stepping in.

Double check the following on your final walk around:

- Check the paint for either swirls or wax residue that may have been missed.

- Ensure there are no streaks in the windows and chrome.

- Keep a keen eye out for any imperfections and address each section as needed.

Inspection And Payment

Ensure you take care of the necessary paperwork or billing before you present the finished car to your customer. Record all future records of the customer's vehicle by using your Retail Billing Receipt Book. This should include the year, make, and model of the car, as well as any special notations or up charges to the customer. Be sure to write clearly as many of your customers will use their receipt as a business write off. This will also help you to maintain clear and precise records for future specials or mailings. You should also get their email address for future correspondence, newsletters, specials, etc. (See sample Invoice at the end of this chapter)

Should you operate at a fixed location, have the car ready for the customer's inspection by opening all the doors, trunk, and hood (if you cleaned the engine). Ensure you allow enough time for the vehicle to thoroughly dry on the inside and out before presenting to the customer. Should this not be an option, I suggest you place a Clear Plastic Seat Protector on the driver's seat and a paper floor mat to keep moisture from coming in contact with the customer's clothing.

Should you be operating a mobile service, be sure your area is clean and all your equipment and bottles are picked up before the customer approaches the car. Don't let the clutter distract them from enjoying the moment when they pick up their clean and spotless vehicle.

Should you provide pick-up and delivery service, be sure to contact the customer beforehand to let them know you are returning their car. Ensure you avoid running into mud puddles, avoid off road driving or any other trouble areas that could mar your detailing job. You may want to consider accepting credit cards for the convenience of your customer. However, the majority of individuals who use this type of service will generally pay with cash or by check. After your customer has had a chance to inspect their car and approve the job, accept payment, hand them their receipt, and on your way to meet your next customer!

Sample Invoice

DETAIL MASTERS OF AMERICA

SERVICE ORDER

Date: 7-4-2010

Customer Name: JOHN DOE City: SALINAS, CA
Address: 1212 SHADY BROOK LANE Zip Code: 90210
Phone: 805-212-4141 Year: 2010 Make: LEXUS Model: LS400
E-Mail Address: JOHNDOE@YAHOO.COM

JOB DESCRIPTION

Super Wash	_____	Exterior Reconditioner	_____
Interior Rejuvenator	_____	(Complete In & Out Detail)	175
Monthly Maintainance Program	_____	Water Spot Removal	_____

EXTRA CHARGES

Heavy Stain Removal	_____	Heavy Oxidation Removal	_____
(Paint Overspray Removal)	20	Tree Sap/Tar Removal	_____
Heavy Scratch Removal	_____	(Excessive Dog Hair)	15

OTHER SERVICES AVAILABLE

Windshield Crack Repair	_____	Headlight Restoration	_____
(Odor Elimination)	40	Paint Chip Repair	_____
RV - Boat - Trailer Estimate	_____	Door Ding Repair	_____

Our Checklist is Your Checklist

Gratuities Optional _____

TOTAL 250.00

- ☐ Interior Vacuumed
- ☐ Trunk Vacuumed
- ☐ Ash Tray Cleaned
- ☐ Windows Cleaned
- ☐ Visor Mirrors Cleaned
- ☐ Headliner Cleaned
- ☐ Carpets Shampooed
- ☐ Doors Jambs Cleaned
- ☐ Interior Dressed
- ☐ Console Cleaned
- ☐ Airs Vents Cleaned
- ☐ Dashboard Cleaned & Dressed
- ☐ Upholstery/Pleats Cleaned
- ☐ Tires/Bumpers Dressed
- ☐ Road Tar Removed
- ☐ Side Mirrors Cleaned
- ☐ Vinyl Top Cleaned
- ☐ Vinyl Top Dressed
- ☐ Chrome Polished
- ☐ Wheels Cleaned & Polished
- ☐ Wheel Wells Cleaned
- ☐ White Walls Cleaned
- ☐ Tooth Brush Cracks
- ☐ Tailpipes Cleaned
- ☐ Interior Fragrance

Dear Customer: Please inspect the car carefully. If anything is not to your satisfaction please let us know right away! We value your business and hope to serve you again soon. *Thank You*

Credit Card Authorization

Card# _____ Exp. Date _____

Signature _____ CVC2# _____

Special Notes Page

Section 19

Recommended Aftermarket Add-On Services

Add-On Repair And Restoration Services For Extra Profits 266

Add-On Repair And Restoration Services For Extra Profits

As you build your business you may want to consider offering additional services to your customers. As you learn these new skills you can increase your average ticket sale to your customer dramatically and at the same time improve the overall value to the vehicle. Think of it. You are already reconditioning the customer's vehicle. This is a perfect opportunity to offer these needed and popular repair and restoration services.

The level and learning skill will vary depending on the service chosen and certain types repair services will require thorough hands on training. Once mastered, you can become a convenient one stop shop for all of your customer's needs. There will be certain services that may not interest you to develop yourself. In this case you can partner up with for example: a mobile Dent repair Service Company and refer out the work to your customer. In this case you can work out an agreement to receive a referral fee or percentage of whatever amount is charged to your mutual customer.

Here are some suggested and most popular profitable add-on Services: I have also added a brief description and a sample you can use on your website, etc.

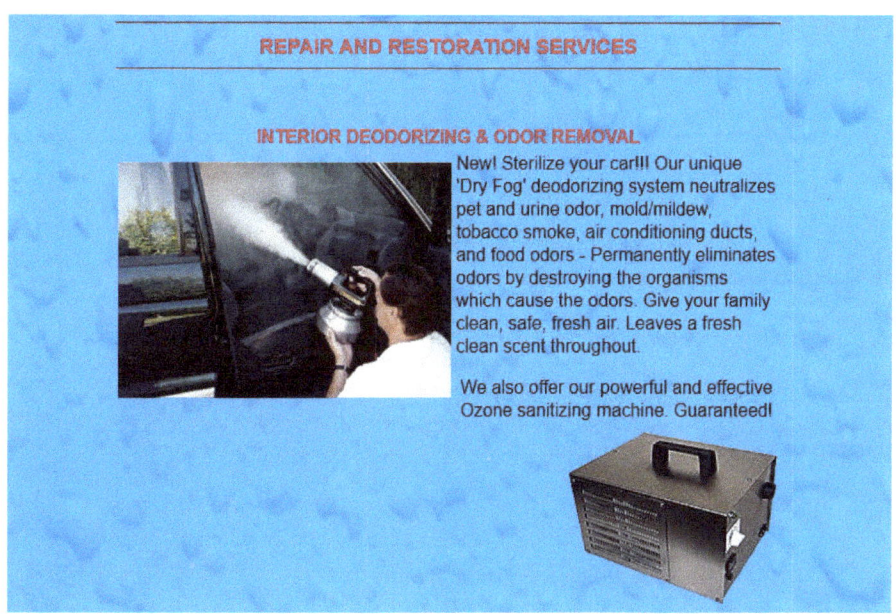

SCOTCH-GUARD FABRIC PROTECTION

Inside Facts: With all the dirt, mud, sand, not to mention the fast foods, cosmetics, gum, crayons, coffee, and soda spills, it's no wonder that the interior is one of the most neglected areas of car cleaning. You can however through a regular cleaning program and an application of our Scotch-guard fabric protectant sealer extend the life and value of your automobile's interior. Scotch-guard is applied to help resist soiling and spill damage from occurring. Scotch-guard fabric protectant is also recommended to treat and protect convertible rag tops from bird droppings and fading. Call for Quote

HEADLIGHT RESTORATION DULL TO NEW

Got old yellow and cloudy Headlights? They are the eyes of your vehicle. They allow you to see at night and be seen by other motorists. Without them, you'd be blind. That's why keeping your headlights clean and clear is so important. With our special process we can make them look brand new. Plastic headlight restoration is a great way to avoid the high cost of replacing them. We carefully mask and wet sand the headlight. A special polishing sequence is then applied. Each headlight is then re-coated with a hard shell UV acrylic sealer to make them look factory new!

- Improve Safety
- Increase Visibility
- Improve Resale Value
- No Disassembling Required
- Substantial Savings
- Enhanced Appearance

Call for Quote

PAINTLESS DENT REPAIR

Before   After

Our convenient mobile service will come to your home or office and remove those unsightly door dings and dents without the hassle of taking your car to a body shop. Our service technicians are highly skilled and trained in PDR. This process requires No down time and No painting. Restore the look and value of your car while saving hundreds of dollars in paint and body work. Dings disappear like magic! Free estimate !

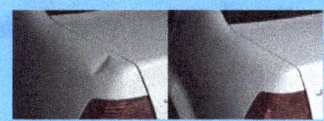

PAINT CHIP AND SCRATCH REPAIR

Our unique mobile service will come to your home or office and repair those unsightly paint chips, nicks, scratches, and bumpers at a fraction of what a typical body shop would charge. Our service will restore the beauty and value of your prized possession!

 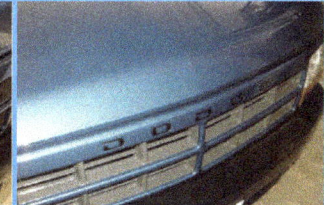

Special Notes Page

Section 20

Conclusion

Congrats 272

Congrats

Congratulations, you've made it through to the end of the book; however you aren't expected to remember everything upfront. With this said, I suggest you review the "Tips and Techniques Glossary" as well as your "Check List". There is also a special notes section at the back of each section to help get your thoughts and study comments noted.

In a short period of time you will start to feel comfortable and have good basic knowledge of how to implement detailing procedures, and the use of your equipment, and products. We have covered a lot of areas and I recommend reading this book a couple of times and then use it as a reference whenever you come up with a situation that needs more study. Keep your book with you at all times for a quick review.

I suggest you first practice on your own vehicle or friends and relatives cars to get comfortable using the equipment and techniques. You may even think of providing an introductory offer to get your customer base started. Be sure to take your time and be thorough. More importantly, enjoy what you do. It will take time to learn how you're cleaning compounds and processes work, however be patient; it will get easier as you go.

Remember that speed and efficiency will come with time and practice.

I certainly hope you enjoyed this training program. We have covered all the secrets of professional detailing to the best of our ability, as well as how to get and keep repeat customers that will help you build a very successful business.

It's up to you now to take the initiative, go out, and get your customer base started. Always be enthusiastic about your business as the next person you meet might very well be your next customer. There will be lots of hard work and long hours, but there's nothing like the satisfaction of owning your own business. Take pride in your work and accomplishments and good luck in your new business venture!

Much success!
GREG DUMOND

Special Notes Page

Section 21

Resource Guide

Product And Equipment Resource Guide 275

Product And Equipment Resource Guide

Products

*National Detail Systems .... 1-800-356-9485 – www.nationaldetail.com
Supplier of waxes, cleaners, soaps, bottles, brushes, buffing pads, towels, etc.

*Auto Geek .... 1-800-869-3011 – www.autogeek.net
Supplier of waxes, cleaners, soaps, bottles, brushes, buffing pads, towels, etc.

*Detailing.com .... 1-888-306-5828- www.detailing.com
Supplier of waxes, cleaners, soaps, bottles, brushes, towels and buffing pads

*One Grand Products .... 1-800-782-3329 – www.onegrand.com
Supplier of waxes, cleaners, soaps, bottles, brushes, buffing pads, towels, etc.

*Stoner Company .... 1-800-227-5538 – www.stonersolutions.com
Supplier of Stoner Trim Shine aerosol cans, bulk vinyl dressing, etc.

*Meguires Products .... 1-800-347-5700 - www.meguiars.com
Supplier of waxes, cleaners, soaps, buffing pads, towels, etc.

*Allbrite Products .... 1-714-666-8683 – www.allbriteusa.com
Supplier of Glass, Chrome Polish, and other detailing chemicals

*Gem Industries .... 1-800-447-4436 – www.gem-industries.com
Supplier of Teflon paint sealants and cleaners

*Auto Magic .... 1-800-826-0828 – www.automagic.com
Supplier of waxes, cleaners, bottles, brushes, buffing pads, towels, etc.

*Car Aroma .... 1-310-834-2682 – www.cararoma.com
Supplier of vacuum crevice and floor tools, towels, bottles, etc.

*S.M. Arnold .... 1-800-325-7865 – www.smarnold.com
Supplier of brushes, wash pads and mitts, chamois, buffing pads, bug sponges, etc.

*Buff & Shine............................ 1-800-659-2833 – www.buffandshine.com
Supplier of brushes, chamois, buffing pads, bug sponges, etc.

*Steam Services Co .... 1-888-278-6630 – www.steamservicesinc.com
Odor removal products for fogging machine. Ask for Firefog 404

*RSC Sales .... 1-800-669-0072 – www.rscsales.com
Paper floor mats, plastic seat protectors, fender covers etc.

*Lil Chizler Products................. 1-800-207-8245 – www.lilchizler.com
Plastic scrapers…Lil Chizler

Equipment
*National Detail Systems .... 1-800-356-9485 – www.nationaldetail.com
Supplier of mobile detailing trailers, pressure washers, water tanks, extractors, etc.

*Gem Industries........................ 1-800-447-4436 – www.gem-industries.com
Manufacturer of Orbital polishers

*Cyclo Manufacturing.............. 1-303-4851990 – www.cyclotoolmakers.com
Manufacturer of the Dual Head Orbital polisher

*Detailing.com .... 1-888-306-5828- www.detailing.com
Supplier of a variety of detailing equipment including buffers, ozone machines, pressure washers and steam cleaners

*ProMotorcar Inc...................... 1-877-460-6032 – www.promotorcarproducts.com
Carries the Pro Paint Thickness Gauge 11

*Electra Inc............................... 1-773-463-4054– www.electraheat.com
Supplier for the Immersion Bucket Heater for cold water extractors

*El Monte Plastics .... 1-626-442-0162 – www.elmonteplastics.com
Manufacturer of Portable Water Tanks

*Radio Shack............................ Check your local store
Supplier of the hand held Paint Magnifier

*Hotsy Pressure Washers .... 1-800-525-1976 – www.hotsy.com
Manufacturer of Pressure Washers

*All American Cleaning Systems.. 1- 800.541.7267 – www.allamericancleaningsystems.com
Suppliers of Pressure Washer Equipment

*Global Industrial. .... 1-888-978-7759 – www.globalindustrial.com
Manufacturer of Portable Tent Canopies

*Mytee Products .... 1- 858- 679-1191 – www.mytee.com
Manufacture of Portable Extractors

*Pep Boys .... Check your local store
Carries the Water Blade and California Car Duster

Training
*Training…National Detail Systems…1-800-356-9485 – www.nationaldetail.com
Supplies Video and Training Manuals, and Hands –On

*Greg Dumond's… Advanced Personal Hands-on Mobile Training School in California
27 years of experience personalized for you! Call for details

Industry Magazines & Forums
*Professional Car Wash & Detail Magazine… www.carwash.com
*Auto Laundry News… www.carwashmag.com
*ICA – International Car Wash Association…1-312-321-5199
*Mobile -Tech News…727-531-7885... www.mobile-technews.com
*Autopia Car Care Forum… www.autopia.org
*Meguiars Products… www.meguiarsonline.com

Aftermarket Services
*National Detail Repair Systems…1-800-356-9485 – www.nationaldetail.com
*Paint Chip Repair Kits… NDS EZ Match Paint…1-800-356-9485 - www.nationaldetail.com
*Gold Plating Kits…Brooktronics Company…1-661-294-1195… www.brooktronics.com
*Windshield Glass Repair…Glass Technology…1-800-441-4527… www.gtglass.com
*Headlight Restoration…Dvelup Corporation…1-800-350-2932… www.dvelup.com
*Odor Removal…Unsmoke Systems…1-800-332-6037… www.unsmoke.com
*Ozone Air Purification...Air-Zone Co…1-800-772-5142… www.air-zone.com
*Paintless Dent Repair…PDQ Tools… 1-888-775-8665... www.pdqtools.com
*Vinyl & Leather Repair…Fitzgeralds…1-800-441-3326… www.fitzgeraldsrestoration.com

*Window Tinting…Sungaurd Company…1-877-273-4364... www.solargard.com
*Car Accessories…Car Cover World…1-800-426-8377… www.carcoverworld.com
*Car Accessories…Griot's Garage…1-800-345-5789… www.griotsgarage.com
*Car Accessories…Star West Floor Mats…1-800-468-7827… www.starwestmats.com
*Eastwood Co.…Body Shop products and Tools…1-800-343-9353… www.eastwood.com

Special Notes Page

www.ingramcontent.com/pod-product-compliance
Lightning Source LLC
Chambersburg PA
CBHW061210230426
43665CB00032B/2974